UNRULY TIMES:

Wordsworth and Coleridge in Their Time

A.S. Byatt

THE HOGARTH PRESS
LONDON

Published in 1989 by
The Hogarth Press
30 Bedford Square
London WC1B 3SG

First published in Great Britain as *Wordsworth and Coleridge in Their Time*
by Thomas Nelson and Sons Ltd 1970

A CIP catalogue record for this book is available from the British Library.

ISBN 0 7012 0857 0

Printed in Great Britain by
Ebenezer Baylis, Worcester

A.S. Byatt was born in Sheffield in 1936 and read English at Newnham College, Cambridge. After two years' academic research in the United States and in Oxford, she finished her first novel, *Shadow of a Sun* (1964). She was a lecturer in literature at the Central School of Art and Design from 1965-69, and then taught English and American literature at the University of London for many years. She is a broadcaster and reviewer and has been a judge on several literary prize panels (Hawthornden, Booker, Betty Trask, David Higham). She was made a Fellow of the Royal Society of Literature in 1983 and awarded an Honorary Degree in Literature from Bradford University in 1987. Her fiction includes the novels *The Game* (1967), *The Virgin in the Garden* (1978) and *Still Life* (1985) and *Sugar and Other Stories* (1987). She has also written widely on 19th and 20th century literature, and has published two studies of the novels of Iris Murdoch: *Degrees of Freedom* (1965) and *Iris Murdoch* (1976). Her most recent novel, *Possession: A Romance*, is published by Chatto & Windus.

Coleridge in 1795
from a portrait by P.Vandyke
(*National Portrait Gallery, London*).

Wordsworth in 1798
from a portrait by W.Shuter
(*Mansell Collection*).

FOR ANTONIA AND CHARLES

Contents

Note to this Edition

This book was first published in 1970. It seems sensible to leave it exactly as it was rather than to rewrite anything. However, if there is anything I feel should be added, or changed, it would be to take account of the discovery of the revelatory correspondence between William and Mary Wordsworth, published in 1982. These letters make it clear that whatever Wordsworth's feelings toward his sister, and hers toward him, the marriage of William and Mary was both deeply loving and steadily passionate.

A.S. Byatt, June 1989

Illustrations

Acknowledgements

I am very grateful to various friends for advice about reading for this book—they are not, of course, responsible for my mistakes and omissions. I should like to thank my sister, Helen Langdon, for help over matters of art history, Henry Roseveare for help with historical reading and general encouragement, and Tim Hilton for much essential information. I am particularly grateful to Brian Inglis, for allowing me to read the manuscript of his book, *By the Sweat of thy Brow: Poverty in the Industrial Revolution*. Finally, I am grateful to John Beer, not only for his book *Coleridge, The Visionary*, but for conversation and ideas over many years.

1 *Introduction*

Wordsworth and Coleridge met briefly for the first time in Bristol, in 1795. Their close friendship, which led to the composition and publication of the *Lyrical Ballads*, began in 1797, when Wordsworth and his sister, Dorothy, moved from Racedown in Dorset to Alfoxden in Somerset, to be near Coleridge, who was living in a cottage in Nether Stowey. Each man had qualities and abilities the other lacked, and at that time needed. The result of the continuous conversation and long walks of that year was, for both of them, an increase in poetic power, and the elaboration of a complex idea of the poetic imagination. It is also true to say that the qualities which brought them together later helped to create the friction and estrangement between them. This introductory chapter is intended to map out, briefly, the pattern of the relationship.

Wordsworth, in 1797, was at the end of an uncertain and miserable period of his life. Both his parents had died when he was young, his mother when he was eight, his father when he was thirteen: Wordsworth and his brothers and sister were cared for by relatives. There were financial troubles—Wordsworth's father had been law agent to James Lowther, First Earl of Lonsdale, who had owed him, when he died, about £5,000, and the family were engaged in prolonged and useless legal struggles to recover this money, which was only finally repaid by the Earl's heir, in 1804, after his death in 1802. William, after going to Hawkshead Grammar School, was sent to Cambridge with the intention that he should take Orders and become a clergyman; after leaving Cambridge he hesitated over this for some time, and was finally saved by a legacy of £900 from a friend, Raisley Calvert, whom he nursed in the last stages of consumption in 1794: this enabled him to set up house with his sister Dorothy and devote himself to poetry. Before this, he had spent the year of 1791–2 in France—a year which had caused

Samuel Taylor Coleridge (1772–1834); detail from a portrait by
Robert Hancock, 1796

him some pain and disillusionment in more than one way.
He had gone to France in the early days of the Republic, full
of revolutionary idealism, and was deeply shocked by the Terror.
He had also got himself into deep emotional trouble: his love-
affair with Annette Vallon in Blois in 1792 had led to the birth
of his daughter Caroline in December. Wordsworth came back
to England leaving Annette, who believed and hoped that he

William Wordsworth (1770–1850), from an engraving after a portrait by Robert Hancock, 1798

would marry her and referred to herself as his wife, in a France internally boiling and soon to be at war with most of Europe, including England. His sense of guilt and bewilderment at this desertion on his own part was expressed in various later poems, such as the tale of *Vaudracour and Julia*, with its seduction and illegitimate child, and, more obliquely, in various descriptions of female vagrants, victims of both men and society, such as the

The second court of St John's College, Cambridge, early in the
nineteenth century

central story of *Salisbury Plain*, written after his solitary walking
tour from Salisbury to North Wales in 1793 and published much
later under the title of *Guilt and Sorrow*.

Wordsworth the young man was on the whole solitary, pain-
fully proud, self-critical and self-suspecting. His letters and other
writings have an overwhelming tone of high moral idealism and
high poetic purpose, sometimes conflicting. He meant, even then,
to be great, and nothing but the best would do, but the circumstances of his life—poverty, lack of family security, lack of
practical vocation, responsibility to Annette—left him in doubt
about when he would achieve or how he would achieve it. In
1791, writing to his friend, William Matthews, about the latter's
decision not to enter the Church but to try to live by travelling
and writing, Wordsworth says

> It is impossible you can ever have your father's consent to a scheme
> which to a parent at least, if not to everyone else, must appear wild
> even to insanity. It is an observation to whose truth I have long since
> consented that small certainties are the bane of great talents.

Wordsworth is torn in this letter between conventional morals and the conflict between small certainties and 'great talents': he tells Matthews that 'I do not think you could ever be happy while you were conscious that you were a cause of such sorrow to your parents', and yet cannot resist adding in the next paragraph that he himself might, without moral obligations to relatives, prefer Matthews' idea to 'vegetating on a paltry curacy'. The relevance of Matthews' situation to Wordsworth's own is clear; Wordsworth recommends Industry to Matthews and assures him he will somehow make a living in London, but in November he writes again to tell Matthews he himself is going to France, and adds gloomily

> I am doomed to be an idler throughout my whole life. I have read nothing this age, nor indeed did I ever. Yet with all this I am tolerably happy; do you think this ought to be a matter of congratulation to me or no? For my own part, I think certainly not.

In 1794 he and Matthews were planning to publish a periodical, and in his letters about this his mixture of self-suspicion and extreme idealism in terms of his own writing can clearly be seen:

> I have not been much used to composition of any kind, particularly in prose, my style therefore may frequently want fluency and sometimes perhaps perspicuity but these defects will gradually wear off; an ardent wish to promote the welfare of mankind will preserve me from sinking under them.

Before the meeting with Coleridge, the only person with whom Wordsworth seems to have been really at ease was his sister Dorothy. Dorothy, a year younger than William, was the only girl in the family; she spent her youth in the care of various relatives before setting up house with William, first at Keswick in 1794, and then at Racedown. She was an energetic, intelligent woman, most of whose considerable passions were spent in devotion to her brothers, particularly John and William. An early letter to a girl friend written from her grandmother's house in 1787 gives an idea of her narrow life, and of the energies repressed by it. Her grandmother, she says, shows so little affection that while I am in her house I cannot consider myself as at home, I feel like a stranger. You cannot think how gravely and silently I sit with her and my Gfr, you would scarcely know me, you are well acquainted that I was never remarkable for taciturnity, but now I sit for whole hours without saying anything except that I have an old shirt to mend, then, my Grandmr and I have to set our heads together and contrive the most notable way of doing it, which I daresay in the end we always hit upon, but really the contrivance its self takes up more time than the shirt is worth, our only conversation is about *work, work*, or what sort of servant such a one's is, who are her parents, what places she lived in, why she left them etc. etc. What my dear Jane can be more uninteresting than such conversation as this? Yet I am obliged to set upon the occasion as *notable* a face as if I was delighted with it, and that nothing could be more agreeable to me; notability is preached up to me every day, such an one is a very *sedate, clever, notable* girl says my Gmr.

It has been argued that William and Dorothy Wordsworth's love for each other was so exclusive and violent in its early days that neither of them were able to give the same amount of emotional energy to any other relationship: Wordsworth's marriage to Mary Hutchinson seems calm, conventional and dutiful by comparison. Their letters preceding their setting up house together are alive with love. Dorothy writes of William

I must be blind, he cannot be so pleasing as my fondness makes him. I am willing to allow that half the virtues with which I fancy him endowed are the creation of my Love, but surely I may be excused! he was never tired of comforting his sister, he never left her in anger, he always met her with joy, he preferred her society to every other pleasure, or rather when we were so happy as to be within each other's reach he had no pleasure when we were compelled to be divided.

And to the same friend, Jane Pollard, Dorothy proudly quotes William's letters to her about their coming meeting and the possibility of setting up house together.

How much do I wish that each emotion of pleasure and pain that visits your heart should excite a similar pleasure or a similar pain

Wordsworth and his wife Mary, from a painting by Margaret Gillies

within me, by that sympathy which will almost identify us when we have stolen to our little cottage!

And

Oh my dear, dear sister with what transport shall I again meet you, with what rapture shall I again wear out the day in your sight. I assure you so eager is my desire to see you that all obstacles vanish. I see you in a moment running or rather flying to my arms.

F. W. Bateson has argued convincingly that Wordsworth's remotely beautiful love poems about the strangely immaterial 'Lucy' are poems about his feelings for Dorothy: he wrote himself in a letter to Coleridge in 1802 that the poem *The Glow-Worm* ('Among all lovely things my Love had been') was written about an incident that had taken place between himself and Dorothy, and Coleridge himself believed that 'A slumber did my spirit seal' was written in 'some gloomier moment' when he fancied that his sister might die. And in a fragment of poetry composed about 1800 Wordsworth described Dorothy as

> The dear companion of my lonely walk
> My hope, my joy, my sister and my friend,
> Or something dearer still, if reason knows
> A dearer thought, or in the heart of love
> There be a dearer name.

It is possible that Coleridge's arrival at Alfoxden to share this intimacy provided a stabilizing influence on the emotions of both brother and sister, who were able to share them with him, and through him: it was Coleridge himself who wrote of them at this time (1797–8) that they were 'Three persons and one soul'. Wordsworth at Alfoxden before the advent of Coleridge seems to have been troubled by obscure guilts and despair: perhaps the best example of this state of mind is a fragmentary poem from his Alfoxden note-book:

> Away, away, it is the air
> That stirs among the withered leaves;
> Away, away, it is not there,
> Go, hunt among the harvest-sheaves.

There is a bed in shape as plain
As from a hare or lion's lair
It is the bed where we have lain
In anguish and despair.

Away and take the eagle's eye,
The tyger's smell,
Ears that can hear the agonies
And murmurings of hell;
And when you there have stood
By that same bed of pain,
The groans are gone, the tears remain.
Then tell me if the thing be clear,
The difference betwixt a tear
Of water and of blood.

The source of this emotion is impossible to trace—guilt over Annette, obscure fear of the nature of his feelings for Dorothy, or some more purely dramatic and fictional impetus have all been suggested—but the emotion itself is clear enough and sharply expressed. With its direct emphasis on sexual pain and guilt, its elaboration of a kind of strained and agonized universal sensuality, and its further religious guilty sense of having committed a crime which is observed by the whole of nature and judged, the poem expresses acute anxiety with an immediacy rare in Wordworth's personal poetry.

Coleridge's life before the meeting at Alfoxden had been more social than Wordsworth's. He was the youngest of nine brothers, the son of an impractical literary clergyman and an ambitious mother. As a little boy he was precocious and clever, which produced in him an anxious desire to display his learning and be admired, and a deeper fear of not living up to what was expected of him. He seems to have been afraid of his brothers, with whom he never managed to be on easy terms—he spent his life alternately shocking them, apologizing abjectly and profusely, and making grandiose gestures and plans to impress them with his seriousness. He describes the child he was with a mixture of self-mockery, self-contempt and showing off which became habitual with him. As a child, he wrote, he was 'fretful and inordinately passionate; and as I could not play at anything and was slothful, I was despised and hated by the boys . . . before I was eight years old I was a *character*. Sensibility, imagination, vanity, sloth and feelings of deep and bitter contempt for almost all who traversed the orbit of my understanding, were even then prominent and manifest.' He extended his self-contempt and mockery even to his Christian name, which he rarely used, preferring to be called Coleridge and sign himself S.T.C.

His father's death, when Coleridge was nearly nine, was the occasion of his being sent to Christ's Hospital, where he had an audience for his brilliance, although he seems to have been lonely in himself and in need of the close affection and steady love provided by a family: separation, which increased the Wordsworths' fierce devotion to each other, simply increased the difference between Coleridge and his respectable elder brothers. Charles Lamb, his junior at the school, wrote a brilliant description of Coleridge's later days there, in an essay called *Christ's Hospital Thirty-five years ago*:

> Come back into memory, like as thou wert in the dayspring of thy fancies, with hope like a fiery column before thee—the dark pillar not yet turned—Samuel Taylor Coleridge—Logician, Metaphysician, Bard!—How have I seen the casual passer through the Cloisters stand still, entranced with admiration (while he weighed the disproportion between the *speech* and the *garb* of the young Mirandula) to hear thee unfold, in thy deep and sweet intonations, the mysteries of Jamblichus, or Plotinus (for even in those years thou waxedst not pale at such philosophic draughts) or reciting Homer in his Greek, or Pindar—while the walls of the old Grey Friars re-echoed to the accents of the *inspired charity boy*!

The capacity for making brilliant and endless speeches lasted the rest of Coleridge's life: so did the learning and the philosophical curiosity and application. Coleridge, too, was intended for the Church, and Coleridge, too, found himself unwilling to commit himself to it. Like Wordsworth, he went up to Cambridge, where his academic career was much more successful than his friend's, and he made much more impression on his contemporaries.

Christ's Hospital, from a print published in 1804

He tried, however, to live the life of a fashionable undergraduate, and ended up in debt: this resulted in flight from Cambridge, and his secret enrolment in the 15th Light Dragoons under the name of Silas Tomkyn Comberbacke. He was a poor horseman and his equipment was rusty: he ended up nursing a man sick with smallpox and had to be ignominiously rescued by his brothers and returned to University. Whilst still an undergraduate he met Robert Southey, with whom he conceived the plan of emigrating to the southern part of the United States and forming an egalitarian colony on the banks of the Susquehanna river—this was Pantisocracy. It was at this time that a Miss Charlotte Poole wrote of him, when he was visiting Thomas Poole of Nether Stowey, who was to remain one of his closest and most stable friends:

> Tom Poole has a friend with him of the name of Coldridge: a young man of brilliant understanding, great eloquence, desperate fortune, democratick principles, and entirely led away by the feelings of the moment.

Jesus College, Cambridge, in the eighteenth century

Coleridge's deepest need was for emotional security, the sense of having a safe place within a group of people he could trust, the love which he had not received from his family, and for which dazzled admiration of his brilliant discourses, or delighted response to his clowning was no substitute. Like many people who demand from those they meet the total response they failed to achieve in childhood, he always demanded too much, and at the same time expected, even provoked, the rejection which was in fact the response he could recognize. He had romantic hopes of both men and women—all men were potentially ideal friends, all women potentially devoted lovers—and at the same time he was obsessed by the fear of living perpetually unloved and solitary. An early sonnet, *On receiving an account that his only sister's death was inevitable*, written in 1791, shifts its central preoccupation from the sister's sufferings to the poet's frightening loneliness:

> Say, is this hollow eye, this heartless pain,
> Fated to rove thro' Life's wide cheerless plain—
> Nor father, brother, sister meet its ken—
> My woes, my joys unshared!

. This is already, more nakedly, the central theme of the great *Dejection* Ode, written eleven years later: the sonnet ends, significantly 'Better to die than live and not be lov'd'. And some cancelled lines from an early poem called *Happiness* combine the clowning at his own expense with the desire for the impossible total love:

> Ah! doubly blest, if love supply
> Lustre to this now heavy eye,
> And with unwonted Spirit grace
> That fat vacuity of face.
>
> Or if e'en Love, the mighty Love
> Shall find this change his powers above;
> Some lovely maid perchance thou'lt find
> To read thy visage in thy mind.

It was the combination of the need for a family group and the need for love that brought about Coleridge's early marriage at the age of twenty-two. During 1794, the year of enthusiasm for Pantisocracy, Southey was the ideal friend, for whose approbation Coleridge poured out all his ideas, plans, politics, philosophy. Southey himself was engaged to a Miss Edith Fricker, a dressmaker, one of the five daughters of a Bristol widow. Edith Fricker's sister, Mary, and her husband, Robert Lovell, were to share in the Pantisocratic expedition: Southey and Coleridge enthusiastically decided that it would be an idealistic convenience if Coleridge married the eldest sister, Sarah Fricker. Coleridge's letters to Southey about this proposed union make it clear that it was primarily enthusiasm for Southey and Pantisocracy which impelled him:

Well, my dear Southey! I am at last arrived at Jesus. My God! how tumultuous are the movements of my Heart—Since I quitted this room what and how important Events have been evolved! America! Southey! Miss Fricker! Yes—Southey—you are right— Even Love is the creature of strong Motive—I certainly love her. I think of her incessantly and with unspeakable tenderness—with that inward melting away of Soul that symptomatises it.

Pantisocracy—O I shall have such a scheme of it! My head, my heart are all alive. . . .

I am longing to be with you—Make Edith my Sister—Surely, Southey! we shall be . . . most friendly where all are friends. She must therefore be most emphatically my Sister.

But even then, in September 1794, he was writing agitated and self-exculpatory letters to Southey excusing himself for not having written to Sarah Fricker—he stayed in London unintentionally and would have written if he had known he was staying:

I told her, I should write the moment I arrived in Cambridge— I have fulfilled the Promise—Recollect, Southey! that when you mean to go to a place—tomorrow—and tomorrow—and tomorrow —the time that intervenes is lost—Had I meant at first to stay in London a fortnight, a fortnight should not have elapsed without my writing to her—If you are satisfied, tell Miss F. that *you* are *so*— but assign no Reasons. I ought not to have been *suspected* . . .

Typically, he takes a high moral line with Southey's indignation on Sarah Fricker's behalf—Southey is *too* virtuous, judges too strictly—he, Coleridge, would be more *sympathetic* in Southey's position. 'Southey! Precipitance is wrong!'

But Coleridge was very much the opposite of precipitate in Miss Fricker's direction. On leaving Cambridge he went to London, where he met a girl called Mary Evans whom he had indeed loved, and was deeply disturbed by the meeting. He lurked in silence in London, distressed by his conscious knowledge that he did not love Miss Fricker, and by Southey's growing ambiva- lence towards Pantisocracy. It was Southey himself, always throughout his life a man of punctuality, precision, duty and moral rectitude, who brought the reluctant bridegroom to a sense of his duties. 'Coleridge,' he said, 'did not come back to Bristol till January 1795, *nor would he, I believe, have come back at all*, if I had not gone to London to look for him. For having got there from Cambridge at the beginning of winter, there he remained without writing to Miss F. or to me till we actually apprehended that his friends had placed him somewhere in confinement.' Coleridge, however indecisive, was always anxious to behave rightly and to be thought well of—when informed by Southey and by Miss Fricker 'with her customary delicacy' that he had compromised her, that she considered herself engaged and had even refused two advantageous offers on his behalf, he submitted to marriage with a good grace. Tom Poole found them the cottage at Nether Stowey; his first son, Hartley, was born in 1796. From this time on he was never free of anxiety about money, and Mrs Coleridge's desire to be a respectable woman in society made life no easier. Family responsibilities are now added to the lack of self-respect and tortuous habit of mind which, combined with high ambition, already made it difficult for him to commit himself to any course of work or piece of writing and carry it through. He was genuinely harassed and bewildered, as is clear in a letter he wrote to the Bristol bookseller Joseph Cottle who befriended him, despite its notes of petulance, exaggeration and over-dramatization:

> I have left my friends: I have left plenty; I have left that ease which would have secured a literary immortality and have enabled me to give to the public works conceived in moments of inspiration and polished with leisurely solicitude and alas! for what have I left them? for [Southey] who deserted me in the hour of distress and for a scheme of virtue impracticable and romantic! So I am forced to write for bread! write the flights of poetic enthusiasm when every minute I am hearing a groan from my wife. Groans, and complaints, and sickness! The present hour I am in a quick-set hedge of embarrassment, and whichever way I turn, a thorn runs into me! The future is cloud, and thick darkness! Poverty perhaps, and the thin faces of them that want bread, looking up to me! Nor is this all. My happiest moments for composition are broken in upon by the reflection that I must make haste, I am too late! I am already months behind! I have received my pay beforehand!

Here again is a theme that recurs throughout the rest of Coleridge's life.

Coleridge was to ascribe many of his later misfortunes to his wife's lack of sympathy with his intellectual needs and aspirations. De Quincey, a sharp observer and psychologist, who worshipped Coleridge as a young man to the extent of making him an anonymous gift of £300, questioned in his *Recollections of the Lake Poets* 'whether Coleridge would not, under any circumstances, have become indifferent to a wife not eminently capable of enlightened sympathy with his own ruling pursuits', and gave it as his opinion that 'neither Coleridge nor Lord Byron could have failed, eventually, to quarrel with *any* wife. . . .' But De Quincey, at the time he wrote that, was given to a slightly malicious touching up and exaggeration of Coleridge's faults, partly at least because he used Coleridge as a kind of public scapegoat for the opium-taking habit with which he was also cursed, and which he alternately glamourized and despised. It is probable that Coleridge would have expected far too much and therefore received far too little from any marriage: but the one he did make was nevertheless certainly far less suitable than many he could have made, and sprang from impractical moral idealism and a terror of disappointing Southey. Writing of how he had, against his principles, allowed himself to be persuaded not to wear coloured clothes when acting as a Unitarian lay preacher in Sheffield, he said

> Indeed I want firmness, I perceive, I do—I have that within me which makes it difficult for me to say, No! repeatedly to a number of persons who seem uneasy and anxious.

And in 1804 he wrote to Southey from Malta:

> I was blasted in my only absolute wish, having married for honour and not for love! Southey! that I think and feel so kindly and lovingly of *you*, who were the sole cause of my marriage, this is a proof to me that my nature is not ignoble—

The Alfoxden year, 1797–8, provided an intellectual and emotional release for both poets. Wordsworth had the qualities

Coleridge most needed and admired. He believed in himself, he was sure of his vocation as a poet, he had immense will-power and tenacity of purpose when it came to getting things done. Dorothy admired and worshipped him, and Wordsworth accepted this as his due: Coleridge's deep need to admire and worship, particularly since Southey's defection from Panti-socracy, found a natural focus within the pattern already set up by the Wordsworths. Wordsworth was resolute and independent: Coleridge, too self-disparaging to be consistently ambitious on his own behalf, could expand his ideals vicariously through Wordsworth, who was going to write the 'great philosophical poem' he, Coleridge, was convinced should be written. The Wordsworths' passionate loyalty to each other, their sharing of ideas about literature, nature and human nature, gave him the sense of naturally belonging within a group which he had lacked, wanted, and failed to create in Pantisocracy. And he was neces-sary to Wordsworth, and expanded into intellectual brilliance and emotional joy as this became clear. He was much more widely read than Wordsworth, much more interested in 'placing' an idea in the history of ideas and in the context of general thought: he was able to give shape and articulation and com-plexity to the views Wordsworth was feeling for about what subjects poetry should treat, and in what manner. He was good for Wordsworth too, in that their emotional needs were com-plementary. Wordsworth, in his innermost self proud, solitary, courageous and self-regarding, was on the surface suspicious and awkward. Coleridge, who lacked self-respect or self-confidence at the deepest level, was on the surface charming, warm, welcoming and quick to relax and involve people he met. Wordsworth in-creased Coleridge's sense of his own value: Coleridge made it possible for Wordsworth to communicate, and thus more precisely to formulate, his solitary thoughts. It is arguable that the beneficial effects on Wordsworth were finally more lasting; and his tribute to Coleridge's humanizing influence at the end of the *Prelude* is precise, eloquent, and beautiful:

With such a theme
Coleridge! with this my argument of thee
Shall I be silent? O capacious Soul!
Placed on this earth to love and understand
And from thy presence shed the light of love
Shall I be mute ere thou be spoken of?
Thy kindred influence to my heart of hearts
Did also find its way. Thus fear relaxed
Her overweening grasp: thus thoughts and things
In the self-haunting spirit learned to take
More rational proportions; mystery
The incumbent mystery of sense and soul,
Of life and death, time and eternity,
Admitted more habitually a mild
Interposition . . .

De Quincey suggested that Coleridge's marriage was not made easier by the advent of Dorothy, 'a young lady whom I will not describe more particularly than by saying that intellectually she was very much superior to Mrs Coleridge'. He describes her as 'the very wildest (in the sense of the most natural) person that I have ever known; and also the truest, most inevitable and at the same time the quickest and readiest in her sympathy with either joy or sorrow . . . with the realities of life or the larger realities of the poets.' Mrs Coleridge, he suggests, was annoyed by the cavalier way in which Dorothy, with her 'Gipsy Tan' and her 'wild and startling' eyes would come in after a long, wet walk and borrow Sarah Coleridge's clothes. But there is little evidence to support the idea, put forward by some romantic biographers, that Dorothy was in love with Coleridge, or he with her: they were both held by the powerful emotion of love for William and the high poetic purpose. Coleridge's admiration for her, and hers for him, were both extravagant and detailed. Coleridge wrote:

Wordsworth and his exquisite sister are with me. She is a woman indeed! in mind I mean, and heart; for her person is such, that if you expected to see a pretty woman you would think her rather ordinary; if you expected to see an ordinary woman you would

think her pretty! but her manners are simple, ardent, impressive . . .
Her information various. Her eyes watchful in minutest observation
of nature; and her taste, a perfect electrometer. It bends, protrudes
and draws in, at subtlest beauties and most recondite faults.

It has been said that Dorothy taught Coleridge to *see*; both
poets drew on her journals for accurate natural descriptions,
and Coleridge's poetry and his poetic theory become much more
involved in the precise 'minute observation' of nature, as opposed
to 'poetic' generalizations, from this time.

Dorothy wrote of Coleridge, to Mary Hutchinson, Wordsworth's
future wife:

> He is a wonderful man. His conversation teems with soul, mind and
> spirit. Then he is so benevolent, so good tempered and cheerful,
> and, like William, interests himself so much about every little
> trifle. At first I thought him very plain, that is, for about three
> minutes: he is pale and thin, has a wide mouth, thick lips and not
> very good teeth, longish, loose-growing, half-curling rough black
> hair. But if you hear him speak for five minutes you think no more
> of them.

She describes, too, the reading aloud that became a regular
occupation: first 'William's new poem *The Ruined Cottage*' and
'after tea he repeated to us two acts and a half of his tragedy
Osorio'. The next morning William read his tragedy *The Borderers*.

Out of these readings, this close attention to the poetic process,
and the long walks in which they encouraged each other to notice
and accurately describe minute natural details, so that the descriptions became part of, and intensified, their feeling for each
other, grew many of the *Lyrical Ballads*, much of Coleridge's
greater nature poetry (*Frost at Midnight, This Lime Tree Bower*)
and the precise analyses of the workings of poetry and the poetic
imagination which made Wordsworth's great preface to the
Lyrical Ballads and, much later, Coleridge's *Biographia Literaria*.
The relationship was prolonged for many more years, but
stresses were already present within it. In 1798 the three went to
Germany together, but separated there, Coleridge to study meta-

Greta Hall and Keswick bridge

physics, and be sociable at Göttingen University, Wordsworth
and Dorothy to a cold and self-contained existence in parsimonious
lodgings in Goslar, where Wordsworth wrote much great poetry.
Back in England, they went to live near each other, Coleridge
at Greta Hall in Keswick, Wordsworth and Dorothy at Grasmere.
By now Coleridge's health was poor—he had gouty swellings
and bowel troubles, and the opium he began to take to relieve
them only exacerbated them. His domestic troubles increased.
Dorothy began to refer to him as 'Poor C.'. In 1802, about a
month after Wordsworth's marriage, she wrote in her journal

> Poor C. left us and we came home together ... C. had a sweet
> day for his ride. Every sight and every sound reminded me of him—
> dear, dear fellow, of his many walks to us by day and by night, of all
> dear things. I was melancholy and could not talk, but at last I
> eased my heart by weeping—nervous blubbering, says William.
> It is not so. O! how many many reasons have I to be anxious for
> him.

A month later she records that they had from him 'a sad
melancholy letter' that 'prevented us all from sleeping'.
By now Coleridge had fallen deeply in love with Sara Hutchin-

son, his 'Asra', Wordsworth's sister-in-law. In 1802 he wrote *Dejection: an Ode*, a great poem inspired by a combination of his despair at his own lack of will and productivity compared with Wordsworth, and the hopelessness of his passion for Sara—the first, unpublished version of the poem is a long, loosely formed, personal verse-letter addressed to her. Dorothy's journal for 21 April 1802 records that

> William and I sauntered a little in the garden. Coleridge came to us, and repeated the verses he wrote to Sara. I was affected with them, and was on the whole, not being well, in miserable spirits. The sunshine, the green fields and the fair sky made me sadder; even the little, happy sporting lambs seemed but sorrowful to me. The pile wort spread out on the grass a thousand shining stars. The primroses were there, and the remains of a few Daffodils. The well, which we cleaned out last night, is still but a little muddy pond, though full of water.

Dorothy's prose captures both the feeling of *Dejection* ('I see, not feel, how beautiful they are') and that of her brother's *Ode on the Intimations of Immortality*, the sense that there has passed away a glory from the earth. The glory had passed away from the relationship too. In 1804 Coleridge went to Malta, partly in search of a better climate for his health than the wet Lakes, partly in order to shelve the problem of his quarrels with his wife and his love for Sara Hutchinson. The Wordsworths thought about him constantly, and awaited his return eagerly: he was needed, for without him Wordsworth seemed unable to embark properly on his 'great philosophical poem', *The Recluse*. When he did return in 1806, they encouraged him to be decisive about making a complete separation from his wife, and to become part of their own close family group. But Coleridge was no longer the same man—increasing addiction to opium had changed him. He lingered indecisively in the south for months after his return, communicating neither with the Wordsworths nor with his wife. Dorothy recorded their shock at the first meeting—he was unhealthily fat and lethargic, would not speak of personal matters, was as different from what they had expected as a stranger would have been. They encouraged him to live with them nevertheless, but the situation became increasingly strained. Wordsworth and Coleridge began to criticize each other, and the qualities which had led to their understanding now became the points of stress.

In 1808 Coleridge was still writing to friends 'That there is such a man in the world as Wordsworth, and that such a man enjoys such a Family, makes both Death and my inefficient Life a less grievous Thought to me'. But in fact Wordsworth's austere existence with his close and worshipping family would not have suited Coleridge even if he had been in good health. He needed wide social contacts, and an audience. Lamb describes him reciting *Kubla Khan*, 'which said vision he repeats so enchantingly that it irradiates and brings heaven and elysian bowers into my parlour when he sings or says it . . . his face when he repeats his verses, hath its ancient glory; an archangel a little damaged'. Crabb Robinson described him holding him 'on the stretch of attention and admiration from ½ past 3 till 12 o'clock' on politics, metaphysics and poetry: De Quincey describes him as delivering more aphorisms and 'weight of truth' in three hours' talk 'than would easily be found in a month's select reading'. But the Wordsworths were not entirely admiring of the skills he had— they undervalued, as will be seen later, his greatest poetic achieve-ments, and Dorothy told Lady Beaumont that he was unwise to lecture since 'a man is perpetually tempted to lower himself to his hearers to bring them into sympathy with him'.

The Wordsworths' increasing impatience with, and criticism of his lack of will-power and decisiveness at this stage of his life coincided with his own self-distaste for the same reason. But Coleridge was a great man and a great psychologist, and beneath both the very real suffering and the hysterical self-pity, self-accusation and self-excusing, was a steady intellectual curiosity about the relationship between body and mind, intellect and emotions (what he called thought and feeling). His greatest need, both as a man and as a thinker, was for a sense of unity and coherence in things: his projected *magnum opus* was to be an organic philosophy which should unite the insights of theology,

Rydal Water and Grasmere

science, the arts, metaphysics and logic; his primary interest as a critic was in the creative imagination of the poet which fused disparate objects into a new 'organic' whole and was an image 'in the finite mind' of the original FIAT or 'I AM' which had created the universe. His great poems—*The Ancient Mariner, Kubla Khan, Dejection*—all present images of worlds in which the vital unifying principle is not functioning or not perceived: the mariner is becalmed, stared at by Life-in-Death, alone on a wide wide sea—

> So lonely 'twas that God himself
> Scarce seemed there to be.

Kubla Khan is an image of a lost Paradise, that sunny dome, those caves of ice, that can only be rebuilt if the visionary poet can 'revive within me' the 'symphony and song' of harmony. In *Dejection* the poet can see, not feel, how beautiful are the natural objects, from which we 'receive but what we give'. And even during the dark years of opium addiction, apparently blasted promise, and apparently hopeless emotional isolation, Coleridge

was observing precisely the effects of illness, opium, frustrated
sexual desire, on his poetry, his metaphysics, his moral being. It
is typical of him that, having been seized in a field with an ex-
cruciating attack of diarrhoea and faintness, he should climb back
onto the stile he had failed to get over and make notes in his
pocket book about the effects on his emotions of the weakness in
his stomach, and the uses of the word 'bowels' in the Bible to
denote the affections.

The theme of his own increasing alienation from any sense
of being connected as a conscious agent to his own immediate
life pervades much of his thinking during this period. The world
of the senses, of natural objects, seems unreal, and so does the
world of normal emotions—domestic affections, family life. He
examines various causes for this. He is sexually confused—he
can feel only dislike for Mrs Coleridge, and cannot allow himself
morally to feel desire for Sara Hutchinson—he watches himself
escaping this predicament by constructing general theories about
the nature of love and the affections, or, more desperately, about
the nature of the universe. He considers his own pain as an agent
of his moral weakness. It confuses his perceptions, tires him and
defeats him. He considers the effects of the opium 'reverie' on
both his thoughts and his sensations—the sense of effortless distance it produces, the endless ramifications of thought without
action. He considers his own predisposition to create complex
abstract structures of ideas as originating in his imaginative but
insecure childhood. In 1800 he wrote to Thomas Wedgwood
that he was oppressed by the state of affairs in France, and remarked gloomily that 'the dedication of much hope and fear to
subjects which are perhaps disproportionate to our faculties and
powers is a disease'. It is probable, he says, reciting Wordsworth's creed, 'that a man's private and personal connections
and interests ought to be uppermost in his daily and hourly
thoughts' but he himself has had the disease of abstract thought
so long 'and my early Education was so undomestic, that I
know not how to get rid of it; or even to wish to get rid of it'.
And he uses the effects of opium as an illustration of his meaning.
'Life were so flat a thing without Enthusiasm—that if for a

Coleridge, from a portrait by James Northcote, 1804

moment it leave me, I have a sort of stomach-sensation attached to all my Thoughts, like those which succeed to the pleasurable operation of a dose of Opium. *Now* I make up my mind to a sort of heroism in believing the progressiveness of all nature, during the present melancholy state of Humanity—'.

On the same kind of subject, he tells Godwin in 1802 that 'partly from ill-health and partly from an unhealthy and reverie-like vividness of *Thoughts* and (pardon the pedantry of the phrase) a diminished Impressibility from *Things*, my ideas, wishes and feelings are to a diseased degree disconnected from *emotion and action*. In plain and natural English, I am a dreaming, and therefore an indolent man—I am a Starling self-incaged and always in the Moult, and my whole Note is, Tomorrow, and tomorrow, and tomorrow.' The causes that have robbed him of will-power have also taken away his power to resist 'Impulses from without'. He is, he says, 'as an *acting* man, a creature of mere Impact. "I will," and "I will not" are phrases, both of them equally, of rare occurrence in my dictionary.'

He even began to construct a theory of the nature of evil and original sin from his observation of the effects of his physical discomforts on his own will-power. The will and the under-standing working together, the equivalence of conscience and consciousness were his ideal, and it was in his own complete helplessness under the stream of delirious images and fantasies created in his consciousness by illness and opium that he glimpsed the workings of something which might be really hostile to philosophy and morality. In 1803 he wrote in a note-book

> I will at least make the attempt to explain to myself the Origin of moral Evil from the *streamy* Nature of Association, which Thinking = Reason curbs and rudders/how this comes to be so difficult/Do not the bad Passions in Dreams throw light and shew of proof upon this Hypothesis?—Explain those bad Passions: and I shall gain Light, I am sure . . .

The innocent sleep of children may contradict the theory that simple passive consciousness and random association offer the point of entry for evil and corruption—'but what is the height, and ideal of mere association?—Delirium.—But how far is this state produced by Pain and Denaturalization? And what are these?—In short, as far as I can see anything in this Total Mist, Vice is imperfect yet existing Volition, giving diseased Currents of association because it yields on all sides and *yet* is—So think of Madness.'

In 1800 he had already touched on the theme of the distortion of consciousness and conscience through pain in a letter to his friend Humphry Davy, the scientist, which shows his typical precise curiosity about the *nature* of his experience:

> Did Carlisle ever communicate to you, or has he in any way pub-lished, his facts concerning *Pain*, which he mentioned when we were with him? It is a subject which *exceedingly interests* me—I want to read something by somebody expressly on *Pain*, if only to give an arrangement to my own thoughts, though if it were well treated I have little doubt it would revolutionize them—
>
> For the last month I have been tumbling on through sands and swamps of Evil and bodily grievance. My eyes have been inflamed to a degree, that rendered reading and writing scarcely possible: and strange as it seems, the act of poetic composition as I lay in bed, perceptibly affected them, and my voluntary ideas were every minute passing, more or less transformed into vivid spectra. I had leaches repeatedly applied to my Temples, and a Blister behind my ear—and my eyes are now my own but in the place where the Blister was, six small but excruciating Boils have appeared, and harrass me almost beyond endurance.

Love too, like evil, is to be defined within the distinction between acts of will and random acts of fantasy, day-dream, sensual preference:

> Love, however sudden, as when we fall in love at first sight (which is, perhaps, always the case of love in its highest sense) is yet an act of the will, and that too one of its primary and therefore in-effaceable acts. This is most important; for if it be not true, either love itself is all a romantic *hum*, or mere connection of desire with a form appropriated to excite and gratify it, or the mere repetition of a daydream.

If love is not an act of the will

> I know not how we could attach blame and immorality to in-
> constancy, when confined to the affections and a sense of preference.
> Either therefore we must brutalize our notions with Pope:—
>   Lust, through some certain strainers well refined
>   Is gentle love and charms all woman-kind:
> Or we must dissolve and thaw away all bonds of morality by the
> irresistible shocks of an irresistible sensibility with Sterne.

Coleridge himself was, in fact, trapped by the conflict between
his own morality and his own experience. In 1801 he wrote to
Poole that he believed 'that deep Thinking is attainable only by
a man of deep Feeling' and declared that the souls of five hundred
Sir Isaac Newtons would go to the making up of a Shakespeare
or a Milton—because in Newton's materialist system *the mind
was passive*—'a lazy Looker-on, in an external world'. Coleridge
was afraid of the passive mind, increasingly connected in his own
view as it was with hallucination and evil, far from the ratiocination
of materialist philosophy—mind for him was 'made in God's
image—the Image of the *Creator*'.

But his own thoughts and feelings could not be connected and
unified. He could not afford, morally, to pay them attention.
In a spate of private letters in 1802 he quotes the famous lines of
Dejection which were not published in the first version of the
poem, but only later, in 1817:

> For not to think of what I needs must feel,
> But to be still and patient, all I can;
> And haply by abstruse research to steal
> From my own nature all the natural man—
> This was my sole resource, my only plan:
> Till that which suits a part infects the whole
> And now is almost grown the habit of my soul.

Coleridge quotes these lines again and again in terms of his
domestic misery—'Ill-tempered speeches sent after me when I
went out of the house, ill-tempered speeches on my return, my
friends received with freezing looks, the least opposition or con-

tradiction occasioning screams of passion—'. But his misery over Sara Hutchinson—the effort he made to turn his reflections on love, desire, sensuality, into abstractions, to keep the relationship Platonic, so that no 'natural man' should corrupt it—this probably told on him much more, as it was much more what he needs must feel but cannot afford to 'think' about. So, as he says of himself in *Biographia Literaria* 'I relapsed into the same mental disease . . . I sought a refuge from bodily pain and mismanaged sensibility in abstruse researches which exercised the strength and subtlety of the understanding without awakening the feelings of the heart.'

Critics who emphasize that Coleridge's philosophical researches are not necessarily an inferior or less valuable mode of thought than his poetic ones are right. But that Coleridge was afraid of the state of mind in which he was capable of endless distant abstract generalization and yet of no action—even if he was also endlessly able to generalize and abstract this very fear—is indisputable. It works on various levels.

At the simplest level it is comic. His nephew, Henry Nelson Coleridge, records him saying 'I have the perception of individual images very strong, but a dim one of the relation of place. I remember the man or the tree, but where I saw them I mostly forget.' His nephew adds a note that there was no man whose opinion of morals or *general* conduct in life he himself would sooner adopt. 'But I would not take him as a guide through streets or fields or earthly roads. He had much of the geometrician about him; but he could not find his way.'

His lack of relation to 'earthly roads', his incapacity to find his way, he also saw in one of his deeper Shakespearean insights:

Hamlet's character is the prevalence of the abstracting and generalizing habit over the practical. He does not want courage, skill, will or opportunity; but every incident sets him thinking; and it is curious, and at the same time strictly natural, that Hamlet, who all the play seems reason itself, should be impelled, at last, by mere accident to effect his object. I have a smack of Hamlet myself, if I may say so.

But beneath his personal problems, his own conflict between thought and feeling, capacity and incapacity to use will and consciousness in meaningful action, lay his preoccupation with wholeness, with the life that seemed to him to unify and pervade all things. And when he and the outside world were in a state of calm his curiosity about the 'feelings' of pain and grief, which could lead to random evil motions of the will, turned in the opposite direction. In poetry and religion a man of deep thought and deep feeling *could* discern meaning and action everywhere: it was negative thought, the human need to be passive, the limitations of consciousness, that produced the sense of death:

> On this calm morning of the 13th of November 1809, it occurs to me, that it is by a negation and voluntary act of no thinking that we think of earth, air, water etc. as dead. It is necessary for our limited powers of consciousness, that we should be brought to this negative state, and that this state should pass into custom; but it is likewise necessary that at times we should awake and step forward; and this is effected by those extenders of our consciousness—sorrow, sickness, poetry and religion. The truth is, we stop in the sense of life just when we are not forced to go on, and then adopt a permission of our feelings for a precept of our reason.

Wordsworth, during the period immediately preceding the quarrel between the friends, was apparently both much more self-confident and much more self-contained. He wrote much upon the theme of Duty, and accepted himself the duty and devotion of the three women of his household. Coleridge, however, wrote, arguably rightly, 'My many weaknesses are of some advantage to me; they unite me more with the great mass of my fellow-beings—but dear Wordsworth appears to me to have hurtfully segregated and isolated his being. Doubtless his delights are more deep and sublime; but he has likewise more hours that prey upon the flesh and blood.' And he saw Wordsworth's personal isolation reflected in his poetry: Wordsworth, like Goethe he said, had 'this peculiarity of utter non-sympathy with the subjects of . . . poetry. They are always, both of them, spectators *ab extra*—feeling *for*, but never *with*, their characters.' There is some truth in this judgment, if not a complete truth. It can be related to Coleridge's view that Wordsworth was 'by nature incapable of being in Love, tho' no man more tenderly attached— hence he ridicules the existence of any other passion, than a compound of Lust with Esteem and Friendship, confined to one Object, first by accidents of Association, and permanently, by the force of Habit and a sense of Duty. Now this will do very well— it will suffice to make a good Husband—it may even be desirable ... that we should have this and no more—but still it is not *Love*—and there is such a passion as Love—which is no more a compound, than Oxygen.'

If Coleridge at this time was distressed by the remoteness from life imposed on him by 'bodily pain and mismanaged sensibility', Wordsworth was building up, in his isolated being, a self-contained poetic 'self' which was to develop into a seer and judge of mankind. His great autobiographical poem, *The Prelude*, usually referred to in his life-time as the *Poem on his own Life*, describes the knitting together of this self from the experience of his childhood and youth, and his conscious organization and acceptance of it. It describes the development of what Keats, in a brilliant phrase called 'the egotistical sublime', although Keats had not read *The Prelude*, which was published after Wordsworth's death. In the beginning this egotism provided a healthy and outgoing energy and curiosity that enabled Wordsworth to do something analogous to, if not the same as, what Coleridge aspired to and missed, the unification of thought and feeling and the sense of life in the world beyond the self. Wordsworth himself was worried by the apparent egotism of the undertaking: he wrote to his friend and patron, Sir George Beaumont, explaining his purpose:

It will not be much less than 9,000 lines, not hundred but thousand lines, long; an alarming length! and a thing unprecedented in Literary History that a man should talk so much about himself. It is not self-conceit, as you will know well, that has induced me to do this, but real humility; I began the work because I was un-prepared to treat any more arduous subject and diffident of my own powers. Here at least I hoped that to a certain degree I should be sure of succeeding, as I had nothing to do but describe what I had felt and thought, therefore could not easily be bewildered.

In the poem on his own life the self-absorption is greedy, curious and creative. His early miseries are wound up in his better self:

> Dust as we are, the immortal spirit grows
> Like harmony in music; there is a dark
> Inscrutable workmanship that reconciles
> Discordant elements, makes them cling together
> In one society. How strange that all
> The terrors, pains and early miseries,
> Regrets, vexations, lassitudes interfused
> Within my mind, should e'er have borne a part
> And that a needful part in making up
> The calm existence that is mine when I
> Am worthy of myself.

But the 'better self' whose creation was marked by the *Poem on his Own Life* contained dangerous elements. The hopeful arrogance of the early letters, the determination to be an extraordinary man, produced some great poetry, and an Olympian 'stance' which is sometimes moving and sometimes maddening. Words-worth writes to Sir George Beaumont about Sir Joshua Reynolds in a high patronizing tone. Reynolds, 'a Man with such a high sense of the *dignity* of his Art', should have paid more attention to the '*nobler* departments of painting' not only because his paintings might have been better but because a great man must set a good example. A man of genius, he says, clearly thinking of Wordsworth as much as of Reynolds, should, 'regardless of temporary gains whether of money or praise', fix his attention 'solely upon what is intrinsically interesting and permanent'. His concluding sentence puts this laudable view about external values slightly differently. Reynolds could have given an example 'of a man preferring the cultivation and exertion of his own powers in the highest possible degree to any other object of regard'. In some way the egotistical sublime, the cultivation of one's *own*

Sir George Beaumont (1753–1827), Wordsworth's friend and patron, from a portrait by G. Dance, 1807

powers, has become equated with 'what is intrinsically interesting and permanent'. This is a common Romantic theme and the consciousness and work of the artist becomes the intrinsic and permanent value of the poetry of the period for reasons outside the scope of this book, and its power can be felt in Coleridge's exaltation of the Creative mind in man and the universe—but it puts a great strain on the character of the individual artist. Wordsworth inevitably became his own isolated sense of the source of value, morality and truth. Crabb Robinson's record of his first meeting with him makes this clear.

He said he thought of writing an Essay 'Why bad poetry pleases'. He never wrote it—a loss to our literature. He said He could not respect the Mother who could read without emotion his poem 'Once in a lonely hamlet I sojourned' . . . He wished popularity for his 'Two voices are there: one is of the Sea' as a test of elevation and moral purity.

Crabb Robinson added

At the end of 40 years since this introduction my admiration and love of this great man is unabated, aye, enhanced.

One's own feelings for this 'great man' aspect of Wordsworth are more mixed. When he says of himself that·

> verse was what he had been wedded to;
> And his own mind did like a tempest strong
> Come to him thus and drove the weary Wight along.

his driven purpose is admirable. And in a sonnet on the evening star the solitary ambition has its splendour, and its candour.

> O most ambitious Star! an inquest wrought
> Within me when I recognised thy light;
> A moment I was startled at the sight:
> And while I gazed, there came to me a thought
> That I might step beyond my natural race
> As thou now seem'st to do; might one day trace
> Some ground not mine—

But in the poems of the later Wordsworth—the *Ecclesiastical Sonnets*, many poems about monasteries in *Memorials of a Tour in Italy 1837*, one or two of the Duddon poems, and even the *White Doe of Rylstone* which he admired himself and defended so fervently—one is struck by a kind of ferocious monastic piety which seems to have overtaken Wordsworth in his inferior poetry. The theme is in another sense a man's retreat into himself: Wordsworth's symbol for the solitary man alone with Nature becomes increasingly the voluntarily confined ascetic in the chosen cell. He can still describe the activity of this man as the exercise of 'natural sympathies' and Keats could still have called it the egotistical sublime. But something is missing—the note becomes increasingly one of conceit, rather than one of self-confidence, and it strikes one that the self Wordsworth is contemplating and praising is increasingly not the creating mind but the created reputation, not energy but responsibility and moral truth. There is an irony in the fact that as he increasingly preaches humility and patience he sounds increasingly remote, arrogant, self-absorbed and self-praising—it is as though he knew that guilt and sorrow were once potent creative forces and is seeking to re-establish them within the conventional framework of official self-chastisement. Only occasionally does the poet admit that this isolation is terrifying. It appears obliquely in his (to me) appalling sonnets on Capital Punishment, when he argues that the terror of the man doomed to lasting solitary confinement is worse than the terror of death. And one poem, composed significantly fairly early, *The Small Celandine*, expresses a much more candid and desperate view of the isolation of age. The poet has seen the celandine, he says, often

> muffled up from harm
> In close self-shelter, like a Thing at rest.

But now it is old and open to storms.

> I stopped, and said with inly-muttered voice
> 'It doth not love the shower, nor seek the cold:
> This neither is its courage nor its choice
> But its necessity in being old.
>
> The sunshine may not cheer it, nor the dew;
> It cannot help itself in its decay;
> Stiff in its members, withered, changed of hue.'
> And in my spleen I smiled that it was grey.

The quarrel between the two poets brewed slowly. Coleridge's very admiration for Wordsworth provided grounds for later differences. He wrote in the early days about the essential happiness of Wordsworth's family—'that it is *I* rather than another, is almost an Accident: but being so very happy within themselves they are too good, not the more for that very reason to want a Friend and common Object of Love out of their Household'. In 1800 he wrote to Poole with truthful enthusiasm, when Poole suggested he abased himself too much before his friend for his own good:

> ... You charge me with prostration in regard to Wordsworth. Have I affirmed anything miraculous of W? Is it impossible that a greater poet than any since Milton may appear in our days? Have any *great* poets appeared since him? ... Future greatness! Is it not an awful thing my dearest Poole? What if you had known Milton at the age of thirty and believed all you now know of him?— What if you should meet in the letters of any then living man, expressions concerning the young Milton *totidem verbis* the same as mine of Wordsworth, would it not convey to you a most delicious sensation? Would it not be an assurance to you that your admiration of the *Paradise Lost* was no superstition, no shadow of flesh and bloodless abstraction, but that the *Man* was even so, that the greatness was incarnate and personal?

He felt admiration, and wistful envy too for Wordsworth's '*practical* Faith', which he himself found so difficult to share, 'that we can do but one thing well, and that therefore we must make a choice . . .'.

But by 1807, desperate with opium and with love for Asra, he was growing jealous of Wordsworth. He wrote in his notebook

> It is not the W's knowledge of my frailties that prevents my *entire* love of them. No! it is their ignorance of the deep place of my being. . . . O agony! O cruel! is he not beloved, adored by two— and two such beings, and must I not be beloved *near* him except as a satellite? . . . W is greater, better, manlier, more dear, by nature to woman than I—I—miserable I!—but does he—O no! no! no! no! he does not—he does not pretend, he does not wish, to love you as I love you. . . .

More coldly, he criticized the effect of Wordsworth's domestic life on his poetry and morals. Wordsworth was

> living wholly among *devotees*, having every the minutest thing, almost his very eating and drinking done for him by his sister or wife—and I trembled, lest a film should rise and thicken on his

moral eye. The habit, too, of writing such a multitude of small poems was in this instance hurtful to him. . . .

Wordsworth had always patronized Coleridge, which had suited Coleridge. But now, when Coleridge was beginning to understand that medical restraint was necessary to cope with his addiction, Wordsworth preached his own bracing morality of self-contained self-control, duty, resolution and independence:

> One thing is obvious, that health of mind, that is, resolution, self-denial and well-regulated conditions of feeling are what you must depend on; . . . Doctors can do you little good and that Doctors' stuff has been one of your greatest curses; and of course, ours through you. You must know . . . better than any surgeon . . . What is to do you good . . . . Do not look out of yourself for that stay which can only be found within.

Coleridge accused him of keeping Sara Hutchinson from him: Wordsworth exculpated himself with dignity, telling Coleridge (with much truth) that he was 'a man in a lamentably insane state of mind'.

Sara Hutchinson left, exhausted: Coleridge finally arranged to travel to London, in 1810, and the quarrel broke. Coleridge was travelling with a certain Basil Montague who wanted him to stay with him: Wordsworth warned Montague of Coleridge's unpleasant habits: and Montague in London repeated the whole warning to Coleridge, who reacted as violently as the complexity and intensity of his worship and dependence and jealousy in regard to Wordsworth would lead one to expect. The Wordsworths tried to ignore his distress but he persisted in it, and would not come north again. In 1811 Dorothy wrote indignantly to a friend

> I do not think he *can* resolve to come if he does not at the same time lay aside his displeasure again William. Surely this one act of his mind out does all the rest.
> William for the most benevolent purposes communicated to a friend a small part of what was known to the whole town of Penrith —sneered and laughed at there, to our great mortification . . .

and William is therefore treacherous!!! He does not *deny* the truth of what William said but William ought not to have said it. . . .

William bears all with calm dignity, neither justifying himself nor complaining of C. . . .

When Coleridge did, in 1812, go to Grasmere, he went past the Wordsworths' house without calling. He was still in a state of great distress and wrote to a friend that Dorothy had 'expressed her confident hope, that I should come to them at once!! I, who for years past had been an ABSOLUTE NUISANCE in the family.' (Wordsworth admitted the use to Montague of the term 'absolute nuisance'—one of his favourite expressions.) A reconciliation was finally arranged, and years later the two poets toured in Germany with Wordsworth's daughter Dora—but the old intimacy was over for ever. Coleridge had admired too much and was too hurt. He wrote—'the *Feeling*, which I had previous to that moment, when the 3/4th Calumny burst like a Thunderstorm from a blue sky on my Soul—after 15 years of such religious, almost super-stitious Idolatry and Self-Sacrifice—O no! no! that I fear, never can return.'

The literary effects of the quarrel were better for Coleridge than for Wordsworth if only because the friendship had been slowly decreasing Coleridge's belief in his own gifts. He had never seen himself primarily as a poet—certainly not as one rivalling Wordsworth. In 1800 he was writing that his literary pursuits were the Northern languages, Slavonic, Gothic, Celtic for amuse-ment and for serious work the investigation of the laws relating human feelings, ideas, and words. 'As to poetry I have altogether abandoned it, being convinced that I never had the essentials of poetic Genius and that I mistook a strong desire for original power.' It was in 1800 that Wordsworth decided to exclude Coleridge's unfinished *Christabel* from the second edition of the *Lyrical Ballads*. At the time Coleridge accepted the judgment—he wrote that 'the poem was in direct opposition to the very purpose for which the *Lyrical Ballads* were published—viz.—an experiment to see how far those passions, which alone give any value to extraordinary Incidents, were capable of interesting, in and for themselves, in

the incidents of common Life.' And in the same letter, to Humphry
Davy, he hastens to add that 'I would rather have written Ruth
and Nature's Lady than a million such poems/but why do I
calumniate my own spirit by saying, I would rather—God
knows—it is as delightful to me that they *are* written—I *know*
that at present (and I *hope*, that it *will* be so) my mind has discip-
lined itself into a willing exertion of its powers without any
reference to their *comparative* value—'.

This is Coleridge over-persuading himself, abasing himself
before Wordsworth—the emphases and the cautious parenthesis
prove it. By 1801 in a letter to Godwin, his distress about his
poetry has itself a real poetry, like that of the *Dejection* Ode:

> You would not know me—! all sounds of similitude keep at such a
> distance from each other in my mind, that I have *forgotten* how to
> make a rhyme—I look at the Mountains (that visible God Almighty
> that looks in at all my windows) I look at the Mountains only for
> the Curves of their outlines; the Stars, as I behold them, form
> themselves into Triangles—and my hands are scarred with scratches
> from a Cat whose back I was rubbing in the Dark in order to see
> whether the sparks from it were refrangible by a Prism. The Poet
> is dead in me—my imagination (or rather the Somewhat that had
> been imaginative) lies, like a Cold Snuff on the circular Rim of a
> Brass Candle-stick, without even a stink of Tallow to remind you
> that it was once cloathed and mitred with Flame. . . .
>
> If I die, and the Booksellers will give you anything for my Life,
> be sure to say—'Wordsworth descended on him like the γνῶθι
> σεαυτόν [know thyself] from Heaven; by shewing to him what
> true Poetry was, he made him know, that he himself was no Poet.'

Not only did Wordsworth insist on the exclusion of the *Christabel*:
he wrote an ungracious prefatory note on the deficiencies of the
Ancient Mariner, which was published in the 1800 edition of the
Lyrical Ballads, although, partly because it aroused a critical fury
in Charles Lamb, who wrote a very intelligent condemnation of
the note to Wordsworth, it was omitted subsequently.

Coleridge had given up his work in order to help Wordsworth with the laborious preparation of Wordsworth's poems for the
press for this 1800 edition. He felt betrayed, but could only as a

Coleridge in later life

The house at Highgate in which Coleridge spent his last years; he occupied the attic room on the right

poet admit the betrayal much later, when in 1818 he began to speak of his own great poems, *Kubla Khan*, the *Ancient Mariner*, *Christabel*, as perhaps a different kind of poetry, one not subsumed in the Wordsworthian definition he quoted at the time. He talked of the Wordsworths' 'cold praise and effective discouragement of every attempt of mine to roll onward in a distinct current of my own—'. And in his later years in Highgate Coleridge became accustomed to reciting these coldly praised poems with enthusiasm, and delivering long speeches on their significance. Lamb records, with admiration, his recitation of *Christabel*, and adds

> But more peculiar in its beauty than this, was his recitation of Kubla Khan. As he repeated the passage
>> A damsel with a dulcimer
>> In a vision once I saw:
>> It was an Abyssinian maid,
>> And on her dulcimer she played
>> Singing of Mount Abora!

his voice seemed to mount, and melt into air as the images grew more visionary and the suggested associations more remote. He usually met opposition by conceding the point to the objector, and then went on with his high argument as if it had never been raised: thus satisfying his antagonist, himself, and all who heard him; none of whom desired to hear his discourse frittered into points or displaced by the near encounter even of the most brilliant wits.

Wordsworth without Coleridge continued self-sufficient; but work on *The Recluse*, that grand philosophical poem on human nature, dragged unproductively—partly perhaps because without Coleridge's sharp, fluid organizing intellect the inspiration for the grand scale was lacking. Although if we read the grandiose plan Coleridge laid out for the work he thought Wordsworth (he himself was naturally incapable, but to Wordsworth all things were possible) should write, it is questionable whether *either* of them had or could have had, any real idea of what the poem should be. In 1814 Wordsworth published *The Excursion*, intended as part of *The Recluse* and very much informed by the recluse's monastic habit of mind and imagery, although it contained the beautiful *Ruined Cottage*. In 1817 Coleridge, partly revitalized by the regular Highgate regime, published his *Biographia Literaria*. He had written in his notebooks

> Seem to have made up my mind to write my metaphysical works as my Life and *in my* Life—intermixed with all the other events or history of the mind of S. T. Coleridge.

The *Biographia*, incomplete though it is, and difficult to follow, with many of its major statements tucked away in footnotes, is one of the central critical documents of our literature, and it is the inclusion of Coleridge's assessment of Wordsworth's poems, including the largely maligned *Excursion** which helps to make it so. He said that he intended to establish Wordsworth's greatness by writing a balanced account of the characteristic merits *and* defects of his poetry, and essentially this is what he did. But the passages on Wordsworth have other meanings within the literary biographies of both poets. Coleridge, by writing a personal

* See below, Chapter 6, for hostile reviews.

account of the inception of the *Lyrical Ballads* and his own part in them, and by writing a balanced, distanced judgment of Wordsworth's *kind* of poetry, detached himself from the over-close, or biased judgments; it gave the work a critical edge and insight that is still largely unequalled, and a certain personal wit that is still amusing. Wordsworth, at that stage of his life wincing from every criticism, and mistrusting Coleridge's motives as well as despising his weakness and his social involvement, was not grateful for the work. As Coleridge had prophesied, he refused to do more than skim the book, and found 'the praise extravagant and the censure inconsiderate'. But it did much to establish his reputation as a major writer during his life-time, and it was the establishment of the reputation that made him able at last to relax a little. Coleridge was aware of this, too, and by 1819 was able to defend Wordsworth's egotism with detached and truthful generosity. Speaking of a parody of Wordsworth, the *True Simon Pure*, he conceded that it was funny and added

> The writer however ought (as a man, I mean) to recollect, that Mr Wordsworth for full 16 years had been assailed, weekly, monthly and quarterly, with every species of wanton detraction and contempt . . . that during all these years Mr Wordsworth made no answer, displayed no resentment—and lastly, that from Cicero to Luther, Giordano Bruno, Milton, Dryden, Wolfe, John Brown, etc. etc. I know but *one* instance (that of Benedict Spinoza) of a man of great Genius and *original* Mind who on those very accounts had been abused, misunderstood, decried and . . . persecuted, who has not been worried at last into a semblance of egotism.

Coleridge's criticism of Wordsworth's poems in the *Biographia* reflects the relationship between the men: the habit of joint detailed commentary on each other's work, the knowledge of character and habits of mind. The following quotation illustrates both Coleridge's shrewdness and psychological accuracy, and his need to reject the Wordsworthian ideal of poetry as the presentation of 'passions, in and for themselves in the incidents of common Life' which he had capitulated to over the rejection of *Christabel*. He is in fact distinguishing between

Wordsworth's personal need to see the strong, self-contained mind as the creator of its own values and the general modes of writing and reading great poetry—which requires a literate and thoughtful public and a poet who knows how to communicate with other minds and needs to do it:

> Who is not at once delighted and improved when the *poet* Wordsworth himself exclaims,
>> O many are the poets that are sown
>> By nature; men endowed with highest gifts,
>> The vision and the faculty divine,
>> Yet wanting the accomplishment of verse,
>> Nor having e'er as life advanced, been led
>> By circumstance to take unto the height
>> The measure of themselves, those favoured beings,
>> All but a scattered few, live out their time,
>> Husbanding that which they possess within,
>> And go to the grave unthought of. Strongest minds
>> Are often those of whom the noisy world
>> Hears least. (*Excursion,* I)
>
> To use a colloquial phrase, such sentiments, in such language, do one's heart good; though I for my part have not the fullest faith in the *truth* of the observation. On the contrary, I believe the instances to be exceedingly rare; and should feel almost as strong an objection to introduce such a character in a poetic fiction, as a pair of black swans on a lake, in a fancy landscape.

And with the great *Immortality* Ode, which had stimulated him into writing *Dejection* he was equally sharp, criticizing Wordsworth's image of the child as the 'Best Philosopher', as the 'deaf and silent' eye reading the eternal deep by asking 'In what sense can the magnificent attributes above quoted be appropriated to a child, which would not make them equally suitable to a bee, or a dog, or a field of corn; or even to a ship, or to the wind and waves that propel it? The omnipresent spirit works equally in them as in the child; and the child is equally unconscious of it as they.'

He goes on to quote four lines which Wordsworth later omitted, and to criticize them on the grounds that children brought up in Christian families do *not* see death in this way, but more conventionally, as sleep—and if they do not, would be terrified of 'the frightful notion of lying awake in the grave'.

The disputed passage speaks of children

> To whom the grave
> Is but a lonely bed without the sense or sight
> Of day or the warm light,
> A place of thought where we in waiting lie.

Coleridge's criticism is apt at the level he is working on. But the passage reminds me, at least, irresistibly, of Wordsworth's later prevalent image of the monastic cell—the spirit retired into itself and its own thought. And Wordsworth's use of this image in this poem brings back the ideas about the human imagination, sensual reality, the unity of both, about which both poets continued to think, and about which their ideas were forever profoundly influenced by each other. Both had had a sense of the world and their minds as united parts of 'an omnipresent Spirit': both wrote most movingly of the gulf between that sense and the opposing sense that they, or the world, or both, were dead, lifeless, disconnected. Wordsworth's biographer tells us that Wordsworth said the *Immortality* ode was based on two recollections—'a splendour in the objects of sense which is passed away' and 'an indisposition to bend to the law of death as applying in our own case'. Far from regarding these intimations as fanciful, he hailed them as the most precious experiences his life had afforded him. And with them he valued something akin to them—the sense of the immateriality of all objects; that state in which everything he saw seemed inherent in himself, 'a prospect in the mind', dreamlike in vividness and solemnity. His song of praise was for 'those obstinate questionings. Of sense and outward things / Fallings from us, vanishings'.

It is in terms of the Ode's sense that as 'a prospect in the mind' sensual things had had 'the glory and the freshness of a dream' that Wordsworth's image even of the solitary confinement of the cell, of the grave as *only* 'a place of thought where we in waiting lie'—not death, not final, but only wisely passive thought—is both moving and appropriate. There is no light or warmth, but there is still the connection to Nature and the spirit of life that the later cell images more fumblingly insist on, and the celandine poem contradicts. Wordsworth also described the withdrawal of this sense of unity. In the *Elegiac Stanzas* on Peele Castle, he explains that once he *would* have painted this storm-beaten castle with 'the light that never was, on sea or land', the 'gleam', the 'Poet's dream' with 'no motion but the moving tide, a breeze/ Or merely silent Nature's breathing life'. This would have seemed 'the soul of truth in every part/A steadfast peace that might not be betray'd'. And then, thinking of his encounter with real death, in the tragic drowning of his brother, John:

> So once it would have been—'tis so no more;
> I have submitted to a new control:
> A power is gone, which nothing can restore;
> A deep distress hath humanized my Soul.

Coleridge's sense of the gulf between life and death was different but analogous. Coleridge, the tortured, the expansive, the believer that the body's pains clogged the immortal spirit feared death less than the essentially pagan Wordsworth, whom Blake called 'the natural man rising up against the spiritual'. Indeed, in his moments of despair and weakness he genuinely desired it, seeing it not as solitary confinement but as expansion into the infinite. Very early he wrote to a friend

> I can *at times* feel strongly the beauties you describe, in themselves and for themselves—but more frequently *all things* appear little— all the knowledge that can be acquired, child's play—the universe itself—what but an immense heap of *little* things?—I can con- template nothing but parts, and parts are all *little*. My mind feels as if it ached to behold and know something *great*,—something *one and indivisible*—and it is only in the faith of this that rocks or waterfalls, mountains or caverns, give me the sense of sublimity or majesty. But in this faith *all things* counterfeit infinity!—'Struck with the deepest calm of Joy I stood
>> Silent with swimming sense; and gazing round
>> On the wide Landscape gaze till all doth seem
>> Less gross than bodily, a living Thing

> Which acts upon the mind, and with such Hues
> As cloath th' Almighty Spirit, when he makes
> Spirits perceive his presence.'—

It is but seldom that I raise and spiritualize my intellect to this height—and at other times I adopt the Brahmin Creed, and say— It is better to sit than to stand, it is better to lie than to sit, it is better to sleep than to wake—but Death is the best of all!

Here too is the sense that the intermittent vision of all things as a 'prospect in the mind' gives meaning to all things. The *Dejection* ode describes Coleridge's opposing vision of the universe of death.

The dying Coleridge is still speculating about the reality of experience, but by now his early sense of visioned unity has been transferred to the spiritual truths of Christianity—both Wordsworth and Coleridge turned to the Church, but whereas Wordsworth needed a cell, a refuge, an outside assurance beyond the bodily failure he experienced, Coleridge took to theology and mysticism in the same way, and with the same needs, as he had taken to artistic vision. Two weeks before his death, he brought his theme together:

> I am dying, but without expectation of a speedy release. Is it not strange that very recently bygone images, and scenes of early life, have stolen into my mind, like breezes blown from the spice-islands of Youth and Hope—those twin realities of this phantom world! I do not add Love—for what is Love but Youth and Hope embracing, and so seen as *one*? I say *realities*; for reality is a thing of degrees, from the Iliad to a dream . . . Yet in a strict sense reality is not predictable at all of aught below Heaven.

And so he wished he had been spared to complete that elusive description of *this* reality,—'my Philosophy'. 'But *visum aliter Deo*, and his will be done.'

Coleridge died in 1834: Wordsworth lived on, outlived by Dorothy (feeble-minded for many years) until 1850. His references to Coleridge towards the end of Coleridge's life already sound with his eternal valuation of him, rather than their temporary differences or imperfections. In 1832 he wrote 'he and my beloved sister are the two beings to whom my intellect is most indebted, and they are now proceeding, as it were, *pari passu,* along the path of sickness . . .'. At his death he wrote to Coleridge's nephew 'though I have seen little of him for the last twenty years, his mind has been habitually present with me, with an accompanying feeling that he was still in the flesh. That frail tie is broken . . .'.

And in 1835 the thought of death, and the death of Coleridge, aroused one of his few great late poems, the *Extempore Effusion on the Death of James Hogg*:

> Nor has the rolling year twice measured,
> From sign to sign its steadfast course,
> Since every mortal power of Coleridge
> Was frozen at its marvellous source;
>
> The rapt One, of the godlike forehead,
> The heaven eyed creature sleeps in earth:
> And Lamb, the frolic and the gentle,
> Has vanished from his lonely hearth.
>
> Like clouds that rake the mountain summits,
> Or waves that own no curbing hand,
> How fast has brother followed brother,
> From sunshine to the sunless land.

The images of the *Immortality* ode and *Elegiac Stanzas* appear in a grimmer context: clouds and waves, once, in their movements symbolic of the life that moved in all things, are now wild and lawless, 'raking' the mountains, uncurbed. Sunlight and the sunless land stand in unqualified contrast to each other, light and dark, life and death—and Wordsworth's own life, like London, partakes of death:

> Our haughty life is crowned with darkness,
> Like London with its own black wreath,
> On which with thee, O Crabbe! forth looking
> I gazed from Hampstead's breezy heath.

Dorothy Wordsworth (1771–1855), from a painting by Samuel
Crosthwaite, 1833

Wordsworth musing on Helvellyn, from a painting by
Benjamin Haydon, 1842

They were great men, and both had an unusually powerful grasp on the relationship of the various aspects of life and nature. I have gone into their ideas and their relationship at such length because to an unusual extent their social beliefs, their political theory, their theories of art and landscape are related to each other and to their fundamental ideas, consciously and in a complex way. The power of their minds still impresses us as strongly as in the days when Lamb wrote, only half-joking, about Coleridge having come to live near him:

> I think his essentials not touched: he is very bad; but then he wonderfully picks up another day, and his face, when he repeats his verses, hath its ancient glory; an archangel a little damaged. ... Tis enough to be within the whiff and wind of his genius for us not to possess our souls in quiet. If I lived with him, or the Author of the *Excursion*, I should, in a very little time, lose my own identity and be dragged along in the current of other people's thoughts, hampered in a net.

2 *Daily Life*

In a time when English domestic architecture and English social life were reaching an elegance and a graceful formality not since equalled, the Wordsworths and Coleridge, constrained partly by poverty and partly by inclination and idealism, lived most of their lives extraordinarily simply. Coleridge at Nether Stowey, and the Wordsworths in Dove Cottage and in their later, larger houses at Allan Bank and Rydal Mount tried to live the simple life—Wordsworth influenced by his own stringent plainness on all fronts, Coleridge more by Rousseauistic idealism and the desire to live close to Nature, indulge in manual labour and grow all his own food. There is a letter written to Cottle two days after his marriage with a detailed and gay list of the 'necessities' still required—riddle slice, candle box, two ventilators, candlesticks, glasses, spoons, tea-kettle, dustpan. He did grow vegetables, and raise pigs and poultry, as the Wordsworths did—their letters and journals are full of loving references to their crops of green beans. When they moved to Allan Bank in 1808 they found it very expensive—coal had to be carried a long way and was dear, and the enormous number of visitors and children made at least two servants necessary. Dorothy was in a state of constant domestic distress, increased by intolerably smoky chimneys—the newly washed dishes, the 'chairs, carpets, the painted ledges of the rooms require endless cleaning and are never clean . . . We are regularly 13 in family and on Saturdays and Sundays [when Coleridge's sons came] 15.' They kept a cow and two pigs and baked all their bread—the cook had to fodder the cow. The enthusiastically frugal Coleridge nevertheless caused trouble by extravagance—one of the servants remembered him as 'a plague' because he wanted roast potatoes and cold meat for supper whilst the Wordsworths never took anything but small basins of new milk from their cow and a loaf of bread.

When they moved to Rydal Mount Dorothy was a little

Above Dove Cottage, from a painting of *c.* 1805
Below Coleridge's cottage at Nether Stowey

defensive about their having 'a *Turkey*!!! carpet in the dining-room and a *Brussels* in William's study. You stare, and the simpli-city of the dear Town End cottage comes before your eyes and you are tempted to say "Are they changed, are they setting up for fine Folks? for making parties, giving Dinners etc. etc."' But they were still frugal, and all had a good time at an auction sale, where they bought 'a stock of Decanters—some glasses—a dozen knives—2 pillows' and 'the beds were sold by candlelight and we all walked home in the bright moonshine, I with a water decanter and Glass in my hand—and William and Mary with a large looking glass—oval with a gilt frame—very cheap £1/13/-.' Even Wordsworth executed domestic commissions—once he bought some curtains, a 'sort of sofa', a meat safe and 'another writing desk' at a sale and in 1833 is buying a new kind of mat—'though I fear you won't like it, it is of a Cocoa tree or nut material and may not perhaps be lasting.'

Southey and his family came to visit Mrs Southey's sister, Mrs Coleridge, at Greta Hall and never moved out again, Southey becoming head of a large household of three Fricker sisters and all their children. Mrs Coleridge's domestic priorities are clearly seen in her complaints of a Mr Dawe who is painting a large picture in Coleridge's study—'subject—A Woman on the point of a high Rock, taking her infant from an Eagle's Nest; the Eagle flying over her head—and this painting business creates a great deal of bustle and running *in* and *out*, windows open to paint the scenery etc. etc. which we can well dispense with in my sister's con-finement—'. Southey himself, in the *Letters from England*, purporting to be the travel journal of a Portuguese gentleman, gives us some of the best contemporary descriptions of the details of life and thought, written with a real novelist's eye for the typical and the curious.

His fictitious Don singles out for special praise in houses the excellent workmanship of English doors and windows, fitted carpets and fleecy hearthrugs. Fireplace and fender amaze him:

The frontal is marble, above is a looking glass the whole length of the mantelpiece . . . divided by 3 gilt pillars which support a gilt

architrave. On each side hang bell-ropes of coloured worsted, about
the thickness of a man's wrist, which suspend knobs of polished
spar. The fender is remarkable; it consists of a crescent basket work
of wire, about a foot in height, topt with brass and supporting 7
brazen pillars of nearly the same height.

Fenders were introduced on account of many newspaper accounts
of women being burned to death. Don Manuel speaks of the new
fashion for mahogany (first imported from Cuba and Honduras
in about 1720) and describes nests of tables, chaises longues,
harpsichords and firescreens made from this wood. He is fascinated
by English Venetian blinds of slatted wood, burglar alarms, and
indeed all sorts of mechanical contrivances towards comfort in
which early nineteenth-century England excelled. He describes
the development of the Patent Compound Concave Corkscrew,
which drew the cork mechanically and discarded it, a revolving

Rydal Mount

machine for stopping candle snuff falling on the table and a proposed mechanical snuffer. Knives and scissors abound—one sort
for fish, another for butter, another for cheese, an instrument to
make pens, one to clip nails; 'a machine for slicing cucumbers,
one to pull on the shoe, another to pull on the boot, another to
button the knees of the breeches'. He describes pocket toasting
forks, a pocket fender, which was to cost £200 (only the customer
refused it and the inventor brought an action against him), and
a pocket hunting razor with which one could shave at full gallop.

Southey's Don is predictably good on kitchens, especially Sir
Benjamin Thompson, Count von Rumford's, with its patent
stove built on scientific principles to channel the smoke and heat
past various iron roasting bars, stoves and boilers, before going up
the chimney and turning the spit on the way out. The kitchen
itself, although underground and lit from an area, he describes as
clean and shining—white wood dresser, copper and tin vessels
burnished, the spit chain bright. His bedroom too is clean and
plain—natural blankets and sheets, the damask bed curtains of the
last generation replaced by linen, the mahogany mirrors and chest
for shaving implements—all he dislikes is the tasteless bedspread
'of white cotton, ornamented with cotton knots in graceless shapes'.

In clothing, too, the Wordsworths and Coleridge were much
more simple than many contemporaries. The Romantic Movement, including Schiller's *Mary Stuart* and Scott's historical
novels, introduced a craze for historical dress and fancy-dress
balls both in France and England—slashed sleeves, ruffs, oriental-
ism of the kind displayed in the Prince Regent's Pavilion at
Brighton, and Egyptian fashions from the Battle of the Nile. But
the lives of these Romantic poets were untouched. An Englishman
who met them in Brussels in 1828 said Coleridge looked like a
clergyman, dressed in black with breeches buttoned and tied at
the knees. Wordsworth, 'tall, wiry, harsh in features, coarse in
figure, inelegant in looks', was roughly dressed in a long brown
surtout, striped duck trousers, fustian gaiters and thick shoes
'like a mountain farmer'. Neither had any real contact with the
high fashion introduced by Beau Brummel, though both had their
troubles with the diminishing use of powdered hair and knee-

breeches and silk stockings as formal wear. Wordsworth describing his youthful follies at Cambridge talks of being 'attired/splendid garb with hose of silk and hair/Powdered like rimy trees . . .'. His school landlady records a purchase of velvet and silk, 5*s*. 6*d*. and 4*s*. 9*d*. respectively, and 1*s*. 10*d*. for making up a velvet evening coat for Cambridge. Later in his life, Keats, calling on him in London, was mortified to find him dressed up in knee-breeches and silk stockings to dine with his official superior at the Stamp Office. As for Coleridge—it was the report that he had been seen wearing 'powder' in London, that made the Wordsworths assured that he was not really grieving over the quarrel. His letters at the time are indignant about this and periodically obsessed by underwear. On one occasion he has caught a cold because 'all the strings but one pair (out of six pairs of Tape strings)' are worn off his undershirt. He has lost three of the six he had and he had stood by mistake on his one remaining one whilst washing himself for a lecture and wetted it. These are the typical plaints of the husband living in lodgings: on another occasion he reproaches his wife for having given him an undershirt which 'was so scanty it left all the lower belly bare and I caught cold in my Bowels . . .'.

Southey's Don complains that English clothes lack variety, and dislikes the 'huge and hideous wig' now worn only by schoolmasters and doctors in divinity. However, he had a whole letter on rapid shifts in fashion, describing the leather breeches worn by Wordsworth's contemporaries as children which required several people to get them on, and 'fitted like another skin; but woe to him who was caught in the rain in them'. He talks of shifts of fashion in boots, and coats—including a transitory fashion for 'oiling the coat and cold-pressing it: this gave it a high gloss but every particle of dust adhered to it'. He writes of the creative language in which fashion autocrats prescribed the colours that were to be fashionable—'the Emperor's eye, Mud of Paris, Le soupir étouffé'—and the fashions in canes, clubs and common twigs for men to carry—'at present the more deformed and crooked in its growth the better'.* He talks of how women have abandoned tight-lacing, tiers of powdered rolls of hair, hoops,

---

* See Chapter 7, p. 245 et seq. for the taste for the 'picturesque' roughness which created this fashion.

bustles, rumps, and 'merry thoughts of wire on the breast to puff
out the handkerchief like a pouting pigeon'; and concludes
grimly 'All these fasions went like the French monarchy and about
the same time: but when the ladies began to strip themselves they
did not know where to stop'. He refers, of course, to the transparent damped muslin of fashionable beauties like Lady Caroline
Lamb.

The two poets did not need and did not have many social
amusements. Wordsworth's descriptions of his early sports in the
Prelude are famous—skating, poaching, playing cards, barn
dances: very much an outdoor life compared with that of
Coleridge, whose chief pleasure was a subscription given to him
by a stranger (who had suspected him of being a pickpocket and
was moved by his explanation that he was acting Leander swimming the Hellespont) to a circulating library, whose entire contents
he went through. Wordsworth was also present at regattas held
on various lakes—the first of these was on Bassenthwaite, in
August 1780. A description of one records that at 8 a.m. a 'vast
concourse' of ladies and gentlemen gathered: there were 400
yards of marquees, races, swimming sweepstakes, 'the sides of
the hoary mountains were clad with spectators and the glassy
surface of the lake was variegated with a number of pleasure
barges'. The chief attraction was a mock sea battle—with 'dreadful discharge of musquetry': afterwards there was dancing in an
assembly room specially built for the purpose. In later years, as
Wordsworth mellowed and his daughter Dora grew up, they all
danced more—at assembly rooms, to fiddlers in their own house,
Dorothy skipping vigorously in late middle age. In 1808 Dorothy
reports a 'PICNIC upon Grasmere Island' where nineteen people
were to have dined but were caught in a thunder-shower. She
asks the derivation of the word picnic and says the Windermere
gentlemen have one almost every day. (The word was introduced
into England in 1800.) John Wilson, the local 'Beau' then aged
twenty-three was present—he was later to be the 'Christopher
North' of *Blackwood's Magazine* who attacked Leigh Hunt and
Keats—and told Dorothy he was glad of the shower. 'For the

Skating, from an
engraving by P. Audinet
after Thomas Stothard

world I would not have had 19 Liverpool persons racketing about
the whole day . . . disturbing those poor sheep.' In 1809 Wilson
took Wordsworth on a 'fishing party' of thirty-two people, including ten servants, tents and baggage carried by ten ponies.
They camped by Wastwater for a week and Wilson wrote a long
poem in honour of the occasion 'consecrated' to Dorothy. By
this time the Wordsworths were living more sociably and visiting
and dining with the nobility: Southey indeed suspected Wordsworth of concealed snobbery. In London in 1807 Wordsworth met
Fox at one of the great Whig houses: Southey wrote 'Wordsworth
flourishes in London, he powders and goes to all the great routs.
No man is more flattered by the attentions of the great, and no
man would be more offended to be told so.'

Coleridge's social life was always gayer—as a young man he
drank 'egg-hot' and smoked 'Oroonoko' with Lamb at a pub
called *The Salutation and Cat*, where he was offered free entertain-

ment for his conversation. In later years he regarded 'dining out' with a mixture of joy and terror that he might be taken ill. In 1814 he records one complete menu:

> Turbot, Lobster Sauce, Boiled Fowl, Turtle, Ham, a quarter of Lamb, Tatas and Cauliflower etc.—then Duck, green Peas, a gooseberry and a currant pie, and a soft Pudding. Desert, Grapes, Pine Apples, Strawberries, cherries and other more vulgar fruits and Sweetmeats. Wines—?[The host] is a Wine-merchant!—Champagne, Burgundy, Madeira—I forget the Commonalty!—Company? not one to make such a dinner less unendurable to me, except a very lovely Woman called Mrs Grove. . . .

Both poets grew blasé about keeping good company—or chose to appear so. Wordsworth in 1831 wrote 'Five times have I dined while at Buxted at the table of an Earl—and twice in the company of a Prince. Therefore prepare for something stately and august in my deportment and manners.'

Their attitude to church-going changed with their attitude to the Church. Coleridge as a young man was a travelling Unitarian preacher—the young Hazlitt heard him and was dazzled by his metaphysical brilliance. In later life both he and Wordsworth supported the Church passionately as a necessary part of national unity and continuity; Wordsworth was furious when a plan to build a magnificent new church at Cockermouth failed for lack of local support. But in 1806 and 1807 their attitudes were critical, and expose some contemporary ecclesiastical shortcomings. Wordsworth took exception to a sermon delivered to a country congregation: 'A most knowing discourse about the gnostics and other hard names of those who were *h*adversaries to Christianity and *h*enemies of the Gospel. How strangely injudicious this is!—and yet nothing so frequent.' He retails a story of Coleridge's, of a sermon delivered to Keswick labourers on the vice of ambition, the shocking desire to be a courtier and wield wordly power, and concludes—'I don't know that I ever heard in a country pulpit a sermon that had any special bearing on the condition of the majority of the audience.' And Dorothy warns a sickly friend not to go to Church too often: 'I speak seriously that I did not read without alarm that you had been at Church four successive Sundays.' The Wordsworths 'are become regular churchgoers . . . that is, we take it by turns, two at a time . . . when the weather will permit.'

Their major pleasure, of course, was walking: the ailing Coleridge walked thirty or forty miles at a stretch, and hundreds across Scotland: De Quincey calculated that Wordsworth, who composed whilst walking, at sixty-five had covered 175,000 to 180,000 miles. Dorothy at forty-one walked '20 miles after 12 o'clock without fatigue' and at forty-six could 'walk 16 miles in 4 hours and ¾ with short rests between on a blistering cold day.' They had also to walk in the ordinary course of things—three miles to Rydale for letters at 10 o'clock at night.

The contrast between country life and London life was not purely one between rocks and lakes and the bustle of the city. The poets noticed, with a mixture of excitement and distrust, the effects of industrialization on the northern landscape. Iron bridges, canals, aqueducts, new metalled roads were admired as great human achievements. The young Wordsworth, walking through the dales, got to know many families who carried on home-spinning of woollen yarn, which survived longer than home-weaving, and admired 'the cylinders of carded wool, softly laid upon each other' at the side of the grandfather, too infirm for any other job. He observed cask-making, basket-making, the local casks of freshly potted char, the charcoal burners and 'the bloomsmithies' for smelting iron ore near Ulverston. He admired ponies carrying panniers of 'beautiful' pale blue slate from Coniston Old Man slate-quarries. These were indigenous and part of local life. But in 1803 Coleridge, at Hawksdale Bridge, was observing 'a plain of ugliest desolation . . . a Sodom and Gomorrah Cotton Factory'. Industrial landscape inspired some poets and painters to see new beauties. Joseph Wright of Derby found the power and the smoke romantic and exciting: John Dyer's poem *The Fleece* (1757) extols the building of factories, 'Industry,/Which dignifies the artist, lifts the swain/And the straw cottage to a palace turns.'

So appear
Th' increasing walls of busy Manchester
Sheffield and Birmingham, whose redd'ning fields
Rise and enlarge their suburbs.

Wordsworth and Coleridge too had artistic curiosity about machinery. Dorothy describes a machine for drawing water out of the mines, seen in Scotland in 1803. 'It heaved upwards, once in half a minute with a slow motion, and seemed to rest and take breath at the bottom, its motion being accompanied with a sound between a groan and *jike* . . . it was impossible not to invest the machine with some faculty of intellect; it seemed to have made the first step from brute matter to life and purpose showing its progress by great power. William made a remark to this effect, and Coleridge observed that it was like a giant with one idea.'

Richard Arkwright's cotton mill at Cromford, Derbyshire, from a painting by Joseph Wright of Derby

But the North Country was growing clogged with smoke, dirt, houses and factories. Even in 1795 Mrs Radcliffe described 'a continuous street of villages' between Stockport and Manchester. Some industrial towns were built where great waste tracts of uncultivated land had been, but they grew increasingly more cramped and ugly, and many rivers became thick black currents of slime. Wordsworth, in *The Excursion*, described how, over the whole region 'continuous and compact . . . the smoke of unremitting fires hangs permanent'. But Coleridge, travelling by coach to Liverpool in 1812, is interested in coal both economically and aesthetically. He describes how it comes from Wigan by canal and is taken to the inhabitants of Liverpool in two horse carts, properly weighed out, and charged at £1 7s. for a double cart-load (35 cwt). In Birmingham he adds, he had seen 'a

Rolling mills at Merthyr Tydfil, from a pen and wash drawing by T. Horner, *c.* 1810

Bartholomew Fair, from Ackermann's *Microcosm of London*, 1811

cluster of enormous Furnaces, with columns of flame instead of Smoke from their chimneys, the extremity of the column disparting itself in projected Balls and eggs of Fire . . .' and 'pools and puddles of water smoking'—a poetic prospect like many contemporary paintings of the sublime and terrible, Milton's Hell or the Fall of Nineveh.

The corrective to this destruction of the countryside was a renewed interest in its history and structure. Wordsworth deeply admired the precise natural history engravings of Thomas Bewick of Northumberland and Gilbert White's *Natural History and Antiquities of Selborne*: he advised a clergyman friend to write a topographical history of his area as a leisure activity. Wordsworth

wrote at a turning point of literary history—he made Nature
respectable, and indeed an ideal force—but from his time on
'nature poetry' had increasingly an element of the preservative
nostalgia for the past of these topographies and natural histories.

Cities, too, were changing. Dorothy Wordsworth observes
Stirling as an eighteenth-century town, with 'intolerable' dirt in
the streets, and a woman throwing tea leaves from an upper window. But in Glasgow there are large shops, and 'the largest
coffee-room I ever saw' with thirty gentlemen sitting in the circular bench of the window, each reading a newspaper. Wordsworth
in *The Prelude* disparaged London, describing gaudy Bartholomew
Fair with its performers, booths, clowns and monstrosities as

All out-o'-the-way, far-fetched, perverted things
All freaks of nature, all Promethean thoughts
Of man, his dullness, madness, and their feats
All jumbled up together, to compose
A Parliament of Monsters. Tents and Booths
Meanwhile, as if the whole were one vast mill,
Are vomiting, receiving on all sides,
Men, Women, three-years' Children, Babes in arms.

And this 'blank confusion' is a 'true epitome', in his view

Of what the mighty City is herself
To thousands upon thousands of her sons
Living amid the same perpetual whirl
Of trivial objects, melted and reduced
To one identity, by differences
That have no law, no meaning, and no end.

Wordsworth, owing to his habit of mind, saw London as a garish
raree-show, a whirlpool of oddities—he noticed beggars and
cripples, fallen women and monsters, but no day-to-day life.
Even the theatre of the day—the theatre of Kemble and Mrs
Siddons—seemed to him a fairly crude, glittery cardboard thing
compared with reading Shakespeare in solitude, or to the 'girlish
child-like gloss of novelty' handed down from theatres in country
barns or the 'crude Nature' of Jack the Giant Killer at Sadler's
Wells. Lamb, who had a comic battle about London with Wordsworth all his life, has described the glory of the theatre in several
essays, and the joy of the movement of life in the streets. He wrote
to Wordsworth

Separate from the pleasure of your company, I don't much care
if I never see a mountain in my life. I have passed all my days in
London, until I have formed as many and intense local attach-
ments as any of you mountaineers can have done with dead Nature.
The lighted shops of the Strand and Fleet Street; the innumerable
trades, tradesmen and customers, coaches, wagons, playhouses;
all the bustle and wickedness round about Covent Garden; the
very women of the Town; the watchmen, drunken scenes, rattles;
life awake, if you awake, at all hours of the night; the crowds, the

very dirt and mud, the sun shining upon houses and pavements, the printshops, the old-book stalls, parsons cheapening books, coffee houses, steams of soup from kitchens, the pantomimes— London itself a pantomime and a masquerade—all these things work themselves into my mind and feast me, without a power of satiating me. . . . I should pity you if I did not know that the mind will make friends of any thing. Your sun and moon and skies and hills and lakes affect me no more, or scarcely come to me in more venerable characters, than as a gilded room with tapestry and tapers, where I might live with handsome visible objects. I consider the clouds above me but as a roof beautifully painted, but unable to satisfy the mind. . . . So fading upon me, from disuse, have been the beauties of Nature, as they have been confinedly called; so ever fresh, and green, and warm are all the inventions of men, and assemblies of men, in this great city.

Lamb's outburst is only one instance of a general attempt to defend London against the crude image, aided by Romantic poetry and the taste for the picturesque, of the city as evil and the country as essentially innocent and beautiful and good—a distinction noticed also by Angus Wilson in the contemporary novels of Jane Austen where sophisticated deceivers come from London to corrupt country paradises like Mansfield Park. Hazlitt wrote an essay on *Londoners and Country People* refuting the Wordsworthian image of the 'natural' virtue of the peasant, in which he describes the pleasures of Cockney excursions to the half-rural inns near Hampstead and Highgate, where people play ball and bowls, drink punch, ale and tea, smoke virginia and oroonoko, bet and talk politics, their imagination 'long pent-up behind a counter or between brick walls' contained by poplar trees and fields 'within gentle limits'.

And if the London of the time was dirty and disease-ridden it was also beautiful. Humphry Repton designed Regent's Park and some of the great squares, Nash's Regent Street was unspoiled in its glory. True, Lamb in 1814 complained that the Regent had let publicans put booths and drinking places in Hyde Park so that 'the whole surface is dry crumbling sand' without 'a vestige or hint of grass ever having grown there' with a 'stench of liquors,

Regent Street early in the nineteenth century

bad tobacco, dirty people and provisions'. But Crabb Robinson going for his first trip in a gig through Regent's Park in 1818 was enthusiastic. 'When the trees are grown this will be really an ornament to the capital and not a mere ornament but a healthful appendage. The Highgate and Hampstead Hill is a beautiful object and within the Park the artificial water, the circular belt or coppice, the bridges, the few scattered villas are objects of taste. I really think this enclosure, with the new street [Regent Street] . . . will give a sort of glory to the Regent's government which will be more felt by remote posterity than the victories of Trafalgar and Waterloo, glorious as these are.'

Travel changed more rapidly in this period than in almost any other. The roadmakers were busy. In 1784 John Palmer of Reading obtained the Post Office contract for organizing mail coaches over the country. They became a symbol of speed—as De Quincey said in his classic essay, *The English Mail Coach*—

A mail coach in a thunderstorm on Newmarket Heath, from an engraving after a painting by James Pollard, 1827

for the glory of motion—grand effects for the eye between lamp-light and darkness on solitary roads, animal beauty and power in the horses and 'the conscious presence of a central intellect that in the midst of vast distances—of storms, of darkness, of danger—overruled all obstacles in one steady co-operation to a national result'. His essay, written already, in 1849, out of the nostalgia of the age of railways, describes the political excitement of carrying the news of Peninsular victories on the galloping coach, hung with laurels, through the night, and the terrors when the coach-man went to sleep and lost control when the coach was 'running at at least twelve miles an hour' or when young men took over the reins for pleasure or a bet.

Coleridge, table-talking about prospective increases in speed, related them prophetically to fashions. 'When balloons, or those new roads upon which they say it will be possible to travel fifteen miles an hour for a day together, shall become the common mode of travelling, women will become more locomotive and the health of all classes will be materially benefitted. Women will then spend less time in attiring themselves—will invent some more simple headgear, or dispense with it altogether.' Southey's Don admires the excellent folding maps, all distances marked, and guide books with 'distances from every place in the Kingdom from London and from each other', the names of the best inns, gentlemen's seats, and objects of interest—produced by the English commercial spirit. But he deplores the cruelty to post-horses, claiming that it is more profitable for postmasters to overwork and kill them in three or four years than to let them live out their natural lives.

Both Coleridge and Wordsworth have interesting memories of stage coaches. De Quincey records the social snobbery associated with the inside and outside of mail coaches—the inside passengers dined at separate tables in inns and considered themselves above the outside passengers—although there was an inverse snobbery of the box, a glamour of air and speed on the outside for young men. Coleridge wrote a graphic description of the Liverpool stage he travelled on in 1812, which suggests that the inside had its hazards:

How pleasant 'tis to travel brisk. At Stratford upon Avon we were only 9 hours behind the Mail, having travelled almost but not quite 4 miles an hour—I breakfasted at Oxford, and stayed more than an hour; but was afraid to send for my nephews, lest they should have been quizzed by their fellow collegiates, such was the Pothouse at which the Stage landed, such the ridiculous appearance of the Coach, with 14 distinct gaudy Pictures painted on it—and we were so followed both in and out of the city by a mob of boys, shouting out—Lazy Liverpool! Lousy Liverpool—! Here comes long, lazy, lousy Liverpool! And truly the Coach deserves its honours—Two *such* wretches were forced in on me all night, half drunk, and their Cloathes crusted over with dirt, the best portion of it from the mud into which they had fallen in a squabble, and the worst part filth of their own making. Two large *ticks* I have found on me.

The bank notes shut in his fob pocket he feared were not safe:

And sure enough in the night, while dozing, I felt a hand at my small Cloathes—and starting up, the *handy* Gentleman said, he was afraid I was cold, and so was only putting up the straw round my Legs. Kind Creature!

In Dorothy Wordsworth's 1820 Journal of a tour on the Continent she records an incident which illustrates the etiquette of stage travelling. On their way south in the Union coach they collected two young ladies outside Canterbury, one of whom had to sit beside the coachman, and 'unwilling to be seen in that situation outside Canterbury dismounted within a mile of the town. *Our* companion—very pretty, and superfine in delicacy—exclaimed from the coach-window "what! walk all the way by yourself! You will have a sad, long dreary walk!" Yet she made no offer to accompany the forlorn pedestrian.' The idea of indelicacy in walking recalls the Miss Bingleys' contempt of Elizabeth Bennet: Dorothy Wordsworth says she recorded the incident for the ludicrous contrast with her own ambition of crossing the Alps on foot.

De Quincey records in terrible slow motion an accident that haunted his dreams where a mail coach with a sleeping coachman ran down a young couple in a stationary gig; Wordsworth himself was run into by the mail coach near Ambleside in 1840 whilst driving a gig, with such force that Wordsworth and his son John, horse and gig were driven right through a stone wall, and the horse, wearing the snapped gig-shafts and traces galloped seven miles to the Grasmere turnpike. Wordsworth adds, gloomily, to this incident, the information that the new modes of transport were no safer. 'In the paper today I read of two railway accidents causing loss of life.'

Wordsworth's relationship with the new railways was not exactly happy. He wrote a sonnet to Steamboats, Viaducts and Railways, addressing them as

> Motions and Means, on land and sea at war
> With old poetic feeling

but assuring them that

> In spite of all that beauty may disown
> In your harsh features, Nature doth embrace
> Her lawful offspring in Man's art—

This is the Wordsworth who, in the preface to the *Lyrical Ballads*, assured his readers that the 'remotest discoveries' of science would become 'as proper objects of the Poet's Art as any upon which it can be employed': it is the artist equally fascinated and repelled by the industrial products of human ingenuity. But Wordsworth the man, whose choice of 'rustic life' to exhibit the simplicity of 'elementary feelings' in simple men aroused protest from Coleridge, Lamb and Hazlitt, was unequivocally against the introduction of railways into the Lake District, and published two letters in 1844, arguing not so much that rustic life would be spoiled as that the resident middle-class gentry of Ambleside would be driven away by 'droves' of working people from Lancashire, who would not appreciate the mountains, a love of which was not to be achieved by 'transferring at once uneducated persons in large bodies to particular spots'. The tone of his letters was snobbish and pompous, and annoyed many of the people who respected him for his understanding of the poor, although his views were a logical consequence of his changing views about the danger of rapid change in societies and the structure of societies.* Dorothy Wordsworth, travelling in a steamboat on Loch Lomond in 1822 was more charitable. She was interested in the difference between the Gentry end and the Steerage end, amused by an 'American' who asked the boatman 'How far does this lake constend navigateable', and moved by a poor woman she talked to who had often walked to Glasgow but never travelled by boat—it was too dear! Dorothy herself would not have been there at all 'had not steamboats been accounted by us so *cheap*'. But they disturbed her serenity and were 'always in a hurry and take noise and commotion along with them'.

Their tours afforded them opportunities of meeting people and observing society. Tours were fashionable, although Dorothy's way of walking and her gipsy-like appearance were a little

* See below, Chapter 3.

indecorous: a Frenchman who had met her and Mary climbing in the Alps, when asked if he had seen two ladies, replied rudely that he had *met two women* a little above. They stayed in many different kinds of inns, from Scottish crofters' hovels to French hotels—Wordsworth's frugality led him into constant bargaining with and beating down of innkeepers and hirers of post-horses, whilst Mary and Dorothy tactfully 'walked forward during the dispute'. On one occasion in Switzerland they slept out in a thunderstorm in their carriage having refused to take excessively expensive beds in an inn: on another, an angry guide impounded the ladies' coats which were only recovered after legal action. Dorothy's description of an inn at Patterdale where her clothes were set to rights for her by a young woman 'very smart in a Bonnet with an artificial flower' who 'did more for me than Mrs Coleridge would do for her own sister under the like circumstances' is moving. So is Coleridge's description of an inn in Letir Finlay in 1803—a 'house of Poverty' where he slept on 'two blankets and a little Fern and yet many Fleas'. One dish of tea exhausted their entire supply, but he made do in the morning with '3 eggs beat up, 2 glasses of Whisky, sugar and $\frac{2}{3}$ of a Pint of boiling water'. But Dorothy in 1822 found good inns in Scotland— carpets everywhere 'even at the villainous Inn at Tarbert'—and a blazing coal fire, and *expensive* furnishings in her room—two washing stands, mahogany tables, and a handsome mirror.

Their records of Continental tours are still vivid and interesting. They shopped—Mary bought a Belgian baby's cap—'it was elastic—would fit the same head for months and needed no ironing'. In Brussels they visited the assembly room where the ball had been given on the night of Waterloo, from which the young officers had hurried away in dancing shoes, 'and of these, how *many* were brought back, in the course of a few hours, dead, dying, or wounded!' At Waterloo they stood upon grass and cornfields 'where *heaps* of our countrymen lay buried beneath our feet. There was little to be seen . . . but something like horror breathed out of the ground.'

In Milan they went to the Opera house, where Dorothy objected to the stage *only* being lit, because of the dullness cast

A steamboat on the Clyde, from William Daniell's *A Voyage round*

over the spectators. But she enjoyed a glass of ice cream in a
lobby coffee house, where she was the only lady, but treated
with courtesy 'and I saw none of those unhappy females so
revolting in the passages of our theatres'. There too they saw
Leonardo's 'Last Supper' and regretted that its 'fading and
vanishing must go on year by year' and saw a marvellous firework
display of the burning of Troy—Dorothy was inclined to be
scornful of the 'thoughtless people having no better employment

Great Britain undertaken in the summer of the year 1813, London, 1818

than gazing at such fooleries' but the rockets, 'twisting, eddying, shooting, spreading' made her ecstatic—'I having never before seen any fireworks better than we sometimes exhibit to children.'

Seventeen years later Wordsworth, touring Italy with Crabb Robinson, wrote a series of letters home that are a marvellous crescendo of tourist grumblings. In Rome he was 'fairly tired' of churches and pictures and statues, too old for toiling and straining and, then as now, finding paintings covered up with curtains, or 'a service going on' or the church closed. By Florence he was beginning to wish 'in spite of all my gratifications' that he was back at home or had never set out. 'I never was good at sight-seeing yet it must be done,' he concludes grimly. By Munich his irritation bursts out over Crabb Robinson, who was 'a most un-suitable companion' as far as Wordsworth's health went. He 'undertook this journey as a *duty* and have gone through with it as such. . . . I have kept duty constantly in my eyes and greatly enriched my mind; and I hope when I get home that I shall find my health not at all worse. So let us all be glad that I have made this upon the whole so delightful journey.'

The mention of health raises the question of medicine in the period. Advances were being made: the Royal College of Surgeons was founded in 1800, and inoculation with cowpox against smallpox had been introduced in 1776. But typhoid and cholera increased as the poor were crowded together in the new manufacturing cities. It has been argued, too, that the deaths of children and others from infection and fevers increased in this period because it was the first where foods such as milk were generally distributed to the population, rather than produced at home.

The Wordsworths and Coleridge observed these evils from a distance; their letters are full of their own medical anxieties of different kinds. A major one was the danger of the death of their children. Coleridge lost a son in infancy, and Wordsworth a daughter aged four, and a son aged six, six months after the daughter. Southey, even more unfortunate, lost three. Whooping cough and measles were not minor irritations—they were dangerous, possibly lethal, plagues: the former seriously weakened Wordsworth's sickly daughter, and the second killed his son. To read their letters about these deaths, not statistics, but real tragedies, is to understand why death-bed scenes of children were such necessary comforters in the novels of the time, and to realize that the Wordsworths never really recovered from these losses—they were always gloomy and over-cautious about the remaining children. And Sara Coleridge wrote to Coleridge (away in

Germany) about the death of the infant Berkely:

> I pray to God I may never live to behold the death of another child. For O my dear Samuel, it is a suffering beyond your conception! You will feel and lament the death of your child, but you will only recollect him as a baby of fourteen weeks, but I am his mother, and have carried him in my arms and have fed him at my bosom, and have watched over him by day and by night for nine months. I have seen him twice at the brink of the grave, but he has returned and recovered, and smiled upon me like an angel— and now I am lamenting that he is gone.

Wordsworth's marvellous sonnet, *Surprised by Joy*, was written to his daughter in the grave, 'that place which no vicissitude can find'. Dorothy grieved intolerably, and her observation in 1822 of a Scottish family with a child corpse in its midst is coloured by her own past anxieties and medical worries. She asked the family —three women and five children—whether they had called in the doctor, to which they replied that it was too far and too expensive. Dorothy adds with a note of envy that they had probably not even thought of it before her questioning, and were 'spared much of the anxiety and perplexity which we are tormented with, who know more of the various diseases that beset all periods of life, and can call in medical help at our pleasure . . .'. These images of child death illuminate Wordsworth's feeling for the innocent surviving children in *We are Seven*, who do not see the grave as an end, but only as a separate existence.

The Wordsworth's chief medical ailments of their own were Wordsworth's weak eyes—he wore a green shade most of the time—and later, Dorothy's feebleness and insanity. It is surprising how many of their circle went mad: Mary Lamb killed her own mother in an insane fit, Charles Lloyd, Coleridge's early pupil, his sister who married Wordsworth's brother, Christopher, Southey's wife and Southey himself were all demented, and Lamb had a period in a mad-house. We have a terrible image of insane houses at the time, but in fact many seem to have been liberal. Lloyd was confined in the Quaker Retreat at

York, an early humane institution for the insane: Mary Lamb
met with sympathy from the newspaper reporters of her crime,
and was allowed out of the asylum on Charles's surety. They.
were reported crossing the fields together towards the asylum
with her case, both weeping, hand in hand.

The other major medical problem of their existence was not
an illness but a supposed cure—opium. Laudanum—a reddish
fluid, a mixture of opium and alcohol—was readily prescribed
for every ailment; toothache, travel sickness, general stimulation,
consumption. Children were 'soothed' with it, and it was sold
under such names as Godfrey's Cordial, Batley's Sedative
Solution, Mother Bailey's Quieting Syrup. Infant mortality from
overdoses was high. Highly praised doctors recommended it.
Dr Thomas Beddoes of Bristol, father of the macabre author of
Death's Jest Book, said to be the best doctor in England, recommended opium to his eminent friends and patients—
Coleridge, De Quincey, Charles Lloyd, Coleridge's friend and
patron Tom Wedgwood. He edited the *Elements of Medicine* of
Dr John Brown of Edinburgh, who believed in it as a stimulant of
the necessary excitability to keep life going. Coleridge and De
Quincey became addicts: Coleridge's letters about the terrible
physical and mental effects of the drug are among the most dreadful and despairing accounts ever written: De Quincey's *Confessions
of an English Opium Eater* is one of the classic descriptions of dream
and nightmare. William Wilberforce, the slave trade abolitionist,
was also an addict, and so was Clive of India: the drug was
respectable, and Coleridge's addiction sprang from a genuinely
well-intentioned medical experiment.

Coleridge's medical curiosity was enormous—he and Wedgwood
experimented also with hashish, and his notebooks are full of
recipes for the loosening of the bowels, ginger and water as a
safer drink than that dangerous stimulant tea, and calming doses.
He and Southey also collected the advertisements of the quack
doctors who abounded. Southey in the *Letters from England*
describes quack cures by 'galvanism' (stroking sores with metal
to 'draw off' the galvanic powers of the illness), magnetic girdles,
to 'attract the iron in the blood and make the little red globules

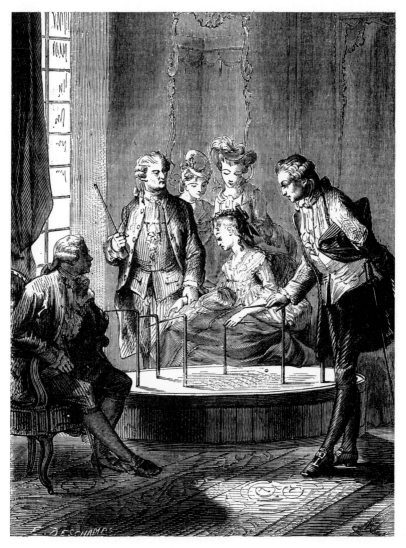

Mesmerism

revolve faster' and animal magnetism. Animal magnetism (or Mesmerism after its founder, Mesmer) attracted a number of devotees, and interested Coleridge, as it was based on a theory of the organic unity of the universe—since all men and all matter were part of the same organic whole one man could cure the illnesses in another's body simply by concentrating on destroying them mentally. Mind and matter were one, and mind had power over matter. Coleridge was interested in the 'cures' produced by men with such theories, and in the true relationship between mind and matter. He is said to have been the first to use the term 'psychosomatic'.

He was also interested in the linguistic absurdities of medical advertising, and collected in his notebooks things like the marvellous advertisement for a 'patent' worm medicine which claimed to have delivered the son of 'The Lord Chief Baron' from 'a Load, which cannot without impropriety be described, but which appeared the Nest of these pernicious animals . . .'.

Fashionable magazines of the time abound in advertisements for false teeth—the fitting of 'real human teeth' to odd stumps. In 1820 Dorothy Wordsworth who had lost all her teeth but three above and three below and had 'a true old woman's mouth and chin' got a new set from a Mr Dumergue for 50 guineas—she seemed satisfied, and remarked stoically that the tooth drawing was 'not half so bad as I expected . . . He is certainly a delightful operator.'

Both poets were also interested in pure science. I have quoted Wordsworth's belief that 'the remotest discoveries of the Chemist, the Botanist, the Mineralogist' were proper objects of poetry, and he equated the scientist's curiosity about truth and creative *pleasure* with the poet's, although in *The Excursion* he criticizes scientists for viewing all objects 'unremittedly/In disconnection dead and spiritless'—'objects as objects fixed and dead' as Coleridge said in *Biographia*, not unified into a living whole by the imagination. Science is good if conducted imaginatively. Indeed, the poets' conception of the universe as an organic whole owed something to an earlier poet, Erasmus Darwin (whom Coleridge met), whose botanical poems about the loves of the plants anticipated the work of his grandson, Charles Darwin, in supposing there were 'living filaments' in common between animals and vegetables. He also talked of the unity of all living things in one life-principle. Coleridge had a life-long friendship with the great Humphry Davy, who, as assistant to Dr Beddoes, administered laughing

Sir Humphry Davy (1778–1829), from a portrait by T. Phillips

gas to him and Southey in Bristol. In 1801 he and Wordsworth and a certain Calvert planned to set up 'a convenient
little laboratory' to study chemistry, and he wrote to ask
Davy's advice on books and equipment, explaining that it
was necessary for Wordsworth to have 'some intellectual pursuit
less closely connected with deep passion'. In 1802 he attended
Davy's lectures on Chemistry at the Royal Institution—in order,
he said, to increase his stock of metaphors—and made copious
notes, particularly noticing the colours of different flames—as
for instance 'Ether, in the same manner, burns bright indeed in
the atmosphere, but O! how brightly whitely vividly beautiful in
Oxygen gas.' Of particular scientific interest was the nature of
perception, and he and Tom Wedgwood—who has been called
the inventor of photography—conducted all sorts of experiments
on their own perceptions, examining their hallucinations, dreams,
and visions, both under drugs and without, in order to write a
book on perception. Wedgwood's posthumous paper on 'Our
Notion of Distance' was concerned with the same ideas.

Lastly, but underlying all other preoccupations and needs,
money. Money for books, money for families. Southey had one
of the largest known collections of books at his death: Coleridge
was too poor to buy so many, but his use of libraries was prodigious.
In 1797, he was writing in rage to the Bristol Library Society who
had asked for the return of two volumes he had had for three
weeks. 'Our learned and ingenious Committee may read through
two Quartos—i.e. *two thousand and four hundred pages of close printed
Greek and Latin*—in three weeks, for aught I know to the contrary:
I pretend to no such intenseness of application or rapidity of
Genius. . . . I subscribe to your Library, Mr. Catcott! not to read
novels, or books of quick reading and easy digestion—but to get
books, which I cannot get elsewhere—books of massy knowledge
—and as I have few books of my own I read with a commonplace
book—so that if I be not allowed a longer period of time for the
perusal of such books I must contrive to get rid of my subscription.
which would be a thing perfectly useless, except as far as it gives
me an opportunity of reading your little notes and letters.' And

in Durham he carried back a load of books from the Cathedral
library to the Hutchinson's home at Sockburn, in a cart.

His own books made him little money. When his tragedy,
Remorse, was produced in 1813 he wrote that the theatre would
make '8 or 10,000£ . . . and I shall get more than all my literary
labours put together, nay, thrice as much, subtracting my heavy
losses in the Watchman and the Friend—400£ including the
Copy-right.' The Wedgwood brothers paid him an annuity of
£150 a year, which went largely to his wife: Josiah withdrew his
share in 1812.

He was in some ways glad to be relieved of the burden of
gratitude and the obligation to produce a great work. But his
financial anxiety increased. In 1813 he wrote to Mrs Morgan,
the friend in whose family he was living:

> Tomorrow, if able, I must transmit 10£ to you, and employ
> Charlotte on a very very awkward Business—to go to the *Depository*
> for me—40 Books, Watch, Snuff Box, in for 6£—the Duplicates
> in the Watch Fob of my old whitey-coloured Small Clothes—the
> same *Relation* of ours as before. How can she do it? And yet who
> else can I employ?

The Morgans were in financial difficulties, and some of Coleridge's
lecture courses on literature and philosophy were undertaken to
help them out financially as well as to support his wife and
children. The lectures were often interrupted by sickness on his
part, and, since he tended to speak from his notebooks, apparently
at random, were sometimes brilliant and sometimes confusing.
Their organization seems to have cost him trouble. He solicits a
friend's interest to procure 'the Great Room at Mangeon's
Hotel, at Clifton', in Bristol, 'from one to three on Monday,
Wednesday and Friday afternoons. . . . As there will be no
Candles necessary, and the Hours such as can not interfere even
with a dinner party, I should not like to exceed 2 guineas a time.'
He wrote to ask Crabb Robinson to get an advertisement for his
London lectures put in *The Times*, and to scatter a few prospectuses
in the Library and Chatting Room of the Russel Institution.
Ladies were to pay two guineas, gentlemen three, 'gentlemen with

power to bring a lady' four—these sums were later reduced to three and two guineas. He talks of the difficulties of procuring a suitable lecture room.

> The Coachmaker's Hall having no literary or philosophical Redolence, or rather smelling somewhat unsavoury to the *nares intellectuales* of all my wealthy acquaintance, partly from past political spouting clubs and partly from its present assignment to Hops and the Instruction of Grown Gentlemen in Dancing, I have at length procured another Room every way answering to my purposes—a spacious handsome room with an academical Staircase and the Lecture room itself fitted up in a very grave poeticophilosophic Style with the Busts of Newton, Milton, Shakespeare, Pope and Locke behind the Lecturer's Cathedra.

He suffered from stage fright and tension, and is constantly hoping to make up for past deficiencies:

> I have sanguine hopes that my second Philos. Lecture will make amends for the dryness of the first and for my own embarrassment occasioned by the tallow candles and the slipperiness of the Table on which I stood which rendered me unable to read my notes.

But even in the midst of these troubles he has a sense of aesthetic unity and admonishes an unknown printer to take care with his prospectuses

> For the commonest address or Advertisement is as susceptible, as an ode or Sonnet, of having its head in the centre of it's folds, Serpent-like, or it's tail in its mouth—aye and requires it too.

But throughout the rest of his life he was haunted by money troubles—he wrote that he lost £200 'by non-payment, from forgetfulness and under various pretexts, by the *Friend*—and for my poems I *did* get—from 10 to 15£. And yet forsooth the Quarterly Review attacks me for neglecting and misusing my Powers!' He had cause to feel himself unjustly denigrated—he had been cheated by a firm of publishers, Gale and Curtis, whom he had chosen for their religious high-mindedness. They had falsified his accounts, and then went bankrupt, leaving Coleridge to buy back his manuscripts and copyright to save them going in the sale of their effects.

Wordsworth too, although he managed his accounts so strictly that he was never in debt and desperation like Coleridge, made surprisingly little money from his work. In 1812 he asked his patron, Lord Lonsdale, to find him some work not incompatible with writing poetry. He had, he said, hoped to meet the 'rational wants' of his family through literature, 'a Life-pursuit justified . . . partly through passionate liking, and partly through calculations of the judgment'. But he admitted his hopes had failed— partly because of economic pressures at the time, when prices, owing to the Napoleonic War, were constantly rising, partly because he had miscalculated 'the degree to which my writings were likely to suit the taste of the times' and partly because his most important works would not be ready to publish for some years.

His own character made these difficulties worse. In 1808 he almost made up his mind to publish the *White Doe of Rylstone* and Coleridge in London was negotiating the terms, when he decided to withdraw it. Coleridge in his embarrassment quoted a letter from Dorothy, pleading with William for publication, in which she shrewdly tries to combat his fear of criticism in the Press of a work not suited to the 'taste of the times':

As to the outcry against you I would defy it—what matter, if you get your 100 guineas into your pocket? Besides, it is like as if they had run you down, when it is known you have a poem ready for publishing . . . And without money what *can* we do? New House! new furniture! such a large family! two servants and little Sally . . . we cannot go on so another half-year . . . we must dismiss one of the Servants, and work the flesh *off our poor bones*. Do, dearest William! do pluck up your Courage and overcome your disgust to publishing. It is but a *little trouble* and all will be over and we shall be wealthy and at our ease for one year, at least.

In 1813 Lord Lonsdale did find a job for Wordsworth: he was appointed Distributor of Stamps for Westmorland. His younger contemporaries thought the post degrading—Leigh Hunt said he was 'marked as government property', and when Mr Kingston, a government official (Comptroller of Stamps) invited himself to a dinner party of the painter, Benjamin Haydon, where Keats and Lamb were present, Haydon—and Keats in all probability— felt that Wordsworth was unpleasantly affected by his superior's presence. 'A man's liberty is gone the moment he becomes an official.' Lamb mocked the pompous official, in a tipsy way, and Wordsworth had to pacify him.

It is generally believed that the post was a sinecure, but this was not so: Wordsworth worked very hard at it, and had responsibility for choosing and supervising sub-distributors all over the county. His duties consisted in collecting the Inland Revenue dues on legal documents, wills, licences, pamphlets, books, papers, insurance policies. He granted licences to pawnbrokers, appraisers, dealers in thread, lace, medicines, persons letting to hire stage coaches and diligences. Amongst dutiable articles were race-horses, gold and silver plate, legacies, penalties and forfeitures. He had to make sure of collecting the duty on these and finding out when there was duty to collect, as his income was a proportion of what he took. He had to pay a secretary (who also did his gardening), and a pension of £100 per year to his retired predecessor; the work, which he had hoped would bring in £400 a year brought in at first more like £200. He made an annual round of his district on horseback, inspecting and collecting. The value of the post declined, in fact, between 1814 and 1829, partly with changes in taxation—£33,200 worth of stamps in 1814 dwindled to £19,000 in 1829. He was worried throughout his later years by the thought of providing for his dependents after his death: one of his sons was a curate, but the other had no secure income.

There were other reasons, as well as comparative poverty, for Wordsworth's despondency in the *Leech Gatherer* about 'mighty poets in their misery dead', and his statement that

> We poets in our youth begin in gladness;
> But thereof come in the end despondency and madness.

But it added to the cold comfort he drew from the self-sufficiency of the extreme poverty of the old leech-gatherer himself. And in this context it is difficult not to sympathize with Coleridge's fury in 1810 with the Christian resignation of Wordsworth's sister-in-law. The two poets are going to leave their house and live simply in a cottage. Their only luxury is tea, and that they will now drink only for breakfast and without sugar—otherwise nothing but water. Coleridge concludes:

> But let any man worthy of that name contemplate William Wordsworth . . . and then say, that men of genius make no sacrifices in order to benefit their fellow creatures. Richard Wordsworth, the attorney, is not worth less than £50,000 made in business—Christopher is Dean of Bocking (1300 per annum) Chaplain to the Archbishop of C. and likely to obtain the theological Professorship of Cambridge. After this Mrs C. Wordsworth declares in a Letter to her Brother—she shall resign herself wholly to Providence and repel from her mind all anxious discontent concerning the advantages of this transitory World!—How exemplary!—What a model of Christian Piety. With 2000£ a year she will take up the Cross of the Lord and mortify the pomps and vanities of the World. Quere. Are such People *conscious* of their Hypocrisy? Answer, No! They take good care, they shall not—and that is the worst sin of the two!

3 *The Structure of Society*

The period during which Wordsworth and Coleridge were thinking and writing about society in England runs from eighteenth-century England, before the French Revolution, through the Napoleonic Wars and the social unrest which followed them and was imaged in the massacre at Peterloo and the Cato Street conspiracy, into Victorian England. At the beginning of their time England was still predominantly an agricultural country. Political power was largely in the hands of the aristocracy (the great landed proprietors), and the squires, the smaller landed gentry. Beneath them were the yeomen, the small independent farmers and tenant farmers, and the peasantry, who were regarded, paternalistically or brutally, depending on the individual landlord, as Property (Coleridge's definition). There was also an increasing number of men, newly made rich by mills or trade, who joined the ranks of the aristocracy—never in fact as rigidly exclusive as the great noble houses of France—and there were the rich Dissenters, men excluded under seventeenth-century laws from political life and some high professional positions, but clever and hardworking, who had put all their energies into trade and into science.

The main social changes and problems in this period concerned two related matters—the changing relationship between the old agricultural sources of power and money and the new industrial ones—mills, machinery, mines—and the condition of the poor. Both of these were aggravated by the rapid increase in population —from seven million in the middle of the eighteenth century to over thirteen million in 1815, and increasing at the rate of about two million every ten years. And these people were, relatively, concentrated in large towns, a completely new feature of English society—Birmingham, Sheffield, Liverpool, Leeds, Manchester and London itself, which in 1815 contained one million people. The birth rate rose, and the death rate fell—hospitals were dangerous places due to lack of medical knowledge and hygiene, but changes in town structure and domestic life helped—timber was replaced by brick in building, sewers were laid, cotton clothes were easier to wash than the old heavy cloth, and the habit of washing the body spread, even though Beau Brummel wrought a minor revolution at Court by his insistence in personal cleanliness, and one of George IV's objections to his bride was that her underwear smelled.

The number of the poor grew too. Both industrial and agricultural workers suffered from poverty—industrial workers from the increasing use of machinery to do work formerly done by men, and agricultural workers, and also the independent tenants and yeomen farmers, because of the increasing tendency of the times to favour the landowners and large tenant farmers who, with improved methods of farming and new enclosures, could afford to increase their livestock and pay tithes and poor rates. These problems had been present before the Napoleonic Wars and the workers had resorted to activities like machine-breaking (as early as 1779), although the wars had temporarily unified the country and made complaints or action seem unpatriotic. Crabb Robinson in 1815 wrote: 'When Buonaparte threatened Europe with his all-embracing military despotism, I felt that all other causes of anxiety and fear were insignificant.' Coleridge in 1814 at the proclamation of the peace noticed popular enthusiasm. The coach bearing the news was dragged by the people through the streets of Bristol, later illuminated with lighted transparent pictures and fanciful allegories. Coleridge designed one himself and was worried about 'the *imminent* danger of Conflagration . . . with three of us constantly watching the abominable Lamps', but was moved by the huge crowd which flowed like 'a vast deep and rapid River' across the square 'and the contrast of this with the thing to be seen! A red Wheel-barrow on men's Shoulders with no one in it—without exaggeration an old Petticoat on a Broomstick would have made as fine a Shew.—O man! man! ever greater than thy Circumstances.'

But Crabb Robinson noted a great lack of deep popular enthusiasm at the news of Waterloo, and both he, Coleridge and

Wordsworth became increasingly worried about the poor in the times immediately succeeding the war. In 1816 Robinson noted five or six cases of arson a week, popular protest against the use of thrashing-machines at Bury, and commented: 'The want of work by the poor, and the diminished price of labour, have roused a dangerous spirit in the common people—when roused the most formidable of enemies.' The poverty was increased by the return of the soldiers, many now unemployed. And the government's attitude was not felt to help.

Throughout the eighteenth and nineteenth centuries there was a strong general feeling that the poor were in the condition to which God had called them. William Paley, in his *Reasons for Contentment* (1781), preached to them their luck. Property entailed responsibility but the poor were in a unique position to develop the Christian virtues of 'dependence and subordination'. In 1849 the *Quarterly* berated *Jane Eyre* for being 'a murmuring against the privations of the poor, which is a murmuring against God's appointment'. Philanthropists had felt otherwise—the Society for Bettering the Condition of the Poor was founded in 1796, and Sir Frederick Morton Eden's three-volume summary of the state of the poor appeared in 1797. But there was a strong party which believed that to help the poor rendered them over-dependent, lazy, prolific, unwilling and unable to help themselves.

The Poor Laws were in an odd state. The Poor Act of 1601 entitled parishes to levy a poor rate—different parishes used this power to very varying degrees. In 1795 the Speenhamland magistrates made their famous decision not to fix the wages of agricultural workers (they feared that more would become unemployed) but to supplement their wages with poor-law allowances tied to the price of bread and the size of the family. This was intended to help, and to preserve the workers' independence, but it had the opposite effect, and resulted in the pauperization of whole rural communities. The landowners paid lower wages, knowing they would be supplemented, and arguing that it was from their pockets that the poor rates came anyway. By 1818 Poor Relief came to £8 millions—and the poorer ratepayers and the Members of Parliament were seriously worried about supporting a lazy army of dependent and greedy paupers. Southey, through his Don Manuel, expresses his indignation at this, and describes the paupers' dread of the workhouse—a place of horror then described in Crabbe's poems, and later in the novels of Dickens, whose characters would rather die than go there. It was a place inhabited indiscriminately by vagrants sent for punishment, unmarried mothers, orphans, and the helpless—idiots, madmen, the blind, the palsied and the senile. And parishes had been known to drive the old to die in the streets and women to give birth there, so that the funeral, or the new baby, should not be at the cost of the parish. As Southey furiously pointed out, the poor-rate wage supplements were parsimonious, lest the poor man indulge in drink or idleness, with the result that none could save, and all labourers, thrifty and lazy, became dependent on the parish in the end.

The Corn Law of 1815 aroused further unrest and resentment. It was introduced to keep up the price of bread, and prohibited the import of foreign corn until English corn reached 80s. a quarter: the intention was to make things safe for landlord, farmer and labourer. But it had various bad effects. Large fluctuations in price were caused by hoarding and rushing in corn from abroad when there was a bad harvest and English prices rose above 80s. The price of the quartern-loaf rose and labourers could no longer afford other agricultural products—bacon, beer, eggs, milk, meat—so they and the farmers suffered. The city-dwellers and industrial workers were also hit by the high price of bread and demanded higher wages. They also began to murmur against the predominant agricultural interest represented by the Members of Parliament, and to urge Parliamentary Reform. Riots and machine-breaking were prevalent, as well as peaceful associations of labouring men to better themselves. The Cato Street Conspiracy of 1820, in which Arthur Thistlewood planned to assassinate all the Ministers of the Crown as murderers of the innocent at Peterloo, only convinced the governing classes that the people were dangerous. Peterloo, where the Manchester Yeomanry and the 15th Hussars over-ran and killed several of the large and

The Peterloo 'massacre', 16 August 1819, from an old print

peaceful crowd agitating for universal suffrage and repeal of the Corn Laws, convinced the people that the Government, with Wellington in the Cabinet, ruled by the sword. Penal reform was slow—as late as 1832 a person could be hanged for sheep-stealing, house-breaking and forgery. Machine-breaking became a capital crime in 1812. It was 1829 before a regular police force (championed by Wellington and Peel) replaced government spies and troops as enforcers of law and order.

Attitudes to all this varied. Cobbett, preaching petitions for reform and believing that England's golden age had been destroyed by the industrial revolution, refused to look at a machine lest he be corrupted. He created a durable image of the vanishing idyllic English peasant on the land, was imprisoned for his radical views, and continued to produce his newspaper in prison. Robert Owen, risen from poverty to great wealth, tried to prove in his model factories in New Lanark that health and fair wages for workers actually provided better economic advantages for the mill-owners as well. There were tentative political attempts to better the condition of children in factories, chimney sweeps and other sufferers, but in spite of the terrible evidence produced by doctors and others about the evils of long hours of child labour, and brutality amongst sweeps, the Bills took years to pass. This was partly because the manufacturers produced evidence in their favour and the agricultural squires in Parliament were unacquainted with conditions in the mills, and did not imagine them. It was also, at a more abstract level of ideas because the beliefs held by the Members of Parliament, such as they were, were against interfering with the right of any individual to run his life and his business his own way. The classical economists believed that economic flows, like rivers, would 'find their own level' without violent interference. Lord Liverpool's government's belief in 'laissez faire'—let us, and things, alone and they will improve— was a reflection of this. Liverpool liked to quote Samuel Johnson:

> How small, of all the ills that men endure
> The part which Kings or States can cause or cure.

Poverty and suffering were acts of divine Providence. In this connection it is worth noting the views of two thinkers who had a powerful effect on the poets, particularly on Coleridge. William Godwin's *Enquiry Concerning Political Justice* inspired the young Coleridge to address a sonnet to him as one 'form'd t'illume a sunless world forlorn', whose

> Voice, in Passion's stormy day,
> When wild I roam'd the bleak Heath of Distress
> Bade the bright form of Justice meet my way
> And told me that her name was HAPPINESS.

Godwin's views of human nature were essentially Utopian and optimistic—remove unjust divisions of property, educate the poor out of ignorance and unreason, and vice and misery would disappear in the clear light of justice. Coleridge was, in his later days, embarrassed by his early attachment to Godwin's republicanism. But it was Godwin's view that 'There is a principle in the nature

of every human society, by means of which everything seems
to tend to its level, and to proceed in the most auspicious way,
when least interfered with by the mode of regulation', coupled
with the consequent belief that 'the number of inhabitants in a
country will perhaps never be found, in the ordinary course of
affairs, greatly to increase beyond the facility of subsistence' that
aroused the intellectual anger of the clergyman Robert Malthus,
whose *Essay on the Principle of Population* was designed to demolish
this easy comfort. Population could, indeed *would*, outrun the
means of subsistence, precisely because men were better off—
the people, particularly the poor, had only been kept in check by
misery (war, famine) and vice (murder and extravagance leading to starvation). He later revised his essay to suggest that
populations could be kept down by 'moral restraint' (abstention
from sex) as well as misery and vice. He aroused great hatred,
including that of Coleridge, who wrote notes all over his copy of
the *Essay*, indignant that Malthus should suggest that sexual
passion was as irresistible as hunger (his own, after all, was not and
he believed in the will), indignant at Malthus's despairing view
of human nature as essentially irrational, corrupt, torpid and
lazy. But although Malthus was hated, his view of the population
problem haunted the governing classes, and gave strength to the
belief that poor relief only made men lazier, more dependent and
more numerous. Indeed it helped towards the Poor Act of 1834,
which diminished outdoor relief and concentrated on workhouse
relief deliberately made unattractive. It took many years to
convince the governing classes that state interference with natural
events and with people was a lesser evil and less dangerous than
simply ignoring them. And, ironically, by the time Dickens came
to write his great black novels *Bleak House* and *Little Dorrit*, the
state was felt to be as much to blame for the suffering of the
helpless as the wicked or unfeeling mill-owner and outdated
aristocrat. The Circumlocution Office strangled the people as
effectively as Sir Leicester Dedlock.

What follows is an account of the poets' attitudes during their
lifetime to this changing social scene.

They record a certain amount of social gossip about the doings of high society. The young Dorothy Wordsworth was wildly excited on a visit to Windsor in 1792 to be introduced to George III and his family. She wrote

> I fancied myself treading upon Fairy-Ground and that the gay company around me was brought there by Enchantment. . . . I think it is impossible to see the King and his Family at Windsor without loving them, even if you eye them with impartiality and consider them really as *man* and women . . . but I own I am too much of an aristocrate not to reverence him because he is a Monarch more then I should were he a private Gentleman.

William Godwin (1756–1836), from an engraving published in 1805

Wordsworth at this stage was a Republican, and believed in what the innocent Dorothy then called the 'new-fangled Doctrine of Liberty and Equality', so it was perhaps fortunate that he was not with her. But George III went mad and the charming but dissipated Prince Regent took over. Coleridge in 1804 was reporting to Southey

> the King will certainly die—Fox's Coalition with the Grenvilles is avowed—and the Prince's Life was last week despaired of from a frenzy fever, the consequence of 3 days' drinking/the two first Claret and Port, did not affect him or his Rivals, the D. of Norfolk and E. of Guildford—on the third day they each drank 2 bottles of Sherry, 2 of Madeira, and a bottle of Noyeau with several Glasses of Brandy—and the Hereditary Earl Marshall waved his flag triumphant over the prostrate Heir Apparent and the Earl—

There was much public grumbling about the Royal expenditure, in which Dorothy joined: in 1816 she says she hopes the Ministers will be 'frightened into more efforts towards economy; but what an immense Royal Family have we to maintain and the Princess of Wales spending her money abroad!' But Wordsworth's sonnet on the death of George III, in 1820, mad and blind, is moving:

> dread Shadow of a King!
> Whose realm had dwindled to one stately room;
> Why should we bend in grief, to sorrow cling
> When thankfulness were best?

Coleridge in 1814 is indignantly disparaging the gossips' and moralists' attempts to denigrate Nelson, whose letters to Lady Hamilton were published that year:

> In the name of God, what have we to do with Lord Nelson's Mistresses or domestic Quarrels? Sir A. Ball [Governor of Malta] himself exemplary in this respect told me of his own personal knowledge Lady Nelson was enough to drive any man wild— He himself once heard her at Nelson's own Table at Breakfast when two Lieutenants were present reproach and worrett him about his *beastly infidelities* in the Mediterranean. She had no sympathy with his acute sensibilities; and his alienation was affected tho' not shewn before he knew Lady Hamilton, by being *heart-starved* still more than by being teized and tormented by her sullens. To the same enthusiastic sensibilities, which made a fool of him with regard to his Emma, his Country owed the victories of the Nile, Copenhagen and Trafalgar—

There is more than a little of Coleridge himself in this picture of the 'heart-starved' hero—but he was purely shocked by Canning's duel with Castlereagh in 1809:

> Good God! what a disgrace to the nation—a *Duel* between two Cabinet Ministers on Cabinet Disputes!! And not a Breathing of its hideous Vulgarity and Immorality in any one of the Papers!. Is it possible that such minds can be fit to govern?

In their early years the poets were deeply, altruistically concerned with the sufferings of the poor, and remained so all their lives, although their political views underwent a sharp change from republicanism to High Toryism. In 1801 Coleridge was berating immigrants to America for grumbling about bad society, vulgar manners and insolent servants in a world where, according to him, there was 'no poverty but as a consequence of absolute idleness', by comparison with England, where 'the laborious Poor are dying with grass within their Bellies!' He noted in his commonplace book in about 1795–6: 'People starved into War.— over an enlisting place in Bristol a quarter of Lamb and piece of Beef hung up.' But the war also impoverished, and Dorothy Wordsworth's Grasmere Journal, which records a steady flow of beggars past her door, gives details of many destitute wounded men, or women whose husbands had been killed in the war. A typical entry is the one about a young woman who had come with 'two shillings and a slip of paper which she supposed a Bank note— it was a cheat. She had buried her husband and 3 children within a year and a half—all in one grave—burying very dear—paupers all put in one place—20 shillings paid for as much ground as will bury a man—a stone to be put over it or the right will be lost— 11/6 each time the ground is opened.' There was the little boy who, when asked if he got enough to eat, 'looked surprised and said "Nay". He was 7 years old but seemed not more than five.' From Dorothy's encounter with a family of beggars came Wordsworth's *Beggars*: and partly from the account in her journal Wordsworth created that monumental, stony figure of pure, poverty-stricken existence, the Leech-gatherer. He was 'an old man, almost bent double. He had on a coat, thrown over his shoulders, above his waistcoat and coat. Under this he carried a · bundle, and had an apron on, and a night-cap. His face was interesting . . .'

He had had a wife and 10 children, all dead but one, from whom he did not hear, a sailor 'His trade was to gather leeches, but now leeches are scarce and he had not strength for it. He lived by begging, and was making his way to Carlisle where he should buy a few godly books to sell.'

Leeches were growing scarcer, owing to a dry summer and being gathered too much; they 'did not breed fast and were of slow growth. Leeches were formerly 2/6 per 100; they are now 30*s*.'

Wordsworth's sympathy for, and capacity to recreate, these solitary, wandering poor men and women is one of his great strengths as a poet. Through him the Leech-gatherer, the Traveller of *Guilt and Sorrow*, discharged from the army, driven by poverty to murder, the Female Vagrant of the same poem, the soldier met on the road in the Lake District, the blind London beggar of *The Prelude*, become symbols—all the more powerful because Wordsworth simply describes them and his emotional response to them—of a basic element in the human condition, one of emptiness, stripped of importance and therefore important. The soldier stands still in the landscape—'in his very dress appeared

> A desolation, a simplicity
> To which the trappings of a gaudy world
> Made a strange background
>   . . . his form
> Kept the same awful steadiness—at his feet
> His shadow lay, and moved not.

And he tells Wordsworth his tale with 'a strange half-absence' like one

> Knowing too well the importance of his theme
> But feeling it no longer.

And the blind beggar, with his story written on paper and pinned to him, seems the isolated, the pessimist, entirely significant:

Caught by the spectacle my mind turned round
As with the might of waters; an apt type
This label seemed of the utmost we can know,
Both of ourselves and of the universe;
And on the shape of that unmoving man,
His steadfast face and sightless eyes, I gazed
As if admonished from another world.

Here Wordsworth's distant capacity to remain, as Coleridge put it, a 'spectator *ab extra*, feeling *for* but not *with* his characters' produces much better poetry than Coleridge's rush of ready personal sympathy. The following is an early poem of Coleridge's, *The Outcast*:

Sweet Mercy! how my very heart has bled
To see thee, poor OLD MAN! and thy gray hairs
Hoar with the snowy blast: while no one cares
To cloathe thy shrivell'd limbs and palsied head.
My father! throw away this tatter'd vest
That mocks thy shivering! take my garment—use
A young man's arms! I'll melt these frozen dews
That hang from thy white beard and numb thy breast.
My SARA too shall tend thee, like a child:
And thou shalt talk, in our fire side's recess
Of purple Pride, that scowls on Wretchedness—

Coleridge's genuine sympathy shows better in the precise economic details collected in his notebooks than in this blend of Shakespearean histrionics, self-aggrandisement, and eighteenth-century abstractions.

Wordsworth's *Ruined Cottage*, incorporated in *The Excursion*, is perhaps the most vivid image there is of the effects on a self-respecting man of loss of employment. Margaret's husband is one of

shoals of artisans
From ill-requited labour turned adrift
To hang for bread on parish charity.

and Wordsworth's picture of his *uselessness* is moving:

> At the door he stood
> And whistled many a snatch of merry tunes
> That had no mirth in them; or with his knife
> Carved uncouth figures on the heads of sticks.

And Coleridge in 1803 was observing the efforts of the families engaged in spinning wool at home:

> 3 and nearly 4 days work for a stout woman, a stout Girl and a feeble old woman, 1 Stone of wool, for which they get £0, 2s, 10d/ spinning from 7 in the morning to 9 at night, of course using Coal and Candle; they can do it in 3 days; but then they have to reel it and carry it . . . at least 5 miles—O women are hardly off!

On the tour of Scotland which they all went on in 1803 they were again close observers of the poverty of the people. Dorothy attributed the constantly repeated 'Ye'll get that' of the Highlands to 'a perpetual feeling of the difficulty with which things are procured. We *got* oatmeal, butter, bread and milk . . .' She describes a whisky hovel, with unglassed windows and half a roof, 'little better than a howling place for the winds' in which at least half a dozen people to her surprise seemed to subsist, 'dealing out whisky to the starved travellers'. And Coleridge grew indignant at the twelve-year-old village of Springfield, built for workmen, mostly weavers, by Sir William Maxwell: 'O what dreary melancholy Things are Villages built by great men / cast-iron Hovels / how ill does the Dirt and Misery combine with the formal regular shapes. Are they cells of Prisons? It is the feeling of a Jail.'

More than Wordsworth's respect for Godwin, his respect for the 'statesmen' of Cumberland and Westmorland led to his early republicanism and also to his poetic idealization of rural life. The 'statesmen' were peasants who owned their own small estates—Cumberland and Westmorland had few resident nobles, and comparatively little of the extreme poverty the Wordsworths observed in the Highlands and Dorset. The people were democratic, independent, and self-respecting. Wordsworth idealized them: they were his education: was it not to be expected

That one tutored thus should look with awe
Upon the faculties of man, receive
Gladly the highest promises, and hail
As best, the government of equal rights
And individual worth?

These 'statesmen' were finding it harder and harder to survive against the economic pressures of the time. Dorothy records a conversation in 1800 with a certain John Fisher who 'observed that in a short time there would be only two ranks of people, the very rich and the very poor "for those who have small estates" says he, "are forced to sell and all the land goes into one hand".' By this time Dorothy, the 'aristocrate' of the meeting with the King, is scornful of riches. An entry in her journal runs: 'We had a pleasant conversation about the manners of the rich—avarice, inordinate desires, and the effeminacy, unnaturalness and the unworthy objects of education. After the Lloyds were gone we walked—a showery evening. The moonlight lay upon the hills like snow.'

They may at this stage have despised the rich and their education, but Wordsworth could not share Godwin's belief that property is a cause of vice. In *The Last of the Flock*, and the later *Michael* he draws a most moving picture of the slow attrition of the personality and energy of the self-respecting smallholder with the loss of his property. With the loss of property, Wordsworth felt, went natural emotions. The hero of *The Last of the Flock* is moved by poverty to 'wicked deeds' and 'wicked fancies'. He is carrying the last lamb of his flock to sell:

Sir, 'twas a precious flock to me
As dear as my own children be;
For daily with my growing store
I loved my children more and more.
God cursed me in my sore distress;
I prayed, yet every day I thought
I loved my children less;
And every week and every day
My flock it seemed to melt away.

In 1808 the Wordsworths organized an appeal for the children of such a smallholder who had been killed in a snowstorm—one of the children they took in themselves. Dorothy's description of their poverty is detailed and distressing:

> They were the poorest people in the vale, though they had a small estate of their own and a single cow. This morsel of land, now deeply mortgaged, had been in the possession of the family for several generations; they were loth to sell it and consequently they had never had any assistance from the parish . . . The cow was grown old, and they had not money to buy another. They had sold their horse and were in the habit of carrying bridles, or anything that they could spare, to barter for potatoes or bread. Luxuries they had none. They never made tea, and when the neighbours went to the children they found nothing in the house but two boilings of potatoes, a very little meal, and a few pieces of lean dried mutton. . . . You will wonder how they lived at all and indeed I can hardly tell you. They used to sell a few peats in the summer which they dug out of their own hearts heart—their land—and perhaps the old man (he was 65 years of age) might earn a little money by doing odd jobs for his neighbours; but it was never known till now (by us at least) how much distressed they must have been. See them when you would they were always cheerful; and when they went from home they were decently dressed. The children too, though ragged, are clean. . . .

Wordsworth's 'Utopian vision' of country people, if it can be called that, appears more in the polemic of his prefaces and that rather polemical and over-designed poem *The Excursion* than in his poems of feeling, where a kind of blank *statement* of the nature of things, poverty, dignity, decay, produces its own emotion. But the criticism of his dogmatic assertions by Coleridge and Hazlitt has its interest and justifications. Coleridge in *Biographia* points out that 'to the formation of healthy feelings and a reflecting mind, negations involve impediments not less formidable than sophistication and vicious intermixture'—but this is the theoretical side of the tragic emotional decay precisely observed by Wordsworth himself in *The Last of the Flock* and *The Ruined Cottage*. But Coleridge goes on to point out that 'education or original sensibility or both' are a prerequisite of the response to 'the changes, forms and incidents of Nature' desiderated by Wordsworth. If these do not exist men may be made 'selfish, sensual, gross and hard-hearted' through the narrowness of the country life. He concludes

> Let the management of the Poor Laws in Liverpool, Manchester or Bristol be compared with the ordinary dispensation of the poor rates in agricultural villages where the farmers are the overseers and guardians of the poor. If my own experience has not been particularly unfortunate, as well as that of the many respectable country clergymen with whom I have conversed on the subject, the result would engender more than scepticism concerning the desirable influence of low and rustic life in and for itself.

Hazlitt bears this out in his essay on *The Character of Country People*, where he opposes the narrow petty life of his own Wiltshire village to Wordsworth's vision of natural feelings. He criticizes Robert Owen, too, for visionary Utopian belief in the goodness of man—borne out in the failure of Owen's attempt to found an ideal Community in America if not in New Lanark. And he defended townspeople. Mr Wordsworth in the Preface to the *Excursion*, he said, 'represents men in cities as so many wild beasts or evil spirits, shut up in cells of ignorance, without natural affections, and barricaded down in sensuality and selfishness.' If man in London *really* did not know his next-door neighbour, 'the feelings (one would think) must recoil upon themselves and either fester or become obtuse'. But of course it is not so; man in London is, as Burke has it, a sort of 'public creature', and has a meaningful communal life, as well, larger and more varied. Therefore he is better equipped, according to Hazlitt, to form political ideals. Hazlitt, the city-dweller, was a Republican, and interested in the development of these independent city minds, with their sense of the government of large communities, into good, reforming Radicals. The City of Westminster was a Radical seat because the social life of its inhabitants led them to understand the ideals of government and the concept of 'the people' as a political force. Wordsworth, and Coleridge too for all his under-standing of Liverpool, Manchester, and Bristol, became con-servative in the true sense of the word. Both saw English life primarily in terms of the proper management of agriculture and organic agricultural communities; both—with, however, many qualifications—saw industry and commerce as threatening forces. They were to some extent justified: even as late as 1851 agriculture still employed one out of four Englishmen over twenty and there were more agricultural labourers than cotton workers, domestic workers, and general labourers. Adam Smith had believed that merchants who became country gentlemen made the 'best improvers' of land and estates and that therefore industry and commerce enriched the country. But many of the traditional landlords were 'improvers' too—Thomas Coke of Norfolk, who never bothered with his title as First Earl of Leicester, was the most famous. Coleridge too was interested in the scientific im-provement of agriculture: in Scotland he had a long conversation with a priest 'concerning the uses and properties of limes and other manures', and when Wordsworth and Dorothy were amused by the incongruous appearance of an 'uncommonly Luxuriant' field of bright gold grunsel next to one of clover and one of potatoes he 'was melancholy upon it, observing that there was land enough wasted to rear a healthy child'.

The reactions of the two poets to the popular agitation about the 1815 Corn Law differed. Wordsworth believed that 'the advocates for the Corn Laws are in fact the friends of the poor; though . . . they may be mistaken as to the best price to fix on'. He thought the price of 80*s.* too high because rents were already unnaturally high, and if they were kept up by this price for corn people would suffer. He thought it possible that the price of corn might fall if it did rise near 80*s.*, if importation became likely 'so that it is possible that the price may answer for the good of the community'. But he does not seem to have foreseen the fluctua-tions in price caused by these drops and the hardship caused by both importation and the artificially high prices of English corn. What he did feel strongly was that the people's dislike of the Corn Laws was unjustified:

Wordsworth in 1817, from an engraving by H. Meyer
after a portrait by Richard Carruthers

> Nothing can be more deplorable than the errors of the mob; who seem never to have had a thought that without a restriction upon importation no corn could be grown in this country, and consequently that it would become insupportably dear; and perhaps could not be got at all.

The poor, the individual peasants, were objects of his detached sympathy, but the other aspect of them, 'the mob', was beginning to make him and many other Englishmen increasingly uneasy. He had, after all, lived to regret his enthusiasm for the French revolutionary people in his disgust at the anarchic Parisian mob. In 1816 there were riots in Suffolk about the Corn Laws and Dorothy wrote to her friend, Catherine Clarkson, wife of the philanthropist Thomas Clarkson, historian of the Quakers and the abolition of the slave trade, about

> the degree of apprehension you might entertain for the property of your Brothers and other Friends . . . I trust that you, being out of the circuit of the Riots, are safe, and surely the Poor could not by any possible means take the fancy that *Mr Clarkson* was their enemy! . . . Perhaps the newspapers exaggerate the mischief; but at best it must be very great. In this part of England we are happy—no public disasters seem to touch us. Labourers feel the benefit of the cheapness of corn; and their wages are not much reduced; so that except for those that have property we have little or nothing of complaints—and they are only suffering under an evil which they can well bear, and which will certainly pass away.

The tone here is moderate; it was not to remain so.

Coleridge, too, was indignant at the thought of the 'mob' and its possible outrages. In 1812, the day after the assassination of the Prime Minister, Spencer Perceval, he wrote to Southey suggesting that Southey should write an article on the 'sinking down' of Jacobinism (democratic, radical beliefs) 'below the middle and tolerably educated Classes into the Readers and all-swallowing Auditors in Tap-rooms etc. of the Statesman Examiner, Cobbett etc.'. He had little or no respect for the working-class Cobbett's radicalism—he called Cobbett the rhinoceros—and a deep suspicion of the popular Radical, Sir Francis Burdett, M.P.

Coleridge in 1814 from a portrait by W. Alston

for Westminster (who nevertheless was a Tory squire and shared Coleridge's beliefs about the sanctity of kingly government and the English constitution). He went on to tell Southey: 'I have ascertained that throughout the great manufacturing Counties . . . [their] Speeches, and the leading Articles of the Statesman and the Examiner are printed in Ballad Form and sold at a half-penny and a Penny each.' Coleridge, who was 'turned numb, and then sick', by the news of the assassination went into the tap room of a large public house to recover, and was dismayed by the 'atrocious sentiments universal among the Populace—and even the lower order of Householders . . . It was really shocking—Nothing but exultation—Burdett's health drank with a clatter of Pots and a Sentiment given to at least 50 men and women—May Burdett soon be the man to have Sway over us! . . . This is but the beginning . . . more of these damned Scoundrels must go the same way— and then poor people may live—'.

But in 1815 he was speaking at a public meeting in Bristol to petition Parliament against the Corn Bill, and declaring his pleasure at being able to show that his support of the Tories had been conscientious, not dictated by interest; he was truly indignant at the Bill's 'Injustice and Cruelty'. Mounted on a butcher's table he 'made a butcherly sort of speech of an hour long to a very ragged but not butcherly audience: for by their pale faces few of them seemed to have more than a very occasional acquaintance with Butcher's Meat. Loud were the Huzzas!—and if it depended on the Inhabitants at large, I believe they would send me up to Parliament.' He saw the Bill as a commutation of the War and Property Taxes to a Poll Tax, 'not proportioned as the Property Tax in some measure was, to the ability of the Payer, but pressing heavier the lower it descends—so that the poorest pays the most, not only *virtually*, as being so much less able to pay it, but actually, as making Bread so very much larger a proportion of his whole sustenance'. He even went as far as declaring that Parliamentary Reform was now necessary since the masters, the landowners and great farmers had dared to establish a minimum price and maximum quantity of 'the Poor Man's cold, dry Dinner'. They assumed the loaf's price would not rise above a shilling—but it would be 'at 16*d*. and may be at 18*d*.'. 'As to the pretext that Wages will rise in proportion, the proper answer, however vulgar, would be—*a Lie*!'

On particular abuses they felt strongly. In 1802 Dorothy recorded a meeting with a sailor who had been pressed into the Navy, and had twice swum from a King's ship in the night and escaped. 'He would rather be in hell than be pressed'. Fishermen were hunted down by soldiers through fields of standing corn where they tried to hide from the press gang. In 1808 both Coleridge and the Wordsworths were writing to influential friends to procure the release of Sara Hutchinson's younger brother Henry, who was pressed after all kinds of adventures—the Navy took from him his own ship after a storm, he was taken prisoner in Mexico for nearly two years, and when he got home was pressed again. This Henry had also travelled on a slave ship, *The Betsey*, and recorded a particularly grisly incident of a slave merchant called Davies who nailed two boys by the ears on his dinner table for bringing him a dirty plate—Henry and the captain of *The Betsey* refused to eat with this man and dined afterwards on deck. The wandering sailor too told stories of atrocities in slave ships— 'one man had been killed, a Boy put to lodge with the pigs and half eaten, one Boy set to watch in the hot sun till he dropped dead . . .'.

Wordsworth wrote a sonnet to Thomas Clarkson on the abolition of the slave trade and Coleridge, describing Clarkson's *History of the Abolition*, praised its 'moral beauty' and called it 'that immortal war—compared with which how mean all the Conquests of Napoleon and Alexander'. He himself wrote a Greek Ode against the slave trade, and a long essay, and Southey wrote twelve sonnets which were very popular. There was an interest in Africans and Negroes: Coleridge writes of a Professor Blumenbach who had 'a complete Library of books written entirely by African Blacks', books in every science and art. When the Queen of Haiti visited the Clarksons the Wordsworths composed a parody of Ben Jonson's 'Queen and huntress', beginning 'Queen and Negress chaste and fair', and referring to the 'holy shade' of 'Wilby' (Wilberforce): they later suffered some embarrassment lest the poem was in bad taste. Wordsworth had to correct the painter, Benjamin Haydon, when he wanted to introduce him into his painting of the Anti-Slavery Society at Freemason's Hall—he 'must on no account be introduced' as he had played no active part, despite his lively interest.

But in later years he was lukewarm about the abolition, declaring that the people of England, whose laws had allowed slavery, could not in strict logic fanatically sweep it away without either the slave or the English people compensating the owner for his loss—and the slave could not do much more than perhaps offer some of his services. He was still troubled by the sanctity of *property*—as Coleridge saw the agricultural workers as property, so Wordsworth saw slaves, and argued from there that to be a man's property might be a better protection than being a free worker, to be exploited. He argued from the analogy of the measures then being considered to prevent cruelty to animals—cruelty was *more*, not less, likely if the law did not consider the animal a man's exclusive property. He refused to contribute to an anti-slavery anthology because he was 'not prepared to add to the excitement already existing in the public mind'. He was on the right side, but he was gloomy about the nature of men in society:

I do not only deplore, but I *abhor* [the slave trade] if it could be got rid of without the introduction of something worse.

In 1801, many years before the Factory Act of 1819, the poets had been interested in the fates of the workers, particularly the children, employed in mills. Coleridge's dangerous acquaintance the revolutionary John Thelwall described the factory children in a poem:

                    a race
        Of infant slaves, broke timely to the yoke
        Of unremitting drudgery—no more
        By relative endearment, or the voice
        Of matronly instruction interspers'd—
        Cheering or sage; nor by the sports relaxed
        (To such how needful!) of their unknit prime
        Once deem'd the lawful charter.

Coleridge in the same year was busy with one of his Utopian plans —for malting acorns for home consumption, as acorns flourish even when harvests are bad:

> Should it be true, that the Oak is fructified by superficial Irrigation, what a delightful Thing it would be if in every Plot adjacent to Mountain Cottages stood half a dozen noble Oaks, and the little red apple-cheeked children in drouthy seasons were turning a small Fire engine into the air so as to fall on them! Merciful God! what a contrast to the employment of these dear Beings by a wheel or machine in a hellish Cotton Factory!

Wordsworth, in *The Excursion*, describes the plight of these children, exhausted by long hours, cramped in mind and body by an imprisonment they carry with them even when they leave the factory, and the plight of the mothers, their domestic rhythms and sense of purpose broken by the departure of the children. There is a touching description of the boy

> His raiment, whitened o'er with cotton flakes
> Or locks of wool, announces where he comes.
> Creeping his gait and cowering, his lip pale
> His respiration quick and audible;
> And scarcely could you fancy that a gleam
> Could break from out those languid eyes—

He introduces this description with the scornful remark:

> Economists will tell you that the State
> Thrives by the forfeiture—unfeeling thought,
> And false as monstrous!

Coleridge was active in the agitation in 1818 for the Cotton-Children Bill. He wrote two tracts on the subject arguing against the principle that it was illegitimate to interfere with free labour and property: 'In what sense, not utterly sophistical, can the labour of children, extorted from the wants of their parents, 'their poverty but not their will consenting', be called free?' Employers have no right to purchase and men have no right to sell the labourer's health, life, and well-being. And in letters he is

Factory children, a cartoon by Robert Cruikshank

indignant about the behaviour of 'that *Scotch* Coxcomb, the plebeian Earl of Lauderdale', who wanted to make a speech, to display his 'muddy three inch depths in the Gutter of his Political Economy. .... Whether some half score of rich Capitalists are to be prevented from suborning Suicide and perpetrating Infanticide and Soul-Murder is, forsooth, the most perplexing Question which has ever called forth his *determining faculties*, accustomed as they are *well known* to have been, to grappling with difficulties.'

In 1817 Dorothy Wordsworth, staying in Halifax, observes the effects of poor trade on the woollen industry. The country she says, is really beautiful except for the 'odious cotton and worsted mills—and steam engines—which are really now no better than encumbrances on the ground'. Some mills are kept going to supply work—but few get more than half work. The population is reduced to pauperism—whole streets kept alive by public charity and families 'broken down—that is their expression'. Dorothy tells her friend that 'making clothes for poor people is a good thing'. In some parts of England women may still be able to sew for themselves, but in Halifax 'the manufactories have kept them ignorant of plain work'. She concludes that it cannot be expected, or even wished, 'that the state of our manufactures should again be what it *has* been—but people and things cannot go on as they are'.

In later years, Wordsworth's fear of the mob and of a popular uprising increased. In 1812 he wrote that for thirty years 'the lower orders have been accumulating in pestilential masses of ignorant population'. In 1817 he warmly approved the suspension of the Habeas Corpus Act, declared himself an alarmist, and said that though he thought a Revolution could be staved off, and the Cumberland and Westmorland population was at present sound —they might not remain so if rebellion grew elsewhere. This he ascribed to the slackening of the community's *organic* sense of the classes' 'vital and harmonious dependence on each other'. There was no longer any vital *feeling* of attachment between landlord, farmer and labourer—the large new farms were worked by gangs of ill-paid and half-pauperized labourers, often without local roots. The 'feelings' Wordsworth so much valued had also disappeared from business relations within country towns. In Wordsworth's lifetime country squires and substantial yeomen had bought from the same shop as generations of their ancestors, breeding 'substantial amity and interchanges of hospitality'. Now 'all this moral cement is dissolved, habits and prejudices are broken and rooted up, nothing being substituted in their place but a quickened self interest, with more extensive views and wider dependencies—but more lax in proportion as they are wider'.

This extensive quickened self-interest is analogous to Carlyle's demon, the Cash Nexus. Coleridge, too, felt that commerce was becoming an end in itself, and not the means to national health, or justice, or happiness. In 1800 he was writing in *The Morning Post* that 'ministerial loans and job work' created vicious speculation: schemes for internal navigation and rendering waste lands useful had not proceeded with their earlier energy. And the numerous soup establishments, the Committees for the labouring poor were in themselves suspicious phenomena. They were highly honourable to the rich—but to the nation? 'Is that a genuine prosperity in which healthy labourers are commonly styled "the labouring *poor*"?'

The conservative Wordsworths grew more afraid of the starving people, the mob. Dorothy complained desperately that 'so many changes are going on, I consider nothing as stable; and do expect that the sovereign people to whom our rulers bow so obsequiously will not long endure the stamp office and its distributors or the national debt or anything else that now is.' Wordsworth declared more grandly in 1835 that he had 'been in the midst of one Revolution in France and recoil with horror from the thought of a second at home. The Radicals and foolish Whigs are driving the nation rapidly to that point that soon alas! it is likely to be found that power will pass from the audacious and wicked to the more audacious and wicked, and so to the still more and more, till military despotism comes in as a quietus.' (The prose in his letters by this time is dull *except* on this subject.)

But in their later years both poets retain a concern for the poor, despite Wordsworth's fear of the mob. Coleridge in 1833, table-talking about machinery, talks about its power to render artefacts cheaper—'a silk gown is now five times cheaper than in Queen Elizabeth's time'. But it cannot in the same way, he believes, cheapen 'the immediate growths of nature or the immediate necessaries of man'. The rich are made incalculably better off by machinery than the poor, whose benefits can be summed up as 'cotton-dresses for maidservants and penny gin to all'.

Wordsworth, gloomy and pessimistic, in 1828 notes that 'misery and privation are fearfully prevalent' but argues that it is 'a thousand to one that the means resorted to to palliate the evil will aggravate it.' The 'means resorted to' include many that *did* help the poor—Benefit Societies, Savings Banks, Infant Schools, Mechanics' Institutes—and Wordsworth's advocation of a 'wise passiveness' seems slightly injudicious here. 'Circumstances have forced this nation to do, by its manufacturers, an undue portion of the dirty and unwholesome work of the globe. . . .' But we 'must bear the sight' of the results, and 'endure its pressure, till we have by reflection discovered the cause . . .'.

Partly, he feared a cheapening and debasing of the things he really cared about through the increase in the power of the people on one hand and commerce on the other. Talking about the sale

Wordsworth in 1832, from a drawing by H. W. Pickersgill

of the Derwentwater estate in 1832 he expresses a fear that the land may be parcelled out which spreads into his double fear:

> If the democratic Spirit be organized in Legislation to the extent now wished for, and aimed at by many, the pecuniary value of every thing in the world of Taste will sink accordingly; and its intellectual estimation will also erelong be proportionately affected. Men will have neither time, tranquillity, or disposition to think about any such thing.

The truth was that Wordsworth, although he spoke truly about being moved by the 'still, sad music of humanity', was moved by the permanent truth of the sadness of the human condition more than by particular abuses, which always became for him emblems of permanent truth, if they did move him, as with the leech-gatherer. For him, solitude, contemplation, and deep thought were necessities of life: and the grudging tone in which he refers to 'democratic legislation' in the quotation above is related to the famous passages in the Preface to the *Lyrical Ballads*, where he speaks of *new* 'causes . . . acting with combined force to blunt the discriminating powers of the mind, and unfitting it for all voluntary exertion, to reduce it to a state of almost savage torpor'. These 'causes' he describes, in part, as 'great national events daily taking place' and 'accumulation of men in cities, where the uniformity of their occupations produces a craving for extraordinary incident'. These complaints—that the pace and uniformity of modern life sap the mind, the will, the necessary sense of being an individual aware of the 'natural' rhythms of life—are still with us, and so, in our fear of bureaucracy, of standardization, is Wordsworth's fear of 'democracy'. It was Wordsworth who wrote

> The world is too much with us: late and soon
> Getting and spending we lay waste our powers:
> Little we see in Nature that is ours;

And knowing what he thought the proper use of 'our powers' to be, we can understand the note of pompous irritation in his letter to Lady Beaumont about criticisms of his *Poems in Two Volumes*:

The things which I have taken, whether from within or without—
what have they to do with routs, dinners, morning calls, hurry
from door to door, from street to street, on foot or in carriage;
with Mr Pitt or Mr Fox, or Sir Francis Burdett, the Westminster
Election . . . in a word, for I cannot stop to make my way through
the hurry of images that present themselves to me, what have they
to do with endless talking about things nobody cares anything for
except as far as their own vanity is concerned . . . It is a truth and
an awful truth, that there neither is nor can be any genuine en-
joyment of Poetry among 19 out of 20 of those persons who live
or wish to live in the broad light of the world . . . This is a truth,
and an awful one, because to be incapable of a feeling of Poetry
in my sense of the word is to be without love of human nature and
reverence for God.

But beside Wordsworth's mistrust of the people and reverence
for 'human nature' must be set Coleridge's assertion, in face of
the 'self-adjusting' economic machine, that persons are not things.
The injustices and inhumanity of thinkers and politicians produced from Coleridge prose as great in its way as all but the
greatest of Wordsworth's poems. They tell us, he wrote, that

things are always finding their level: which might be taken as the
paraphrase or ironical definition of a storm. . . . But persons are
not things—but man does not find his level. Neither in body nor
in soul does man find his level. After a hard and calamitous season,
during which the thousand wheels of some vast manufactory had
remained silent as a frozen waterfall, be it that plenty has returned
and that trade has once more become brisk and stirring: go ask
the overseer, and question the parish doctor, whether the workman's
health and temperance, with the staid and respectful manners best
taught by the inward dignity of conscious self-support, have found
their level again? Alas! I have more than once seen a group of
children in Dorsetshire, during the heat of the dog-days, each with
its little shoulders up to its ears and its chest pinched inward—the
very habit and fixtures as it were that had been impressed on their
frames by the former ill-fed, ill-clothed and unfuelled winters. But
as with the body, so or still worse with the mind. Nor is the effect
confined to the labouring classes, whom by an ominous but too
appropriate change in our phraseology we are now accustomed to
call the labouring poor!

4 *Political Views*

Three main themes can be traced in the political views and writings of both Wordsworth and Coleridge. These are their early belief in the rationality and goodness of human nature, leading to support of revolutionary and republican politics: the effects on their beliefs and attitudes of the wars with France, the French conquest of Europe and the character of Napoleon: and their later belief, in differing forms, in a hierarchical society, a national Church and an inherited English constitution which made them appear largely as supporters of the High Tory interest. Browning's reproach to Wordsworth, the 'lost leader', is well known:

> Shakespeare was of us, Milton was for us,
> Burns, Shelley, were with us,—they watch from their graves!
> He alone breaks from the van and the freemen,
> He alone sinks to the rear and the slaves!

The reproach was to a certain extent justified—Wordsworth's fear of the rising mob, leading to fear of any social change at all, did become exaggerated political timidity and rigidity towards the end of his life, and Browning's lines

> Deeds will be done,—while he boasts his quiescence,
> Still bidding crouch whom the rest bade aspire.

touch a note of criticism already touched by his friends and contemporaries. But the poets' later profound conservatism springs as powerfully from their studies of human nature and their interest in the nature of things, in man's relationship to his environment and to Nature, as their earlier sympathetic republicanism. However, the view of human nature has changed. It is a literary cliché that the 'Romantic Movement' appeared more or less with the French Revolution and that it celebrates bursting individual energy as opposed to the eighteenth century's celebration of neo-classical order, harmony and constraint. It is thus revolutionary and anarchic. This cliché is truer of the French Romantics, born in a later generation than Wordsworth and Coleridge, than it is of the English—Stendhal admired the bursting energy of Napoleon whilst Wordsworth and Coleridge loathed him, Victor Hugo celebrated the French Revolution as a human event and a human blessing analogous to Homer and Shakespeare. The English Romantics never were a 'movement' and differ very greatly in their beliefs. It has been pointed out that on the day the Bastille fell, Crabbe and Blake were over thirty, Wordsworth just nineteen, Scott close on eighteen, Coleridge and Southey sixteen, whilst Byron was eighteen months old and Shelley and Keats unborn. And it was the later generation— Byron and Shelley, with the older Blake—who shared the belief in unleashing human *energy* with the French—Byron's sexual misdemeanours and Alfred de Musset's were part of *a* Romantic mythology. But Coleridge and Wordsworth had seen the French Revolution as a dawning of a new *order*, and they were later to change their views about the possibility of forming an order in that way.

An interest in medieval life was part of Romanticism: everyone knows that ivy-covered ruins, ballads, and the glamour of the past were major poetic props and themes from *Christabel* to *St Agnes Eve*. Sir Walter Scott's historical novels, Coleridge's researches into the lost theology and philosophy of the Dark Ages, Southey's antiquarian interests grew from more than a romantic nostalgia for fancy dress and deeds of blood and gallantry—of which, after all, they had enough in their lifetime. It has been argued that fears of mob violence and disillusionment with the self-seeking rulers of England caused these writers to feel nostalgia for what they imagined to have been the rigid rules and personal relationships of feudal England—a point to which I want to come back. But the interest in history revealed also an aspect of human nature ignored by the hopeful utilitarian and socialist reformers like Bentham and Owen, who believed that enlightened self-interest would produce harmony and happiness. It revealed savagery and unrestrained energy—analogous to that

Sir Walter Scott (1771–1832), from an engraving after a portrait
by G. S. Newton

revealed by the French Terror—and this helped Wordsworth,
Coleridge and Southey to develop a 'pessimistic' view of human
nature which implied political structures and controls very
different from those envisaged by their youthful enthusiasms.
Feudal rigidity was the corollary of unleashed human energy.

Writing on human nature in the world of Scott's historical novels, Hazlitt observed that these

> carry us back to the feuds, the heart-burnings, the havoc, the dismay, the wrongs and the revenge of a barbarous age and people . . . As we read, we throw aside the trammels of civilisation, the flimsy veil of humanity. . . . The wild beast resumes its sway within us. We feel like hunting animals, and as the hound starts in its sleep and rushes on the chase in fancy, the heart rouses itself in its native lair, and utters a wild cry of joy, at being restored once more to freedom and lawless, unrestrained impulses. Everyone has his full swing, or goes to the Devil his own way. Here are no Jeremy Bentham's Panopticons, none of Mr Owen's impassable Parallelograms, no long calculations of self-interest—the will takes its instant way to its object.

Hazlitt, the Radical and the profound admirer of Napoleon, was less disturbed by the possible political effects of releasing the 'impulses' and the 'will' than either his subject, Walter Scott, or Wordsworth and Coleridge—although all of these were believers in releasing the real human passions from the trammels of 'civilization' in some way or another. And there is a note of caution in Hazlitt's own remarks. But it was the shift of interest from the naturally 'good' human passions to the naturally 'destructive' human passions which underlay the poets' change of position on political belief. This shift of interest is still with us—it produced Freud's pessimistic view of man's underlying irrational passions and drives, controlled only by reason and civilization: it produced the current interest not in medieval but in animal patterns of aggression as a means of understanding the behaviour of groups of human beings. A reassessment of Coleridge's political psychology is illuminating.

I have described Browning's criticism of Wordsworth: both Coleridge and Southey also suffered in their public lives from the shift of their views. In 1817 Southey's republican play, *Wat Tyler*, was republished when the poet was Laureate and a respectable conservative figure: the Whig newspapers abused him as 'turncoat Southey'. Coleridge made several attempts to water down his past views as his position changed, but was politically suspected by both sides as a result of his history. He wrote a great deal of excellent political journalism, and talked and thought more, but was never recognized fully as a political thinker. This was partly because of the complexity of his more serious style and his belief that all political views should be seen to be derived from true philosophical principles. In 1817 he wrote a long letter to Lord Liverpool, then Prime Minister, who endorsed it with what is in fact a neat and honourable summary of an extraordinarily abstruse piece of writing:

> From Mr Coleridge, stating that the object of his writings has been to rescue speculative philosophy from false principles of reasoning, and to place it on that basis, or give it that tendency which would make it best suited to the interests of religion as well as of the State; at least, I believe this is Mr Coleridge's meaning but I cannot well understand him.

In 1814 Coleridge was complaining with some justice to the editor, Daniel Stuart that

> I have too sad an account to settle between my Self that is and has been and my Self that *can* not cease to be, to allow me a single Complaint that for all my labors in behalf of Truth, against the Jacobins first, then against military Despotism abroad, against Weakness, and Despondency, and Faction, and factious *Goodness* at home—I have never received from those in power even a verbal acknowledgement—tho' by mere reference to dates it might be proved, that no small number of fine Speeches in the House of Commons and elsewhere originated directly or indirectly in my Essays and Conversation.

Crabb Robinson was fond of quoting Southey's saying that he was no more ashamed of having been a Republican than of having been a child. And of Godwin's *Political Justice*, the book that inspired part of Coleridge's revolutionary fervour, Crabb Robinson wrote:

> I never became an atheist, but I could not feel aversion or contempt towards anything that Godwin was. In one respect the book had

the best of effects on my mind—No book ever made me feel more
generously. I never before, nor have I ever since, I fear, felt so strongly
the duty of not living to one's self, and that of having for one's sole
object the welfare of the community.

Although Wordsworth and Coleridge rejected Godwin's views
of reason as a guiding light to perfect justice and perfect society
they both remained personal friends of Godwin himself throughout his later unpopularity. And they, like Crabb Robinson, were
ready to admit that Godwin's work had made them feel generously
and unselfishly. The young Coleridge, lecturing in Bristol in
1795, praised 'thinking and disinterested patriots' as men who
had discovered that vice lay not in men but 'in the surrounding
circumstances; not in the heart but in the understanding'.

But he was abandoning Godwinism the next year, and placing
emphasis in man's struggle for justice and freedom on qualities
Godwin mistrusted or disbelieved—natural private affections and
the Christian religion with its prescription, not of enlightenment,
but of love and duty.

Coleridge's state of mind during this early part of his career as
a political thinker is best gauged by looking at the plan for the
Pantisocracy, that ideal scheme to which he gave so much passion
and turned out to have sacrificed so much. The idea was that
twelve men of liberal political views should emigrate to Pennsyl-
vania, to the banks of the Susquehanna river, to form an ideal
society governed by all equally. Southey's brother-in-law, the
Quaker Robert Lovell, is said to have described the scheme as
based on a belief in human perfectibility—they would 'realize a
state of society free from the evils and turmoils that then agitated
the world, and present an example of the eminence to which men
might arrive under the unrestrained influence of sound principles'.
The structure would work in a Godwinian way 'by not establishing
formal laws, but by excluding all the little deteriorating passions',
such as injustice 'wrath, anger, clamour and evil speaking'.
Cottle said that Coleridge's preference for the Susquehanna
seemed to rise 'solely from its imposing name, which, if not classical
was at least poetical', but this is not quite true. Coleridge had read

Coleridge in 1795, from a portrait by P. Vandyke

various pamphlets about colonizing that part of the world: and the scheme itself was only one of many, several of which went much further than the planning stage. Robert Owen, so successful in reforming the mills at New Lanark, set out to found a visionary community, New Harmony, in the New World, and failed miserably. But Coleridge's extravagant enthusiasm for the scheme was a powerful emotional determinant in his life. His early love, Mary Evans, wrote to dissuade him from it, accusing him of 'an Eagerness in your Nature which is ever hurrying you into a sad extreme'. This distressed him greatly but did not disillusion him: it was Southey's defection which did that. At the time he was writing in a generally idealistic and iconoclastic mode to his friends, that despite Mary's plea 'where Justice leads I will follow—though her path be through thorns and roughness—The Scotts desire their compliments. *Compliments*: cold aristocratic Inanities—! I abjure their nothingness. If there be any whom I deem worthy of remembrance—I am their Brother. I call even my Cat Sister in the Fraternity of universal Nature. Owls I respect and Jack Asses I love: for Aldermen and Hogs, Bishops and Royston Crows I have not particular partiality—; they are my Cousins, however, at least by Courtesy. But Kings, Wolves, Tygers, Generals, Ministers and Hyaenas, I renounce them all— or if they *must* be my Kinsmen, it shall be in the 50th Remove— May the Almighty Pantisocratizer of Souls pantisocratize the Earth and bless you and S. T. Coleridge.'

Wordsworth's early republicanism was equally fervent if less extravagant. His passage on his early feelings about the French revolution is almost too famous to need quoting:

> Bliss was it in that dawn to be alive,
> But to be young was very Heaven! O times,
> In which the meagre, stale, forbidding ways
> Of custom, law and statute, took at once
> The attraction of a country in romance!
> When Reason seemed the most to assert her rights
> When most intent on making of herself
> A prime enchantress—to assist the work,
> Which then was going forward in her name.

But Wordsworth, like Coleridge at the same time, was concerned to believe that Godwinian reason led not to fantastic Utopias but to sober reality and reform. Both the meek and the lofty, he claimed

> Were called upon to exercise their skill,
> Not in Utopia,—subterranean fields—
> Or some secreted island, Heaven knows where!
> But in the very world, which is the world
> Of all of us—the place where in the end
> We find our happiness, or not at all!

And Wordsworth's first political pamphlet, written probably early in 1793 but not published in his life-time was as republican as any of Coleridge's fiery addresses. *A Letter to the Bishop of Llandaff* is a reproach to that Bishop who had supported the Revolution in its early days but publicly recanted after the execution of Louis XVI. Wordsworth was at this time as much of an egalitarian as the Coleridge of the letter quoted above. He argued that monarchy implied nobility and that leisured classes encouraged racing, gambling and prostitution: they were parasitic and became richer as the poor became poorer. At this stage Wordsworth was extreme enough to advocate the abolition of the monarchy and of all titles, and the institution of universal suffrage.

The Anti-Jacobin Magazine issued a parody of Coleridge and Lamb which caught well enough the hostile image of the sources of their political sympathy and its relationship to the soft sensibility of their early verses:

> See! faithful to their mighty dam,
> C-dge, S-th-y, L-d, and L-b,
> In splay-foot madrigals of love,
> Soft moaning like the widow'd dove,
> Pour side-by-side their sympathetic notes;
> Of equal rights, and civic feasts,
> And tyrant kings and knavish priests
> Swift through the land the tuneful mischief floats.
> And now to softer strains they struck the lyre,
> They sung the beetle or the mole,

The dying kid, or ass's foal
By cruel man permitted to expire.

During the unrest in England at the time of the French
Revolution, the government took various steps to stamp out the
possibility of revolution at home; the Habeas Corpus Act was
suspended in 1794 and various measures were taken against
meetings for political purposes or propagation of doctrines leading
to sedition. Spies and informers were also very active. Coleridge,
in *Biographia Literaria*, related that when they were in Somerset
'the dark guesses of some zealous quidnunc met with so congenial
a soil in the grave alarm of a titled Dogberry of our neighbourhood
that a spy was actually sent down from the government *pour
surveillance* of myself and friend. There must have been not only
abundance, but variety of these 'honorable men' at the disposal
of ministers: for this proved a very honest fellow.' Research among
the Home Office papers proved that Coleridge's claim was no
extravagant fantasy. In August 1797 a Mr Lysons had written
to the Duke of Portland about 'a very suspicious business concerning an emigrant family who have contrived to get possession
of a Mansion House at Alfoxton'. The man and the 'woman who
passes for his sister' had been observed to make nocturnal and
diurnal excursion around the countryside carrying camp stools
and a portfolio, in which they entered observations for which
they had been heard to say they should be rewarded. A spy was
despatched to Stowey to observe the 'French people'. His reports
contained several suspicious circumstances—the French people
had been seen washing and mending *on Sunday*. The most suspicious
circumstance was reported by a man named Mogg ('by no means
the most intelligent Man in the World' the spy thought). The
French people had been enquiring whether the brook was navig-
able and had afterwards been seen examining its course 'quite down
to the sea'. Coleridge in *Biographia* explains this: he was writing
a poem entitled *The Brook* and the brook itself 'traced from its
source in the hills among the yellow-red moss and conical glass-
shaped tufts of peat' to the hamlet, town, manufactories and sea-
port was to form a natural connecting link between the parts of a

poem concerned with 'description, incident and impassioned reflections on man, nature and society'. Coleridge ended mockingly by saying that had the work been finished he intended

> to have dedicated it to our then committee of public safety as containing the charts and maps with which I was to have supplied the French government in aid of their plans of invasion. And these too for a tract of coast that from Clevedon to Minehead scarcely permits the approach of a fishing boat!

Although the spy came to the conclusion that the inhabitants of Alfoxton House were 'a Sett of violent Democrats'—partly because of the presence of Thomas Poole (who ran a Poor Man's Club in Nether Stowey), Coleridge, and the democrat Thelwall—the trouble died down. Coleridge *said* that the spy had engaged him in conversation and Coleridge had, when asked about Jacobinism 'plainly made it out to be such a silly as well as wicked thing, that he felt ashamed, though he had only put it on'.

Coleridge was good at describing his past views as though they had been more virtuous and consistent than was the case. But various events had disillusioned both him and Wordsworth with the new French government. In 1798 the French government suppressed the Swiss cantons, which also represented democracy in the minds of men like Coleridge: the result of revolution and republicanism was turning out to be tyranny. *France, an Ode*, was Coleridge's poetic statement of this change. It describes his adoration of 'the spirit of divinest Liberty':

> When France in wrath her giant-limbs upreared
> And with that oath, which smote air, earth and sea
> Stamped her strong foot and said she would be free
> Bear witness for me, how I hoped and feared!
> With what a joy my lofty gratulation
> Unawed I sang, amid a slavish band.

He had opposed the British participation in the war against France. But he has to continue

Forgive me, Freedom! O forgive those dreams!
I hear thy voice, I hear thy loud lament,
From bleak Helvetia's icy caverns sent—
I hear thy groans upon her blood-stained streams!
Heroes, that for your peaceful country perished,
And ye that, fleeing, spot your mountain-snows
With bleeding wounds; forgive me, that I cherished
One thought that ever blessed your cruel foes!

Both in *France, an Ode* and in *Fears in Solitude* Coleridge turns away
from the search for freedom, which he declares never 'didst
breathe thy soul in forms of human power' to the consolation of
the different freedom of nature, symbolized in both poems by
trees which are unmoved by distant gusts of wind:

May the vaunts
And menace of the vengeful enemy
Pass like the gust, that roared and died away
In the distant tree: which heard, and only heard
In this low dell, bowed not the delicate grass.

Wordsworth in his early days as a student of the French language
in France felt that the Revolution was 'nothing out of nature's
certain course/A gift that was come rather late than soon'. But
on his way back to England through Paris after the September
massacres he lay awake at night feeling that 'the fear gone by/
Pressed on me almost like a fear to come'. And the sleeping city
seemed, like Macbeth's world, haunted by a voice that cried 'sleep
no more': Wordsworth called it 'Defenceless as a wood where
tigers roam'. Tigers had replaced reason as the image of the
French people in his mind, and he later compared the greed of
the tyrants for 'Head after head and never heads enough' to a
small child playing with a toy windmill, running against the wind
to make the thing whirl faster. Wordsworth who had received in
proud isolation the news of England's declaration of war against
France and 'fed on the day of vengeance yet to come' came to
rejoice deeply at the news that Robespierre was dead. His summing up, in the *Prelude*, of his new attitude to the events is a
masterly piece of psychology, balance, and verse:

> If from the affliction somewhere do not grow
> Honour which could not else have been, a faith,
> An elevation and a sanctity,
> If new strength be not given nor old restored
> The blame is ours, not Nature's. When a taunt
> Was taken up by scoffers in their pride,
> Saying 'Behold the harvest that we reap
> From popular government and equality,
> I clearly saw that neither these nor aught
> Of wild belief engrafted on their names
> By false philosophy had caused the woe,
> But a terrific reservoir of guilt
> And ignorance filled up from age to age
> That could no longer hold its loathsome charge
> But burst and spread in deluge through the land.

It was the reversal of views on France which caused both poets to develop a respect for Edmund Burke, the political thinker who was later to influence their theories of nationality and the con- stitution of the state very profoundly. Coleridge, in *Biographia*, describes Burke in terms which he would ideally have liked to see applied to his own work too. He points out that Burke's speeches and writings at the beginning of the war with the American colonies (in which Burke supported the Americans) and at the beginning of the French Revolution, were constructed from the same *principles* 'but the practical inferences almost opposite in the one case from those drawn in the other; yet in both equally legitimate and in both equally confirmed by the results'. This success Coleridge attributes to Burke's capacity to understand the general laws of human behaviour.

> Edmund Burke possessed and had sedulously sharpened that eye which sees all things, actions and events in relation to the laws that determine their existence and circumscribe their possibility. He referred habitually to principles. He was a scientific statesman; and therefore a seer. For every principle contains in itself the germs of a prophecy; and as the prophetic power is the essential privilege of science, so the fulfilment of its oracles supplies the outward and (to men in general) the only test of its claim to the title. Wearisome

as Burke's refinements appeared to his parliamentary auditors,
yet the cultivated classes throughout Europe have reason to be
thankful that

> he went on refining
> And thought of convincing while they thought of dining.

Burke believed that the French revolutionaries with their
egalitarian principles had abolished all distinctions of class and
privilege only in order to create from their mass of equal—and
therefore undifferentiated—*individuals* the lawless mob. In-
dividualism of this kind produces anarchy, and anarchy tends
to throw up absolute dictators (in the name of 'the people' or in
their own name) to produce a kind of order. Burke foresaw the
military rule which succeeded mob rule in France. The violence
and disorderliness of the new French state alarmed him more than
the dangerous democratic beliefs themselves. 'The effect of
erroneous doctrines may soon be done away with; but the example
of *successful pillage* is of a nature more permanent.' The new state
had rejected at one blow all the principles of order which had
governed human society; it had 'made a schism with the whole
universe'. He described this State in his marvellous prose: a
'strange, nameless, wild, enthusiastic thing'.

Coleridge, writing in *The Morning Post* about Bonaparte's
elevation to First Consul, was cautiously approving. He pointed
out that 'in all great cities and in all countries, much more therefore in a revolutionary country' the possessors of *new wealth* were
likely to be more powerful, more active, more widely experienced
than the men of hereditary wealth, and that these people with the
real power were unlikely to want to restore the monarchy. It was
true that Bonaparte's methods were undesirable, but the man
himself seemed possibly the right man for the times. 'In this
usurpation, Bonaparte stabbed his honesty in the vitals; it has
perished—we admit that it has perished—but the mausoleum
where it lies interred is among the wonders of the world.' Bonaparte
was a 'man of commanding genius' (a favourite term of Coleridge
for the *active* man of imagination) whose interest in art and letters
was genuine, and who seemed likely to be broadly tolerant of
varied views amongst all his supporters and thus employ all the

available talent. Coleridge concluded: 'He is a despot indeed, but not a tyrant.' The question was whether he would 'act with true greatness and make the happiness of the nation, rather than personal power, his object'. Time alone could decide that. However, 'if his virtues be as great as his genius he may do for the old world what Washington has done for the new'.

He changed his mind very quickly. In 1803, when England was under the threat of immediate French invasion he wrote to his brother praising himself for having forced himself away from 'the abstruse Researches in which I am engaged, to embark on this stormy Sea of Politics—but I felt it my Duty to write essays and Alarum-trumpets in the Morning Post'. He claimed that his writings had 'extravagantly irritated the First Consul'. In 1800 he had published a long and very severe Character of Pitt and promised to follow it up with one of Bonaparte. He claimed that an emissary from Bonaparte himself had been enquiring about the *Character of the First Consul*—'which no doubt he expected would be pure eulogy'. Coleridge's editor, Daniel Stuart, was in high spirits about this, but, Coleridge claims, he himself was gloomy:

'Stuart, that man will prove a Tyrant, and the deadliest enemy of the Liberty of the Press.' 'Indeed?' 'Yes! a man, the Dictator of a vast Empire, to be so childishly solicitous for the *panegyric* of a Newspaper Scribbler—! will he not be equally irritable at the *Abuse* of newspaper Scribblers!—I am sick and sad, to feel how important little men become, when madmen are in power.'—Stuart has often talked of publishing this conversation of mine as an instance of political prophecy.

Coleridge continued to be an object of Bonaparte's resentment; he was warned by the Prussian plenipotentiary at Rome when he visited that city in 1806 and had to leave, he said, in a hurry—a warrant was out for his arrest. He may have spoken deprecatingly of newspaper scribblers and compared himself to a leveret or a fieldmouse under the telescopic eye of the 'true vulture', Napoleon, but in fact he believed deeply in the power of the press and of free discussion. In 1816 he wrote to Daniel Stuart claiming that Stuart 'did more against the French Scheme of Continental Domination than the Duke of Wellington has done—or rather, Wellington could neither have been supplied by the Ministers, or the Ministers supported by the Nation, but for the Tone first given and then constantly kept up by the plain *un*-ministerial, anti-opposition, anti-Jacobin, anti-Gallican, anti-Napoleonic spirit of your writings.' It was very important, he believed, that newspapers should not become 'Ministerial organs' but should remain independent. Ministers 'do not *love* Newspapers in their hearts, not even those that support them. Indeed it seems epidemic among Parliament men in general to affect to look down upon and despise Newspapers, to which they owe $\frac{999}{1000}$ of their influence and character, and at least 3/5ths of their knowledge and phraseology.' He carried his belief that political thought entailed a grasp of philosophical principles into his journalistic world too. He recorded that he had 'undertaken the literary and political department of the Morning Post' on condition 'that the paper should thenceforwards be conducted on certain fixed and announced principles, and that I should be neither obliged or requested to deviate from them in favour of any party or event.'

His judgment of particular men was apt, for this reason, to be severe. His *Character of Pitt* is a splendid piece of prose. Pitt, according to Coleridge, fundamentally lacked what Coleridge most cared about—imagination, a sense of the unity and causes of things. Pitt had been created by his father's ambition: the elder Pitt used to make the younger stand on a chair and declaim to large gatherings, a process which must, Coleridge believed, by diverting his attention from the *thing* on which he spoke to the praise to be gained, have given him 'a premature and unnatural dexterity in the combination of words, which must of necessity have diverted his attention from present objects, obscured his impressions, and deadened his genuine feelings'. Pitt was a very young man, and early very successful. 'He was always full grown: he had neither the promise nor the awkwardness of a growing intellect.' At Cambridge he avoided 'that revelry and debauchery which are so often fatal to the powers of intellect . . .', which was a pity, Coleridge thought, as in his case they might have given him a sense of reality and humanity. 'But Mr Pitt's conduct was correct.'

William Pitt addressing the House of Commons, 1793, from a painting by Karl Anton Hickel

Coleridge, one of whose major interests was the relationship between individual psychology, the history of thought and the
creation and use of language, saw Pitt as a man controlled by
abstract *words* and eloquence, unrelated to the feelings and facts
which create words. 'Press him to specify an *individual* fact of
advantage to be derived from a war and he answers, security.
Call upon him to particularize a crime, and he exclaims—
Jacobinism! Abstractions defined by abstractions! Generalities
defined by generalities!' Coleridge's portrait has literary qualities
of precisely the opposite kind—it is concrete and curiously vivid.
There is a kind of sympathy, a wish to understand *how* Pitt, as he
saw him, came about, even in his condemnations:

> The influencer of his country and his species was a young man,
> the creature of another's predetermination, sheltered and weather-
> fended from all the elements of experience; a young man whose
> feet had never wandered; whose very eye had never turned to the
> right or the left; whose whole track had been as curveless as the
> motion of a fascinated reptile.

In 1806, however, when both Pitt and his great rival Charles
James Fox died, Coleridge was busy preparing to answer *The
Morning Chronicle*'s assertions 'that Mr Fox was the greatest and
wisest Statesman . . . that Mr Pitt was no Statesman'. Both,
Coleridge said, were undeserving of that high character, but Pitt
was the better, as 'the evils which befel him were undoubtedly
produced in great measure by blunders and wickedness on the
continent . . . While the effects of Mr Fox's measures must in
and of themselves produce calamity and degradation.'

Coleridge himself was enlightened about the character of
practical politicians during his work to assist the Governor of
Malta, Sir Alexander Ball. He said many years later that 'it was
not until I had to correspond with official characters myself that
I fully understood the extreme shallowness and ignorance with
which men of some note too were able, after a certain fashion, to
carry out the government of important departments of the empire'.
He seems to have been an efficient administrator himself. In 1805
he wrote to Southey that he had spent nine months on the affairs

of Egypt, Sicily and the Coast of Africa, and described his fear that France, if she took over the African coast, would become a second Rome. He was bothered by the British inefficiency. The Egyptians, he said, 'were eager for France, only more, far more eager for Great Britain'. But what they really cared for was '*Hats* at all events!—(*Hats* means Europeans in contradistinction to Turbans!)'.

Wordsworth and Dorothy, too, observed the political and military events from a distance. Wordsworth wrote at Pitt's death that although he was generally regarded as a great loss he, Wordsworth, had never been quite happy about him:

His first wish (though probably unknown to himself) was that his Country should prosper under his administration; his next that it should prosper: could the order of these wishes have been reversed, Mr Pitt would have avoided many of the grievous mistakes into which, I think, he fell.

His opinion of the hero, Nelson, was equally measured. His poem, *The Happy Warrior*, a eulogy of the man of commanding genius, was written on Nelson's death. But he believed that Nelson's 'public life was stained by one great crime'—the crushing of the Neapolitan rebellion and hanging the patriot Caracciolo from the yardarm of *The Minerva* 'in a manner which was a clear breach of faith'.

Wordsworth wrote of his death: 'Considering the matter coolly there was little to regret. . . . Few men have ever died under circumstances so likely to make their death of benefit to their country; it is not easy to see what his life could have done comparable to it.'

Both poets came to feel real personal animosity towards Napoleon. Coleridge grew indignant about the inevitable comparison with Alexander. 'Napoleon was an APE', and war *within* a civilization for no reason other than aggrandisement was not glorious but 'contemptible, vulgar, the dotage of second childhood'. After Napoleon's imprisonment on Elba Coleridge made a prophetic 'transparency' for the Bristol peace celebrations depicting 'a Vulture with the Head of Napoleon chained to a rock, and Britannia bending down with one hand stretching out the wing of the Vulture and with the other clipping it with Shears, on the one blade of which was written Nelson, on the other Wellington. The motto:

> We've fought for Peace and conquer'd it at last.
> The ravening Vulture's Leg is fettered fast.
> Britons, rejoice! *and yet be wary too*!
> The Chain may break, the clipt wing sprout anew.

The Wordsworths were—to put it mildly—irritated by Napoleon's escape from Elba, which prevented Dorothy from attending the wedding of Wordsworth's daughter, Caroline, in Paris as she had planned to do. She at first hoped that he would not reach Paris, owing to 'the ludicrous and ragamuffin way in which he has proceeded'. When he did reach Paris she was indignant and mocking. 'Buonaparte's conduct, in direct contradiction to former practice and profession proves his weakness—Did you not smile with scorn when you read his decree of Abolition of the slave trade and Liberty of the press?—Then his fine professions of renouncing Conquest after his first declaration that he was come to avenge the Cause of France stripped of her Conquests!— These villainous Sunday newspapers are my abhorrence—I read in one the other day the following sentiment 'Surely it would be wise that the Allies should at length give Buonaparte time to show whether he is sincere or not!' In other words give him time to be quite prepared to fence himself in in his wickedness.' She was still indignant when she saw a paper affixed on the Ambleside coach proclaiming 'Great News. *Abdication of Buonaparte*'. 'What right,' she demanded, 'has he to abdicate or to have a word to say in the business! I am only afraid that the armies have stopped too soon as they did before.' The English tendency to find the deposed Emperor glamorous or sympathetic annoyed William too. In 1816 he was castigating Brougham, the Lonsdales' political opponent, who was 'not content with scribbling in the *Edinburgh Review* to the praise and glory of the Corsican but he must insult the people of England by expressing in their House of Legislature . . . his hope that the great man may be *kindly* treated in his insular prison'. In 1831, writing to the painter, Benjamin Haydon, who had finished a portrait of Napoleon on St Helena, he summed up his views:

> I think of Napoleon pretty much as you do but with more dislike probably; because my thoughts have turned less on the flesh and blood man than yours and therefore have been more at liberty to dwell with unqualified scorn upon his various liberticide projects and the miserable selfishness of his spirit. Few men of any time have been at the head of greater events; yet they seem to have had no power to create in him the least tendency towards magnanimity.

Wordsworth's tract *On the Convention at Cintra*, written in 1809, is an excellent example of the way he attacked political issues with the use of general principles and an interest in the imaginative workings of the mind. The occasion was the behaviour of the English generals, Sir Hew Dalrymple, Sir Harry Burrard and Sir Arthur Wellesley, after they had defeated the French at the Battle of Vimiero in Portugal. They had agreed, without consulting their Spanish or Portuguese allies, to convey the French forces, with all their arms and artillery, back to France and release them, to be at Napoleon's disposal again. Wordsworth wrote out of indignation at this, as he saw it, disloyal and dishonourable behaviour. The British in general had little love for their Spanish allies, disliking their Catholicism, their historic enmity with England, their guerrilla tactics and their fading away from pitched battles. Wordsworth defended them: their mode of warfare existed because 'the whole people is their army and their true army is the people and nothing else'. He himself intensely disliked Catholicism, but in this context he saw it as what it was— a faith which could hold a people together and give them a focus for value and a motive for action. What 'superstition' there was 'must necessarily have been transmuted by that triumphant power which grows out of intense moral suffering from the moment in which it coalesces with fervent hope ... and the types and instruments of error ... must have become a language and a ceremony of imagination'. The English leaders, he considered, had betrayed this energy and imagination of the Spaniards. In

1809 he was asking De Quincey to review the letters of Sir John Moore from Corunna 'as proofs of the miserable state of public spirit upon the Peninsula', in their prejudiced view of the Spaniards. Idealism caused him to make an unusual brutal pun: De Quincey was not to criticize Moore personally as 'this the People of England would not bear, he being a Commander-in-Chief, shot, and of course in their tender estimations, *cannonized*'. As for the generals of the Convention, the people 'were compelled by a necessity involved in the very constitution of man as moral Being to pass sentence upon them'. What he meant by this was that the feelings which led to patriotic loyalties and social cohesion were *natural* to human beings, and that therefore the morality which appealed to these loyalties was not imposed from above, but an organic part of human nature—thus *the people* could and must judge the generals. Patriotism was the highest conscious extension of the biological instinct to make home and family—from the 'sentient, the animal, the vital', higher principles of benevolence were evolved. Wordsworth used a beautiful image of a web to describe the interdependence of the needs of the self and the outgoing devotion to society:

The outermost and all-embracing circle of benevolence has inward concentric circles which, like those of the spider's web, are bound together by links, and rest upon each other; making one frame and capable of one tremor; circles narrower and narrower, closer and closer, as they lie more near to the centre of self from which they proceeded and which sustains the whole.

In his descriptions of the human soul involving itself in loyalty to its country and the human race he uses the conflicting images he uses in his poetry—the mind in solitary confinement, in a single cell as opposed to the mind joined, through imagination, with the unity of being. 'All that is *creative* in art and science and all that is magnanimous in virtue' come from communion with the outside world:

Despair thinks of *safety* and hath no purpose; fear thinks of safety; despondency looks the same way:—but these passions are far too selfish, and therefore too blind, to reach the thing at which they aim . . . All courage is a projection from ourselves; however short-lived, it is a motion of hope. But these thoughts bind too closely to something inward—to the present and to the past—that is to the self which is or has been. Whereas the Vigour of the human soul is from without and from futurity—in breaking down limit, and losing and forgetting herself in the sensation and image of Country and of the human race; and when she returns and is most restricted and confined, her dignity consists in the contemplation of a better and more exalted being which, though proceeding from herself, she loves and is devoted to as to another.

Thus Wordsworth's patriotism has the same roots as his poetic theory: the enhancing of vital energy through contemplation of a larger world. In *Cintra* he claimed explicitly that he as a poet, detached from 'the exclusive and artificial' situation of politicians was better equipped to 'assert the sanctity of principles and passions which are the natural birthright of man'. He felt about politicians very much as Coleridge felt about the younger Pitt. The nature of their calling, of their relationship to daily life and natural objects, of their manipulation of language made them blind and insensitive to 'the instincts of natural and social man'. Therefore revolutions could not liberate mankind. Coleridge had accused Pitt of using words without any relation to life or objects, in an abstract void. Wordsworth, in *Cintra*, suddenly produced Coleridge's image of the failure of the fusing imaginative power to describe the statesmen:

They have not a right to say—with a dejected man in the midst of the woods, the rivers, the mountains, the sunshine and shadows of some transcendent landscape—
I see not feel how beautiful they are!

The statesman lacked even the poets' capacity to see without feeling—had neither vision nor life. 'These spectators neither see nor feel,' Wordsworth wrote grandly.

There was perhaps something a little remote from practical politics in the grandeur and generality of Wordsworth's views—although Canning declared of *Cintra* that he could not deny that

Wordsworth had spoken with the 'bone of truth'. When the pamphlet was published, however, he became practical in a very worried way and harrassed De Quincey, who was seeing it through the press, with corrections and revisions. He became terrified that he would be imprisoned for attacking Wellington—that the passages about the People's judgment might be libellous. The women were more stoical. Dorothy wrote to De Quincey: 'William continues to haunt himself with fancies about Newgate or Dorchester or some other gaol, but as his mind clings to the gloomy, Newgate is his favourite theme.' Nothing came of these fears, and the pamphlet came out so late that it was no longer very topical.

But although Wordsworth here appealed to the conscience of 'the people', neither he nor Coleridge was any longer at all democratic. Coleridge spent much time and imagination in working out the implications of belief in Rousseau's social contract, with its assumption that society 'must be framed on such principles that every individual follows his own reason while he obeys the laws of the constitution, and performs the will of the state while he follows the dictates of his own reason'. This ideal reason could hardly be shown to exist: it was a dangerous dream of impossible perfection. What *did* exist was the evidence of the ways in which men had formed societies in the past. Coleridge saw a society not as an additive accumulation of equal individuals but as something analogous to an organism, the parts subserving the whole— like a poem. 'Unlike a million of tigers, a million of men is very different from one man. Each man in a numerous society is not only co-existent with, but virtually organized into, the multitude of which he is an integral part. . . . This is strictly analogous to what takes place in the vital organization of the individual man.' He believed that there never had been a state which was unified by 'absolute co-ordination of each to all and of all to each'. What republics there had been had slavery as an indispensable part of them—witness Athens. 'Subordination of classes and offices' made slavery unnecessary and actually created freedom. The Jacobin ideal of equality in fact meant a government founded on the belief that people had *rights*—in practice, the *right* to choose the government, which implied universal suffrage. Coleridge believed that more emphasis should be placed on *duties* of those in power. He also argued that a vote was not necessarily the best thing a man could have, or the most just or most useful. Writing in 1814 he criticized democrats, 'citizens of the world . . . the demagogues of the "enlightened age"', as he had criticized Pitt, for being *abstract*, setting up a bleak 'idea' of a state instead of one that was a natural growth. The result would be a democratic tyranny more absolute and inescapable than any tyranny by one person or class. They

> *commenced* by worshipping the sanctity of abstraction MAN, in the divinity of that other abstraction, the PEOPLE. But alas! the scheme *concludes* by mortising and compacting the scattered and sooty fragments of the *Populace* into one living and 'multitudinous idol', a blind but hundred-armed giant, of fearful power, to undermine the foundations of the social edifice and finally perchance to pull down the all-sheltering roof on its own head, the victim of its own madness! Thus, in order to sacrifice the *natural* STATE to PERSONS, they must concorporate PERSONS into one *unnatural* state; the deluded subjects of which soon find themselves under a dominion tenfold more oppressive and vexatious than that to which the laws of GOD and NATURE had attached them.. . . Shut up in the labyrinthine prison of forms and by-laws, of engagements by oaths and contributions by compulsion they move in slavish files beneath a jealous and ever-neighbouring control which despotizes in detail; in which every man is made his brother's keeper; and which, arming the hand and fixing the eye of all against each, merges the free will of the individual in the merciless tyranny of the confederation. . . .

It was a gloomy prediction of police states and bureaucracy, with a large measure of truth in the vision of what abstract ideals and totalitarian states can do to human nature.

This view of democratic idealism as pure fantasy did not stop Coleridge from criticizing the government of his own day. Both he and Wordsworth were attracted to the idea of existing English political and social institutions as naturally growing organisms, which had developed to suit the needs of the people. This was backed up by their medievalism and nostalgia for what they felt to have been the organic social links of benevolence and dependence, authority and duty, in the feudal system. Coleridge castigated 'those who commence the examination of a system by identifying it with its abuses or imperfections': no-one should criticize an institution until he had worked out what it was *ideally* designed for.

'How fine, for example, is the idea of the unhired magistracy of England, taking in and linking together the duke to the country gentleman in the primary distribution of justice, or in the preservation of order and execution of law at least throughout the country! Yet some men seem never to have thought of it for one moment, but as connected with brewers and barristers and tyrannical Squire Westerns.' But he was perfectly prepared himself to criticize the actual Government and Opposition. If the Whigs, he said in 1818, had not grievously misconducted themselves, the Government 'could not have remained in the hands of such simpleton saints as the Sidmouth Sect or of such unprincipled adventurers as the Castlereagh gang.' He lamented the 'awful deterioration of the lower classes, spite of Bible Societies and spite of our spinning jennies for the cheap and speedy manufacture of reading and writing'. But the blame was not wholly, or indeed largely, with the lower classes. The gentry were alarmist and full of self-interest. 'I see an unmanly spirit of alarm, and of self-convenience, under many a soft title, domestic comfort, etc. etc. in our gentry. The hardihood of English good sense in the shape of manly compromise (on the which, by the by, all our institutions are founded) seems to me decaying.'

Wordsworth's respect for the Constitution of England, like Coleridge's, derived from a vision of it as something evolved, worked out through manly compromise and real experience. This was what gave it its almost religious grandeur in his eyes: writing in 1831 out of fear of the Reform Bill, he said:

The Constitution of England, which seems about to be destroyed, offers to my mind the sublimest contemplation which the history of Society and Government have ever presented to it; and for this cause especially, that its principles have the character of preconceived ideas, archetypes of the pure intellect, while they are in fact the results of a humble-minded experience.

Much earlier in 1816 he was condemning the Whig opposition with grand rhetoric for lacking the human feeling necessary to understand and imagine the unity of England, church and state, which was the flower of the patriotism he desiderated:

> Suppose the opposition as a body, or take them in classes, the Grenvilles, the Wellesleys, the Foxites, the Burdettites and let your imagination carry them in procession through Westminster Hall, and thence let them pass into the adjoining Abbey, and give them credit for feeling the utmost and best that they are capable of feeling in connection with these venerable and sacred places, and say frankly whether you would be at all satisfied with the result. Imagine them to be looking from a green hill over a rich landscape diversified with Spires and Church Towers and hamlets, and all the happy sensations come much nearer to what one would desire; in a word, have they becoming reverence of the English characters and do they value as they ought, and even as their opponents do, the constitution of the country in *Church* and State.

The metaphor of organic growth of ideas permeates their political thought, as their poetic thought—Coleridge's nationalism, like Wordsworth's, assumed an organic relation between a man's senses, his *feelings* and his beliefs, and this led naturally to organic imagery for his beliefs. 'The cosmopolitanism which does not spring out of, and blossom upon, the deep-rooted stem of nationality, is a spurious and rotten growth.'

The high idealism of their views—particularly Wordsworth's—about the old forms of government and life produced some attitudes whose narrowness irritated broader-minded friends like Crabb Robinson, who wrote in 1845 'How many topics of the day are excluded at Rydal Mount. The Maynooth and Irish Colleges Bills. The Dissenters Chapels' Act. The American Questions— Slavery, Texas and Repudiation.' He later said he found it a relief to get away from 'the perpetual effort to preserve my independence' in this High Church, Tory atmosphere. Wordsworth's sonnets on the punishment of death, advocating the retention of capital punishment, are ringing with a rather nasty idealism—he considers the condemned alone within his cell *lucky* to have been given the chance of repentance by 'the solemn heed' of the State and the chance to avoid 'fresh offences'. He writes that the legislator

> feels how far the act would derogate
> From even the humblest functions of the State;
> If she, self-shorn of Majesty, ordain
> That never more shall hang upon her breath
> The last alternative of Life or Death.

Here the image of the imprisoned single man in a cell and the sympathy with the whole which produces love of nature or patriotism produces an unpleasant respect for a rigidly authoritarian State.

Since both poets' respect for the old state included a belief in a National Church as part of the unified feelings and loyalties of the nation, they felt strongly on religious issues. Coleridge's view was that the Church existed to provide the spiritual respect for the individual that the law and the body politic could *not* provide—thus giving meaning to the idea of lords spiritual, lords temporal as parts of a whole. Wordsworth saw the Church as authority: for this reason he was violently opposed to the movement for Catholic emancipation. Southey was with him on this—although Coleridge's clever daughter, Sara, was brave enough to argue about it.

The other measure which agitated them and everyone else was the issue of Parliamentary Reform. Both poets were against the Reform Bill of 1832. Coleridge disliked the particular measure —partly because it artificially extended the franchise only as far as £10 renters and he felt that logically one either did or did not admit universal suffrage. If £10 freeholders, why not everyone— why not even women? He also felt that the government was acting from 'fear of the mob' and that no measure of vital importance should be rushed through out of fear. There was cause for this fear—the Spa Field Riots in 1817 brought about the suspension of Habeas Corpus for a year. In 1819 was the famous massacre of Peterloo and in 1820 the Cato Street Conspiracy to murder all the ministers—as justified assassination. Wordsworth (though not Crabb Robinson or Coleridge) believed the Manchester magistrates had some right on their side in charging on the quiet crowd at Peterloo. He based his own opposition to Reform on what he called Burke's aversion to '*hot* Reformations . . . every sudden change in political institutions on a large scale'. He believed rotten boroughs should only be abolished if they could be shown to be corrupt. As for the large cities, the vote would do them little good—'but e'en let them have their humour in certain cases and try the result'. But the proceeding should be *tentative*, not wholesale. He feared that reform of the franchise would produce frequent parliaments which 'would convert the representatives into mere slavish delegates, as they now are in America, under the dictation of ignorant and selfish numbers, misled by unprincipled journalists who, as in France, will—no few of them—find their way into the House of Commons and so the last traces of a deliberative assembly will vanish'. He felt also that the proposals ignored the rights and responsibilities of holders of *property*. 'When I was young,' he said 'giving myself credit for qualities which I did not possess, and measuring mankind by that standard, I thought it derogatory to human nature to set up Property in preference to Person as a title for legislative power. That notion has vanished.' Part of his respect for property as entitlement to power came from his increasingly close association with Lord Lonsdale, promoting 'the Lowther interest' by journalism and electioneering at various elections against the candidature of Henry Brougham, a reforming lawyer who tried to appeal not only to voters but to those without votes who influenced voters—women and children. Wordsworth's activities on this front were not always pleasant—in 1818 he was busy buying up estates to be converted into freehold properties for safe Lonsdale voters 'as many persons, gentlemen, my friends and relations, who could be depended upon'. He informed the Lonsdales of his neighbours' political convictions. Brougham in his 1818 campaign directly attacked the poet, and at a banquet quoted Wordsworth's own poem on Rob Roy against him:

> For why? Because the good old rule
> Sufficeth them; the simple plan
> That they should take who have the power
> And they should keep who can.

But the Lonsdales kept: Brougham was never elected in West-morland.

There may have been a narrowness and timidity in certain of the poets' political views, but the basic thought patterns of their political logic and psychology are still of great interest. Coleridge argues brilliantly against Major Cartwright's belief that 'Laws to bind all must be assented to by all' on the ground that the same logic suggests that all have an equal right to property. 'Therefore unless he carries his system to the whole length of common labour and common possession, a right to universal suffrage cannot exist: but if not to universal suffrage, *there can exist no natural right to suffrage at all*' [my italics]. He produces, criticizing Major Cartwright's abstractions, a beautifully written summing-up of his own position:

> For his universal principles, as far as they are principles and universal, necessarily suppose uniform and perfect subjects, which are to be found in the ideas of pure geometry and (I trust) in the realities of Heaven, but never, never, in creatures of flesh and blood.

Wordsworth, in *The Excursion*, describes the wanderings of the Solitary in America—the America of Coleridge's dream of the Pantisocracy, home of the naturally pure and good Noble Savage, who is 'free as the sun and lonely as the sun', viewing 'with mind that sheds a light on what he sees'. But the noble savage, like Major Cartwright's universal principles, proves to be an abstraction, not a creature of flesh and blood:

> But that pure archetype of human greatness,
> I found him not. There, in his stead, appeared
> A creature squalid, vengeful and impure;
> Remorseless, and submissive to no law
> But superstitious fear and abject sloth.

The appeal to Nature had come full circle: the best that could be hoped was that habits and prejudices and inherited patterns of behaviour would produce some kind of motive to behave well. They came to understand what Burke meant in his appeal from reason to 'prejudice' as a guide to moral and political action—it was more consistent with human nature as they found it:

> We are afraid to put men to live and trade each on his own private stock of reason; because we suspect that this stock in each man is small, and that the individuals would do better to avail themselves of the general bank and capital of nations and of ages. Many of our men of speculation, instead of exploding general prejudices, employ their sagacity to discover the latent wisdom which prevails in them. If they find what they seek, and they seldom fail, they think it more wise to continue the prejudice, with the reason involved, than to cast away the coat of prejudice, and to have nothing but the naked reason; because prejudice, with its reason, has a motive to give action to that reason, and an affection which will give it permanence. Prejudice is of ready application in the emergency; it previously engages the mind in a steady course of wisdom and virtue and does not leave the man hesitating in the moment of decision, sceptical, puzzled and unresolved. Prejudice renders a man's virtue his habit; and not a series of unconnected acts. Through just prejudice, his duty becomes a part of his nature.

5 *Education and Childhood*

The child is father of the Man;
And I could wish my days to be
Bound each to each by natural piety.

Some of Wordsworth's greatest poetry deals with the relationship between the experience of the child and the experience of the adult —development of consciousness, modes of learning. *The Prelude, or the Growth of a Poet's Mind* traces Wordsworth's own progress in detail: the *Immortality* ode explores the philosophical and poetic implications of Wordsworth's awareness of his own states of consciousness in childhood. The interest in the child as a child, not a miniature adult, developed generally in this period, but some of Wordsworth's insights—and Coleridge's—are much deeper than was usual amongst poets or educational theorists. The precision of the *Immortality* ode's description of the child's awareness of the unreality of the external world could not be bettered. Wordsworth's own note on the poem describes his own experience of this state:

> I was often unable to think of external things as having external existence, and I communed with all that I saw as something not apart from, but inherent in, my own material nature. Many times while going to school have I grasped at a wall or tree to recall myself from this abyss of idealism to the reality. At this time I was afraid of such processes.

From this precise understanding of the way in which the child only gradually establishes an identity separate from the world around him—and thus only gradually becomes conscious that the world, and objects, and people are independent of his own consciousness—comes the famous passage in the *Immortality Ode*, where Wordsworth gives thanks for 'our past years' *not* indeed

> For that which is most worthy to be blest;
> Delight and liberty, the simple creed

> Of childhood, whether busy or at rest,
> With new-fledged hope still fluttering in his breast:

What Wordsworth is thankful for is

> those obstinate questionings
> Of sense, and outward things,
> Fallings from us, vanishings
> Blank misgivings of a Creature
> Moving about in worlds not realized—

Lionel Trilling has compared Wordsworth's interest in the child's changing sense of reality—literally the realizing of worlds—with Freud's. And Wordsworth understood well enough the connection between his experience of the 'abysses of idealism' as a child and his adult sense of the tension between the adult conscious identity, the prisoner of mortality in the individual cell or grave, and the poet's sense of the consciousness which expanded to relate to everything.

At this level where sensuality, instinct, emotions and mind are indistinguishable his awareness of childhood is rarely equalled.

It followed that he attached great importance to the education and upbringing of children. In *The Prelude* he contrasts the fate of the over-educated clever child with the free-running 'natural' boys who were his companions at Hawkshead Grammar School. Wordsworth's bright child is rather like Coleridge's image of Pitt. As with Pitt, virtuous conduct does not spring from *feeling* or from the whole human being:

> This model of a child is never known
> To mix in quarrels; that were far beneath
> Its dignity; with gifts he bubbles o'er
> As generous as a fountain; selfishness
> May not come near him, nor the little throng
> Of flitting pleasures tempt him from his path;
> The wandering beggars propagate his name,
> Dumb creatures find him tender as a nun,
> And natural or supernatural fear,
> Unless it leaps upon him in a dream,
> Touches him not.

This child is replete with knowledge—'a miracle of scientific lore'. He knows how to guide ships, 'he can read/the inside of the earth and tell the stars' he knows politics,

> Can string you names of districts, cities, towns,
> The whole world over, tight as beads of dew
> Upon a gossamer thread; he sifts, he weighs;
> All things are put to question; he must live
> Knowing that he grows wiser every day
> Or else not live at all, and seeing too
> Each little drop of wisdom as it falls
> Into the dimpling cistern of his heart:
> For this unnatural growth the trainer blame,
> Pity the tree.

Wordsworth deals with this 'unnatural growth' by placing it immediately next to one of his most famous and successful pieces of writing—'There was a Boy: ye knew him well, ye cliffs/And islands of Winander.'

This Boy is natural—his skill is to imitate the owls who halloo and scream back to him—but Wordsworth manages to convey the feeling that boy, owls and landscape are part of a spiritual experience all the greater for being unsought. The boy has, what the scholarly child has not, a sense of the unity of things. As he *is* the owls, so his mind and the water and sky are fused into one:

> Then sometimes, in that silence while he hung
> Listening, a gentle shock of mild surprise
> Has carried far into his heart the voice
> Of mountain torrents; or the visible scene
> Would enter unawares into his mind,
> With all its solemn imagery, its rocks,
> Its woods, and that uncertain heaven, received
> Into the bosom of the steady lake.

And Wordsworth and his companions at school were, he felt

> A race of real children; not too wise
> Too learned or too good; but wanton, fresh

And bandied up and down by love and hate;
Not unresentful where self-justified;
Fierce, moody, patient, venturous, modest, shy;
Mad at their sports like withered leaves in winds;
Though doing wrong and suffering, and full oft
Bending beneath our life's mysterious weight
Of pain, and doubt, and fear, yet yielding not
In happiness to the happiest upon earth.

Whilst at Hawkshead, at the age of fourteen he wrote a school exercise in praise of Education, which he said himself was 'but a tame imitation of Pope's versification and a little in his style'.

But what he most remembered of his schooldays was his continuing relationship with 'rivers, fields and groves' and in *The Prelude* he addressed a sympathetic paragraph to Coleridge who in his days at Christ's Hospital was educated in a very different way—more academic, more confined, and more stringent. He

Hawkshead Grammar School

envisages Coleridge 'yet a liveried schoolboy' lying on the leaded
roof of 'that wide edifice, thy school and home' watching the
movements of the clouds, the only visible natural object, or using
the 'internal light' of imagination to

> See trees and meadows and thy native stream,
> Far distant, thus beheld from year to year
> Of a long exile.

Coleridge, in fact, was not as Wordsworth pictured him. He did
take intense delight in natural scenery but it was not to him, as
it was to Wordsworth, an inbred necessity—most of his great
nature poetry and notebook descriptions come when he was
living through Wordsworth. In fact he enjoyed city life and was
peculiarly able to cope with the academic education system,
since he was extremely gifted and much more excited by pure
ideas—geometric, linguistic, philosophic—than Wordsworth
would ever be. Sent away to Christ's Hospital at nine years of
age he was undoubtedly bewildered and homesick—Lamb uses
his dreams of his native town in his picture of 'a poor friendless
boy' at the school. But he was inventive and stimulated: in 1791
he sent his brother, the Reverend George Coleridge, an amusing
poem on an equilateral triangle, written, he said, because mathe-
matics 'the quintessence of Truth' had found few and languid
admirers—this because it appealed to reason only—and 'whilst
Reason is luxuriating in its proper Paradise, Imagination is
wearily travelling on in a dreary desert'. The result is grotesque
but curiously memorable, and for all its heavy-headed humour
does *imagine* the tension between lines and angles:

> And from the point C.
> In which the circles make a pother
> Cutting and slashing one another,
> Bid the straight lines a-journeying go.

From Lamb's memories and Coleridge's own we have a very
vivid picture of Christ's Hospital at this time. Lamb, writing
under his pseudonym Elia about 'Christ's Hospital Five and Thirty

The annual oration given by senior pupils at Christ's Hospital, from
Ackermann's *Microcosm of London*, 1811

Years ago', describes how the diet of the child, Charles Lamb,
was improved by gifts from home compared to the general school
food:

He [Lamb] had his tea and hot rolls in a morning, while we were
battening upon our quarter of a penny loaf—our *crug*—moistened
with attenuated small beer, in wooden piggins, smacking of the
pitched leathern jack it was poured from. Our Monday's milk
porritch, blue and tasteless, and the pease soup of Saturday,
coarse and choking, were enriched for him with a slice of 'extraordinary bread and butter' from the hot-loaf of the Temple. The
Wednesday's mess of millet, somewhat less repugnant (we had
three banyan to four meat-days in the week)—was endeared to his
palate with a lump of double-refined, and a smack of ginger (to
make it go down the more glibly) or the fragrant cinnamon. In
lieu of our *half-pickled* Sundays, or *quite fresh* boiled beef on Thurs-

days (strong as *caro equina* [horseflesh]) with detestable marigolds floating in the pail to poison the broth—our scanty mutton scrags on Fridays—and rather more savoury, but grudging, portions of the same flesh, rotten-roasted or rare, on the Tuesdays (the only dish which excited our appetites, and disappointed our stomachs, in almost equal proportion)—he had his hot plate of roast veal or the more tempting griskin (exotics unknown to our palates) cooked in the paternal kitchen (a great thing) and brought him daily by his maid or aunt!

Lamb also records the story of a 'gageater', a boy who was thought to be gorging himself on gags—the fat of fresh beef boiled—but was in fact carrying them off to feed his starving parents in Chancery Lane.

Lamb gives a vivid picture of the inhumanities of punishments at the school. At the age of seven, on his first day there, he saw a boy in fetters—the punishment for running away. If a boy ran away a second time he was put in the dungeons—'little square, Bedlam cells, where a boy could just lie at his length upon straw and a blanket . . . with a peep of light, let in askance from a prison orifice at top, barely enough to read by'. Boys were kept there day and night—the porter brought bread and water but was forbidden to speak: the beadle came twice a week to administer the 'periodical chastisement'. If a boy ran away for a third time he was expelled after a state flogging in front of all his schoolfellows. 'Scourging was after the old Roman fashion, long and stately.' Lamb felt, he says, very sick.

Monitors were tyrannous, lashing the younger children, keeping them from fires, exacting fines of bread for various trumped up crimes—one of them, a 'petty Nero', *branded* some little boy, and took his bread to feed a donkey which had been smuggled onto the leads of the roof. Masters, too, were tyrannous. Both Lamb and Coleridge have left records of the Reverend James Boyer, who deeply impressed them. Lamb's picture deserves full quotation:

He had two wigs, both pedantic but of different omen. The one serene, smiling, fresh powdered, betokening a mild day. The other, an old, discoloured unkempt angry caxon, denoting frequent and bloody execution. Woe to the school, when he made his morning appearance in his *passy*, or *passionate wig*. J.B. had a heavy hand. I have known him double his knotty fist at a poor trembling child (the maternal milk hardly dry upon his lips) with a 'Sirrah, do you presume to set your wits at me?' Nothing was more common than to see him make a headlong entry into the schoolroom from his inner recess or library, and with turbulent eye, singling out a lad, roar out 'Od's my life, Sirrah (his favourite adjuration) I have a great mind to whip you,' then, with as sudden a retracting impulse, fling back into his lair—and after a cooling lapse of some minutes (during which all but the culprit had totally forgotten the context)

Punishment in school, a cartoon by George Cruikshank

drive headlong out again, piecing out his imperfect sense, as if it had been some Devil's Litany, with the expletory yell—'*and I* WILL *too.*' In his gentler moods, when the *rabidus furor* was assuaged, he had resort to an ingenious method, peculiar, for what I have heard, to himself, of whipping the boy, and reading the Debates, at the same time; a paragraph and a lash between; which in those times when parliamentary oratory was most at a height and flourishing in these realms, was not calculated to impress the patient with a veneration for the diffuser graces of rhetoric.

Lamb records that when Coleridge heard Boyer was on his death-bed he expressed the hope that he might be 'wafted to bliss by little cherub boys, all head and wings, with no *bottoms* to reproach his sublunary infirmities'.

But Coleridge's encounters with Boyer, when he was a 'Grecian' in the upper school, working for a university scholarship were intellectually stimulating and left their marks on much of his later works. Boyer's mind was clearly rigorous, complex and precise. He had no patience with the vague exclamatory phrases of the poetry of the time. Coleridge, twenty-five years later, wrote: 'In fancy I can almost hear him now exclaiming "Harp? harp? lyre? Pen and ink, boy, you mean! Muse, boy, Muse? Your Nurse's Daughter, you mean! Pierian spring? Oh, aye! the cloister-pump, I suppose."' Coleridge the poet in his slacker moods was always given to rhetorical flourishes, but his great poetry and his precise responses as a critic to particular poems show that he had well learned Boyer's lesson about the value of the real, the precise, the concrete. From Boyer too he learned something still more important; that poetry had its own coherence of form, its own mode of thought:

I learned from him, that Poetry, even that of the loftiest and, seemingly, that of the wildest odes, had a logic of its own, as severe as that of science; and more difficult, because more subtle, more complex, and dependent on more, and more fugitive causes.

Even in Coleridge's youth Boyer's arbitrary harshness and the torturous punitive system at Christ's Hospital were felt to be out-dated. Views of education—and parenthood and child psychology —at the time were undergoing sweeping changes largely through the influence of one book—Jean Jacques Rousseau's *Emile*, first published in 1762. It was translated into English as *Emilius and*

Sophia or A New System of Education: over two hundred treatises dealing with its views were published in England before the end of the century. It is generally assumed that what Rousseau recommended was a return to a 'State of Nature' because mankind was born free and good but became corrupted by social pressures and habit. It is true that, unlike many of his predecessors, Rousseau did not believe in original sin—that children were born corrupt. Janeway's *A Token for Children* (1671) recommended that parents 'take some time daily to speak to your little children one by one about their miserable condition by nature' because 'they are not too little to die; nor too little to go to hell'. Rousseau, on the contrary, wrote: 'Let us lay it down as an incontrovertible rule that the first impulses of nature are always right; there is no original sin in the human heart; the how and why of the entrance of every vice can be traced.' But Rousseau's State of Nature is not primarily one of automatic virtue: he is more concerned with his belief that man is *not* essentially or originally a social being: his 'natural' impulses are self-regarding, his 'natural' desires in conflict with the society in which, unless he retreats into an artificially primitive seclusion, he must live. What Rousseau was concerned to demonstrate was that each modern man, like his savage ancestors, had to *learn* to be social, and that the learning process must be suited to the nature of the individual human being. Children, he believed, had no powers of reasoning before the age of twelve, no social needs or capacities before fifteen. It was therefore useless to teach them the usual 'school subjects' before they were capable of the mental processes which made them able really to understand them—book-learning was actually harmful. Rousseau's ideas of a child's actual capacities may have been a bit wild, but his general theory was illuminating and seminal. In the preface to *Emile* he wrote:

We are not sufficiently acquainted with a state of infancy: the farther we proceed on our present mistaken ideas, the farther we wander from the point. Even the most sagacious instructors apply themselves to those things which man is required to know without considering what it is children are capacitated to learn. They are always expecting the *man* in the *child*, without reflecting what he is before he can become a man. . . .

Nature, he argued, intended children to develop their bodies before exercising their minds:

Children are always in motion; quiet and meditation are their aversion; a studious or sedentary life is injurious to their health and growth; neither their minds nor their bodies can bear constraint.

This belief caused him to feel strongly about contemporary nurses as well as about the undesirability of books before adolescence. Mothers who unnaturally sent their babies away to wet nurses in the country perhaps did not realize how these babies were kept quiet:

How often is the little innocent, when its nurse is in the least hurry, hung on a peg like a bundle of clouts, there to remain crucified . . . Such children as have been found in this situation have been observed to be always black in the face; the stomach being violently compressed, preventing the circulation of the blood and forcing it into the head: in the meanwhile the poor little creatures were supposed to be very patient, because they had not the power to cry.

Rousseau remarked cynically that he did not know how long such children were likely to live—but, he imagined, not very long, and that this was one of the conveniences of swaddling clothes.

Emile, Rousseau's model pupil, was to be brought up in isolation in a state of innocence and learn skills as and when they were appropriate to him. No books—except *Robinson Crusoe*—before the age of fifteen. *Robinson Crusoe* was excepted because it showed man learning social, economic and scientific skills practically and from scratch, as Emile must do. Emile's natural talents were to be brought out of him, not imposed as ideas or technique from outside authority—the tutor was to run races with him and allow him to evolve his own methods of winning; walls were to be decorated only with Emile's own drawings which were improved by critical comparisons with his own earlier work.

Rousseau's views on education, like his views on politics, were simplified by being popularized. The *idea* of the Social Contract worked magically in France at the time of the Revolution: in the same way the idea of allowing a child to develop naturally without prejudicing influences led many people who had never read *Emile* to believe that Rousseau wanted to turn everyone back into a noble Savage. Rousseau was indeed pessimistic about man's influence on things in general:

> All things are good as their Creator made them, but everything degenerates in the hands of man. By human art is our native soil compelled to nourish exotick plants, and one tree to bear the fruits of another. Improving man makes a general confusion of elements, climates and seasons: he mutilates his dogs, his horses and his slaves: he defaces, he confounds everything, as if he delighted in nothing but monsters and deformity. He is not content with anything in its natural state, not even with his own species. His very offspring must be trained up for him, like a horse in the menage, and be taught to grow after his own fancy like a tree in his garden.

But this condemnation of art as opposed to Nature does not lead Rousseau to reject education and society:

> Without this indeed, in the present state of things matters would be still worse than they are and mankind be civilized by halves. Should a man, in a state of society, be given up, from the cradle, to his own notions and conduct, he would certainly turn out the most preposterous of human beings.

Rousseau had a vision, an honourable vision, of what human beings should aim at—a kind of integrity of personality:

> To be something, to be consistent with one's self, and always the same individual, our words and actions should agree; we should be always determined in the part we ought to take; we should take it with a high hand and persevere. If such a prodigy could be found we might then know whether he be a man or a citizen or how he can so manage as to be, at once, both the one and the other.

But—contrary to the general view of Rousseau's beliefs—this could *not* be achieved by having 'man in the bosom of society, retain the primitive sentiments of nature'. If he did this he would be hopelessly torn between man and citizen, inclination and duty —not an integrated personality but defined by his place of origin or his function. Rousseau and Coleridge come together in their hatred of the abstract definitions of human nature. 'Like men of the present time, the Englishman, the Frenchman, the citizen,' Rousseau wrote scornfully, 'he would be in reality nothing at all.'

But Coleridge the young man apparently took pleasure in mocking Rousseau's more extreme attitudes: he had after all benefited himself from authoritative teaching. When his friend Thelwall, the notorious democrat, called to see him in Nether Stowey and announced his intention of 'preserving the minds of his children from any bias in favour of notions which they could not appreciate or even understand' Coleridge showed him his 'Botanic Garden'. When Thelwall exclaimed that it was a wilder- ness of weeds and had so many capabilities that it seemed a shame, Coleridge replied that the weeds were indigenous and the garden was being educated on the Rousseau Plan, preserved from all artificial insemination—and therefore full of those natural growths, nettles, hensbane, nightshade, Devil's Bit, Fool's Parsley and Cox-Comb. The soil was not to be prejudiced towards roses and strawberries.

Despite caution and mockery Rousseau's ideas had a deep effect on Coleridge and Wordsworth. Wordsworth and Dorothy, who were employed to look after little Basil Montague at Alfoxden, attempted to bring him up as a child of Nature, running about in the open: Wordsworth's poem to Dorothy addressed 'To a Young Lady' who had been reproached for taking long walks in the country addressed her as 'Dear Child of Nature', and the concept of this child haunted both Wordsworth's rural poems and Coleridge's supernatural ones: the child symbolized innocence and youthful energy as a natural power. But association with Basil brought out a natural shrewdness about childish behaviour in Wordsworth. The poem *Anecdote for Fathers* recounts neatly and dramatically an encounter which is based on one between Wordsworth and Basil in which the father persists in demanding *why* the child would rather live at Kilve than Liswyn farm. Cornered and inarticulate, the child in the end happens to catch sight of the weathercock:

> Then did the boy his tongue unlock
> And eased his mind with this reply
> At Kilve there was no weather-cock;
> And that's the reason why.

Wordsworth suggests gently that insisting that 'there surely must some reason be' produces wild answers and lies—for which less wise adults reproach the child.

In 1806 he wrote a long letter to a friend who had asked for his advice on dealing with a gay and selfish child who craved for sympathy. This letter shows the same shrewdness and is pompous and perceptive both at once. He points out the dangers of the new interest in children as children to their characters. 'Formerly, indeed till within these few years, children were very carelessly brought up; at present they too early and too habitually feel their own importance from the solicitude and unremitting attendance which is bestowed upon them.' Wordsworth is nevertheless very firmly determined that the child's temperament is not to be *mortified* 'which is the course commonly pursued with such tempers'. Nor should she be preached to about her own defects, or her infancy overrun with 'books about good boys and girls and bad boys and girls and all that trumpery.' He goes on to supply a fascinating list of educational matter chosen on the basic criterion of being 'interesting for its own sake; things known because they are interesting, not interesting because they are known'. Behind his list again lies his vision of the human spirit and personality expanding through contemplation of images which contribute directly to its growth and can be assimilated as personal experience. It was Wordsworth who said 'Two things we may learn from little children from 3 to 6 years old; that it is a characteristic, an instinct, of our human nature to pass out of self. . . . And not to suffer any one form to pass into me and become an usurping self.' The volatile child in need of constant affection from outside will benefit from being left at liberty 'to luxuriate in such feelings and images as will feed her mind in silent pleasure.'

There were two categories of things to learn which fed the mind. The first and most important was found in 'fairy tales, romances, the best biographies and histories and such part of natural history relating to the powers and appearances of the earth and elements, and the habits and structures of animals as belong to it, not as an art or a science but as a magazine of form and feeling.' Form and feeling—both necessary to the growth and integrity of the mind. The second group of laudable lessons consisted of those which combined the pleasure of exercising bodily and mental gifts and being praised for them—dancing, music, drawing, grammar, languages, botany probably. What was to be avoided at all costs was the acquisition of useless knowledge, interesting 'almost solely because it is known and the knowledge may be displayed'—and this, Wordsworth believed, covered 'three fourths of what, according to the plan of modern education, children's heads are stuffed with'—minute, remote, trifling facts in geography, history, natural history, conventional 'accomplishments'.

There is something essentially Rousseau-like in this opposition between what could be said to feed the mind and what was imposed from without. And much later in life, writing to the inspectors appointed by a committee of the Council on Education he was even more dogmatic. He asked whether the council placed too much value on knowledge inculcated by the teacher as opposed to their occupations out of doors, learning through nature. Also too little attention was paid to 'books of imagination' —a common fault. 'We must not only have knowledge but the means of wielding it and that is done infinitely more through the imaginative faculty assisting both in the collection and application of facts than is generally believed.'

Coleridge also believed that education should be a process of aiding natural development and natural curiosity. He used the organic metaphor in this instance too, defining education as 'to call forth; as the blossom is educed from the bud'. Children should not be crammed with knowledge—a child must be child-like.

'Touch a door a little ajar or half-open and it will yield to the push of your finger. Fire a cannon-ball at it and the door stirs not an inch; you make a hole through it, the door is spoilt forever, but not *moved*. Apply this moral to Education.' And he, like Wordsworth, believed that imaginative literature helped to develop a whole human being as pure information did not. A letter from Lamb to Coleridge illustrates their concern about this and dislike of the current compendiums of useful facts:

'Goody Two Shoes' is almost out of print. Mrs Barbauld's stuff has banished all the old classics of the nursery; and the shopman at Newbery's hardly deigned to reach them off an old exploded corner of a shelf, when Mary asked for them. Mrs Barbauld's and Mrs Trimmer's nonsense lay in piles about. Knowledge insignificant and vapid as Mrs Barbauld's books convey, it seems, must come to a child in the *shape* of *knowledge*; and his empty noddle must be turned with conceit of his own powers when he has learned that a horse is an animal, and Billy is better than a horse, and such like; instead of that beautiful interest in wild tales, which made the child a man, while all the time he suspected himself to be no bigger than a child. Science has succeeded to poetry no less in the little walks of children than with men. Is there no possibility of averting this sore evil? Think what you would have been now, if, instead of being fed with tales and old wives' fables in childhood, you had been crammed with geography and natural history.

And Lamb's picture of the 'modern schoolmaster' indicates mockingly some of the strains of instilling useful knowledge:

The modern schoolmaster is expected to know a little of everything, because his pupil is required not to be entirely ignorant of anything. He must be superficially, if I may say so, omniscient. He is to know something of pneumatics; of chemistry; ... an insight into mechanics is desirable, with a touch of statistics; the quality of soils, etc.; botany, the constitution of his country, *cum multis aliis*. ... He must seize every occasion—the season of the year—the time of the day—a passing cloud—a rainbow—a waggon of hay— a regiment of soldiers going by—to inculcate something useful. He can receive no pleasure from a casual glimpse of Nature, but must

catch at it as an object of instruction. He must interpret beauty into
the picturesque. He cannot relish a beggar-man, or a gipsy, for
thinking of the suitable improvement. Nothing comes to him not
spoiled by the sophisticating medium of moral uses. The Universe—
that Great Book as it has been called—is to him, indeed, to all
intents and purposes, a book out of which he is doomed to read
tedious homilies to distasting schoolboys. . . . Wherever he goes
this uneasy shadow attends him. A boy is at his board, and in his
path, and in all his movements. He is boy-rid, sick of perpetual
boy.

In this passage one can clearly see the realization of a problem
increasingly pressing in the conduct of education—the growing
quantity of possible subjects for learning, the growing impossibility
of covering them all, of being a fully educated man. Coleridge
himself seems a monumental figure in retrospect because he was
still trying to bring together and synthesize enormously varying
modes of knowledge—and had the intellectual capacity and the
vast memory to achieve great things. But the idea of the 'whole
man' growing through learning was already a bit of a dream—
so emotional integrity and developed personality became more
important.

Coleridge's notebooks make it clear that he was a precise and
loving observer of his own children's development. He believed
children should be *happy*—his own childhood anxieties had left
marks on his character which he associated with his adult failures
and illnesses. 'The great importance of breeding up children *happy*
to at least 15 or 16 illustrated in my always dreaming of Christ's
Hospital and when not quite well having all those uneasy feelings
which I had at School/feelings of Easter Monday etc.' Writing
to his wife he suggested that she teach Hartley to read out of
Practical Education—a joint work by Maria Edgworth and her
father which appeared in 1798—but felt compelled to add that
'J. Wedgwood informed me that the Edgworths were most
miserable when Children and yet the Father, *in his book*, is ever
vapouring about their *Happiness*.' His own descriptions of his
sons—the volatile Hartley and the staid Derwent—suggest a
bliss and a capacity for joy which their later lives did not bear out.

Hartley Coleridge (1796–1849)

They represented to him the innocence of the Child of Nature:

> The wisdom and graciousness of God in the infancy of the human species—its beauty, long continuance etc. etc. (Children in the wind—hair floating, tossing, a miniature of the agitated Trees, below which they play'd—the elder whirling for joy, the one in petticoats, a fat Baby, eddying half willingly, half by the force of the Gust—driven backward, struggling forward—both drunk with the pleasure, both shouting their hymn of Joy.)

Hartley in particular had inherited much of Coleridge's own temperament, the brilliance, the excitability, the curiosity.

Coleridge 'sent him naked into a shallow of the river Greta; he trembled with the novelty, yet you cannot conceive his raptures'. Coleridge told Humphry Davy that this son was 'a spirit that dances on an aspin leaf—the air which yonder sallow-faced and yawning Tourist is breathing is to my Babe a perpetual Nitrous Oxyde'. As the father experimented with laughing gas with Davy and became dependent on stimulants, so did the son. Hartley was dismissed from a Fellowship at Oriel College, Oxford for drunkenness and immorality and spent most of his short life wandering the Lake District cadging drinks. The precocious child and the philosopher father had long conversations about 'Life, Reality, Pictures and Thinking' in which the analytic Coleridge and the visionary operated together:

> He pointed out without difficulty that there might be five Hartleys, real Hartley, Shadow Hartley, Picture Hartley, Looking Glass Hartley and Echo Hartley/and as to the difference between his Shadow and the Reflection in the Looking Glass, he said, the Shadow was black and he could not see his *eyes* in it. I asked him what he did when he thought of anything—he answered—I look at it and then go to sleep. To sleep?—said I—you mean, that you *shut your eyes*. Yes, he replied—I shut my eyes and put my hands so (covering his eyes) and go to sleep—then I WAKE again, and away I run—
>
> That of shutting his eyes and covering them was a Recipe I had given him some time ago/but the notion of that state of mind being Sleep is very striking, and he meant more, I suspect than that people when asleep have their eyes shut—indeed *I know* it from the tone and *leap up* of Voice with which he uttered the word WAKE! Tomorrow I am to exert my genius in making a paper-balloon/the idea of carrying up a bit of lighted Candle into the clouds makes him almost insane with Pleasure.

Coleridge's passionate interest in the operations of consciousness and language made him a stimulating teacher. He tells how he tried to teach Derwent how his senses worked: Derwent had never connected sight with eyes, or speech with his mouth (he was 2 years and 10 months old within 8 days, Coleridge recorded). He was passive when his father held his tongue to show how he could not speak without it but when the experiment was repeated with Derwent holding his *own* tongue, 'finding that he could not speak he turned pale as death and in the reaction from fear flushed red and gave me a blow in the face'.

Mixture of emotions—in himself and others—always fascinated Coleridge. He was as fascinated by Hartley's reaction to pain as by Derwent's fear and anger. 'Pain with him is so wholly transubstantiated by the Joys that had rolled on before, and rushed in after, that often times five minutes after his Mother had whipt him, he had gone up and asked her to whip him again . . .'. And in the Conclusion to Part II of the unfinished *Christabel*—at first sight irrelevant to the central narrative of supernatural good and evil—Coleridge discusses the relationship between innocence and human destructiveness in terms of the relationship between father and son. It has been suggested that Coleridge left *Christabel* unfinished because he could not solve its central philosophical and moral problem—that of the relationship between innocence and the experience of evil. Blake presented the gulf between innocent goodness and the goodness based on the knowledge of good and evil, *conscious* goodness, in the opposed *Songs of Innocence* and *Songs of Experience*, which present two contradictory, if not mutually exclusive, modes of consciousness. Coleridge in *Christabel* seems to have intended that the dove-like innocence of the heroine should have prevailed over the daemonic serpent-woman, Geraldine, and her goodness have been strengthened by the knowledge of and contact with evil. In his description of the complex mixture of rage and delight in his own relationship with Hartley he is conducting the same kind of enquiry into the original forces behind human conduct that he made into his own opium dreams and sensual responses to Sara Hutchinson.* In the imperfect world of human passions, which is not the pure and complete world of geometry or of heaven, love is inevitably distorted into bitterness—which in its turn creates love. Coleridge describes what is in fact a common experience of parenthood— the sense of delight in the child so intense that out of reaction one snaps at it. Hartley, like Christabel, is the Child of Nature,

---

* See Chapter I, p. 34.

> A little child, a limber elf
> Singing, dancing to itself,
> A fairy thing with red round cheeks
> That always finds and never seeks—

self-sufficient, living in the moment. The father's heart is so overwhelmed with joy

> that he at last
> Must needs express his love's excess
> With words of unmeant bitterness.

As with the 'streamy association' which might have held a clue to the origin of evil, this forcing together of 'thoughts so all unlike each other' holds a clue to the nature of experience. The reaction is valuable:

> Perhaps 'tis tender too and pretty
> At each wild word to feel within
> A sweet recoil of love and pity.

And, even more deeply, perhaps the experience is an indication that in this life we perhaps can only know good through the distorting vision of anger and evil. The poetic simplicity covers a deal of profound speculation about pain:

> And what if, in a world of sin
> (O sorrow and shame should this be true!)
> Such giddiness of heart and brain
> Comes seldom save from rage and pain,
> So talks as it's most used to do.

Coleridge, long before modern psychological studies of innate aggression and its inextricable relationship with the positive emotions of love and protection, recognized the value of Derwent's rage with him, and the nature of his own anger with Hartley. When nervous, or later guilty about neglecting his children, he could over-act the heavy Victorian father in an embarrassing way, lecturing Hartley on his tendency to show off and prevaricate as though this was a black sin, becoming wildly over-emotional about the children's duty to their mother who had fed them with her blood and later with her milk. But, at his best, he was intelligent, relaxed, curious and shrewd, and his views of what 'natural' children and happy children should be were unusually complex.

Mrs Coleridge was as conventional as a parent as Coleridge was unusual. She was clearly a devoted and affectionate mother of babies—Dorothy Wordsworth was extremely scornful over the amount of time she spent on suckling Derwent and remarked that she was, to be sure, a sad fiddle-faddler. She was conventionally ambitious for the boys—touchingly overjoyed and uncomprehending at Hartley's academic successes, shattered by his disgrace. When the Southeys came to Greta Hall the whole *ménage* became an academic hothouse of which she was exceedingly proud. In 1814 she was explaining

> we keep regular School from ½ past nine until 4 with the exception of an hour for walking and a half-hour for dressing—Mrs Lovel keeps school in a small room for English and Latin—and the writing and figures—french—italian etc. are done with me in the *dining room* with the assistance of Aunt Eliza—and Southey teaches his wife and daughters to read spanish and his son Greek—should we not all be very learned!

Coleridge's youngest child, his daughter Sara, perhaps benefited most from the parental combination of brilliance and thoroughness. She grew up to be beautiful, scholarly and extremely serious, married her first cousin Henry Nelson Coleridge, and devoted much of her life to the editing and publishing of her father's scattered works. She applied herself intelligently and energetically to the education of her small son, Herbert, and can be seen putting Wordsworth's and Coleridge's educational principles into practice. Lessons were made into games—Latin was taught with cards, each with a Latin word on one side and the English on the other. Geography was made meaningful with stories and visual aids—Sara and Herbert traced Napoleon's campaigns, or the journey of the Chosen People to the Promised Land on maps: Sara insisted sensibly on using maps of the whole world so that the child early developed a sense of relative distances and positions. When she was warned by a doctor that she might be overtaxing the mind of a child of four she replied that she never *insisted* on his learning—he looked at maps for sheer amusement and was allowed to run away the moment he was tired. Like the poets she appealed to the imagination: 'Give him classical Fairy Tales instead of modern poverty-stricken fiction—show him the great outlines of the globe instead of Chinese puzzles and spillikins. Store his mind with facts rather than prematurely endeavour to prepossess it with opinions or sophisticate it with sentiment based on slippery ground.' She published a romantic fairy tale called *Phantasmion* and *Pretty Lessons in Verse for good children* which made history easy with mnemonic rhymes. Bloody Mary is presented thus:

> One thousand five hundred and fifty three
> Began Queen Mary's fiery reign;
> The worst of counsellors had she
> And an evil spouse in Philip of Spain.

The Wordsworths were less successful with the academic education of their children than the Coleridges. They seem to have left them free and hardy as toddlers—Dorothy describes John, the eldest son, in 1805, living all day in his great-coat and running in and out of the house in all weathers—'he is the best endurer of wet and cold I ever saw—in the frostiest weather he never complains'. And there is a sense of real family unity and gaiety in Dorothy's descriptions of all the neighbourhood children dancing in their kitchen to the music of the Grasmere Fiddler going his rounds. 'It is a pleasant sound they make with their little pattering feet upon the stone floor, half a dozen of them, Boys and Girls; Dorothy is in ecstacy and John looks as grave as an Old Man.' But the unfortunate John (and later the other surviving son, William) turned out to be academically very slow—and Wordsworth made the mistake of trying to teach him himself all through 1819. By then Wordsworth was morbidly anxious about the welfare of his three surviving children, and John's slowness and the fact that he was, as Sara Hutchinson put it, 'diseasedly shy' drove Wordsworth into fits of irritability and impatience. This had a

Sara Coleridge (left), with Edith May Southey, one of Robert Southey's daughters; from a miniature by an unknown artist

bad effect on John. Sara wrote 'it was a sad error ever to despair of him as his father did at one time'. John and Wordsworth both recovered to some extent—John, responsible and conscientious, felt freer away from his anxious father and Sara was able to report: 'Now even he has thrown off much of the fear that he had of his father—and does talk freely with him at times.'

Wordsworth, Coleridge and Southey all became involved in various ways in the great educational controversy surrounding the new teaching methods of Doctor Andrew Bell. Dr Bell's system had been introduced at the Military Male Orphan Asylum at Madras, in 1795. The military male orphans were the half-caste abandoned children of British soldiers and Indian women. This system promoted self-respect and learning amongst the boys by introducing self-tuition: the more advanced boys taught the younger and slower ones, thereby increasing their own understanding and skill. They were self-reliant—they made their own pens and ruled their own paper and kept their own individual accounts of their progress, so that their work was their own achievement, not imposed from above. Punishments, too, were allotted by the boys, and Dr Bell said he 'never had reason to think their decision partial, biased or unjust, or to interfere with their award, otherwise than to mitigate or remit the punishment, when he thought the formality of the trial and of the sentence were sufficient to produce the effect required'. He was determined to prevent occasions for punishment—the teachers were told to make the boys happy, and bad boys were assigned to care of particular good boys, who were instructed to 'treat him kindly, reconcile him to the school, and render him happy like the rest in his situation'.

This emphasis on happiness, responsiblity and development of the whole personality appealed to the poets. Southey wrote a book, *The Origin, Nature and Object of the New System of Education*, to defend Bell against later copiers and rivals. Coleridge lectured eagerly on his work in Bristol—De Quincey accused him of talking endlessly about Ball and Bell, Bell and Ball.* In 1811 Dr Bell visited Keswick with Southey and met the Wordsworths. 'Johnson the Curate' was running the Grasmere school on the Madras system—Bell took him to run one of the new Central or National Schools in London. Wordsworth himself taught at the Grasmere school regularly two or three hours every morning and evening. It was a low, dark, and poor building with a few tables and forms and a chair at the end for the master. 'The children came up individually 4 times a day and managed some way or

* Sir Alexander Ball, Governor of Malta during Coleridge's stay there.

Dora Wordsworth (1804–47), from an engraving after a portrait
by Margaret Gillies, 1839

Joseph Lancaster (1778–1838), from a portrait by J. Hazlitt

other to get through as many lessons.' Later, he seems to have handed this work over to his devoted women. Dorothy indeed helped Bell to prepare a new edition of his book, but he later rejected her version and changes and reverted to his own. Words-worth was anxious that his children should be educated at the Charterhouse largely because it practised the Madras system—

William the younger did spend an unsuccessful time there after attending the Central School in London under Mr Johnson, the former curate of Grasmere. Wordsworth, writing to his brother in 1819 about William's shortcomings, complains that a teacher who had rejected William did not seem to grasp the importance of the Madras system for *slow Boys*. 'One Boy advances *more rapidly* than another, but *all* are made to advance according to their talents—I conclude then either that Mr Russell does not perceive this principle of the system, or he is content to have his school managed with as much of the new scheme as suits his fancy, and to fall below the point of its characteristic excellence, or that not questioning but my Son might benefit to a certain degree, he apprehends that striking a balance between loss and gain the account would be against the Boy.'

Another reason for the poets' approval of Dr Bell's Madras system was that Bell believed the schools should be Church-controlled, whilst his great rival Joseph Lancaster the Quaker believed in 'free education on general Christian principles'. This battle between the Established Church and Dissent contributed to the delay of any plans for State education for two generations.

Southey's *New System of Education* is sharply mocking about Lancaster, both as an 'experimental' teacher and as a theorist about the nature of children. Dr Bell in the Military Male Orphanage had taught children to write, economically, by getting them to trace letters in a tray of sand. Lancaster also introduced this innovation but used wet sand and skewers instead of dry sand and fingers. The result was messy, heavy and awkward. The sand 'required great care in wetting; if wetted either too much or too little it was equally useless and inconvenient'. When Dr Bell told him it should be *dry* sand, Lancaster remarked that this fully showed 'how essential a minute detail is to the ready practice of any experiment'.

Southey said that the same necessity for minute directions was shown by the English Christmas pudding cooked in France according to a receipt that forgot to specify it should be boiled in a cloth—'the unhappy pudding made its appearance all abroad in a soup dish'.

Lancaster's teaching methods did not entail the growth and grasp of knowledge provided by Bell's self-tuition and exposition. Boys were gathered in groups round a monitor who dictated a sum which they wrote on their slates. He then dictated the answer, which they again took down by rote, and the slates were inspected for copying errors. Southey quoted an 'Edinburgh critic' who admired Lancaster for 'enabling a boy to communicate to others that of which he is ignorant himself.' If there was any merit, Southey wrote scornfully, in inventing an ignorant teacher surely 'there would be much more in superseding him by a Teaching Machine such as Lord Stanhope could supply with much less ingenuity than was required for his reasoning one'.

Lancaster's system of rewards and punishments also aroused Southey's—and Coleridge's—furious scorn. Rewards were competitive—boys received numbered leather tickets to wear, and pictures pasted on board to be hung on their breasts and surrendered to the boy who overtook them. Bats, balls, books of prints, were given to boys who received more than a certain number of prize tickets, and the highest reward was a silver medal on a plated chain. Southey thought this Honours system was a contradiction to Lancaster's Quaker principles and bad for the desire for knowledge itself.

Lancaster's punishments, as described by Southey, show a certain perverted psychological insight, and a horrible inventiveness. He believed in variety. 'Any single kind of punishment continued constantly in use becomes familiar and loses its effect. . . .' He was a kind of artist in devising punishments to suit crimes which 'could be inflicted so as to give much uneasiness to the delinquents without disturbing the mind or temper of the master'. Boys were put in sacks or baskets hoisted onto the roof of the school in sight of all the other boys who 'smiled at the *birds in the cage*'. Others were yoked by a piece of wood fastened to all their necks and made to parade the school, walking backwards 'being obliged to pay very great attention to their footsteps for fear of running against any object that might cause the yoke to hurt their necks'. This instrument of torture was jokingly called the Caravan. Lancaster believed that the punishments should be made 'a matter of diversion and laughter for the spectators'. Boys whose reading voice developed a singing tone were marched round the school 'hung with ballads and dying speeches to provoke risibility'. Slovens were publicly washed and slapped in the face by a child of the opposite sex. Labels, like that worn by Jane Eyre, were affixed to children—they read 'Idle', 'Noisy', 'Suck-finger baby', and 'tell-tale tit'. An idle boy had a feather pillow ostentatiously placed on his desk: a boy who wandered from his seat was caged in a hen-coop.

Southey, quite rightly, believed that the effect of all this was very bad on both audience and sufferers. Lancaster's 'diversion and laughter' he compared to 'the beneficial consequences arising to an English mob from regarding an execution as a holiday . . .'. Dr Bell's boys judged cases of delinquency and were responsible for justice. Lancaster's boys, as Southey put it, had the liberty of acting as executioners, which was bad for their characters—as it was bad for the 'decency, reserve and modesty of the female character' to be called on to smack boys' faces in public. And all these punishments of exposure to ridicule and mockery would have a progressively worse effect on the *best* boys. Shame was a more severe punishment than pain, but, this was particularly true in the case of boys with a strong moral sense. Dr Bell's system taught boys humanity in a practical way. Southey described Coleridge in a lecture at the Royal Institution hurling Lancaster's book away from him in contempt, exclaiming that 'No boy who has been subjected to punishments like this will stand in fear of Newgate or feel any horror at the thought of a slave ship'.

It was a time that led to the production of theories about how children should be brought up. The poets' friend, Tom Wedgwood, Coleridge's benefactor, at one stage decided that the most proper use for his riches was the finance of the education of a genius. His letter about his project written to Godwin shows a belief that a carefully devised educational theory *must* produce a perfectly qualified human being: beside Coleridge's and Wordsworth's belief in natural growth his ideas suggest mechanical control. 'My aim is high. I have been endeavouring some master-stroke which should anticipate a century or two upon the large-paced progress of human improvement. . . .' His idea was to control the sense-impressions of the small child and the resulting emotions and ideas completely to avoid distractions and pain. To this end 'the nursery should have plain grey walls with one or two vivid objects for sight and touch'. Children should acquire manipulation sooner— 'Hard bodies' should be hung round them to 'irritate their palms'. Uncontrolled exposure to Nature was dangerous—the child should therefore never go out of doors or leave his room. And productivity could be greatly increased by making the child *think* rationally during periods most human beings wasted on reverie and daydreaming. The education was to be planned by a committee of philosophers. The only people Wedgwood thought suitable for the job of actually superintending the child were Wordsworth and Coleridge. It is perhaps fortunate that the scheme came to nothing—neither poet could have liked its determinism and both were aware of the value of periods of lassitude, wise passiveness, reverie, to the creative mind. But it is indicative of a whole contemporary experimental atmosphere.

Wordsworth, in *The Excursion*, had written an eloquent plea for statutory universal education. The state should

> admit
> An obligation on her part, to *teach*
> Them who are born to serve her and obey;
> Binding herself by statute to secure
> For all the children whom her soil maintains
> The rudiments of letters, and inform
> The mind with moral and religious truth.

But in his laters years he was more often to be found in opposition to practical plans to extend education. His comments on the subject show a mixture of the expected practical shrewdness about the *actual effects* of infant schools and adult education, as opposed to the ideal theory behind it, and that timid and narrow conservatism that made him unduly pessimistic and rigid in his social views.

In 1808 he was pointing out the difficulties of a uniform national system of education when the needs of the rural agricultural communities and the city workers were so different. His old political enemy Henry Brougham was campaigning vigorously for opportunities for education for working men—publication of cheap books, forming of book clubs and reading societies, the arrangement of public lectures, particularly in the sciences which required demonstration to be fully understood. He, with Dr George Birkbeck, was a promoter of the Mechanics' Institutes (in Glasgow, in London and the large cities—the London Mechanics' Institute became Birkbeck College), where working men for a fee of about £1 a year could come to lectures on Chemistry, Geometry, Hydrostatics, the application of Chemistry to the Arts, Astronomy, French and many other subjects. Brougham was also instrumental in forming The Society for the Diffusion of Useful Knowledge in 1826. There is no doubt that these efforts transformed many lives. Wordsworth, however, was dubious. He attacked Brougham for thinking that 'sharpening of intellect and attainment of knowledge are things good in themselves'—Bacon may have said knowledge was power, but it could be power for evil as well as good. He was dubious about the London College—University College, the new London University of which Crabb Robinson was a benefactor; Wordsworth argued that cheaper medical education was *not* required—'we have far more doctors than can find patients to live by'. Lectures he thought an absurd mode of teaching except possibly in scientific subjects—there is perhaps some later truth in this, but less when students are too poor to afford books. He attacked the Mechanics' Institutes and the London University with the favourite distinction, used politically by Coleridge and himself, between abstractions and living organic growth. There was in one case (the Mechanics' Institutes where knowledge was *imposed* from above) 'a sudden formal abstraction of a vital principle and in both an unnatural and violent pushing on'. This may be a half-truth—half-educated people do tend to flounder in unmanageable abstractions—but showed little knowledge of the real *need* for intellectual growth and information that existed. He added to this argumentative blow a snobbish and intolerant social judgment. 'Mechanics' Institutes make discontented spirits and insubordinate and presumptuous workmen.'

Religion was excluded, which made the instruction itself dangerous, and, more than that, the subjects taught were distasteful to Wordsworth. 'I cannot look without shuddering on the array of surgical midwifery lectures to which the youth of London were invited at the commencement of this season by the advertisements of the London University.' Hogarth, he said, understood human nature better than professors—*he* showed the dissecting room as the final stage of cruelty. And if poor people were encouraged to train as doctors they would naturally *lack* the qualities of the present class from which doctors were drawn—absence of 'meanness and unfeeling and sordid habits'.

Infant education, too, he regarded with increasing suspicion. He was highly critical of the party of young ladies, 'sour-looking teachers in petticoats' who wanted to set up a Madras school for girls in Ambleside, 'confidently expecting that these girls will in consequence be less likely to go astray when they grow up to be women'. Here, if not conclusive, his criticism of the Utopian idealists is perhaps valid. He asked whether the women's new knowledge, far from *improving* their lot and character, might not be bad for it. They would be unsettled without any real change in circumstances. 'What demand is there for the ability that they may have prematurely acquired? Will they not be indisposed to any kind of hard labour or drudgery? And yet many of them must submit to it or do wrong. . . '. In a long letter to the Reverend H. J. Rose, Wordsworth argues that infant education is destroying the ties of family affections and loyalties out of which, in the pamphlet *On the Convention at Cintra* he had argued that patriotism and many other virtues sprang. Rousseau, in *Emile*, had described how different societies produced different ideals of value in personality, and had cited the case of the Spartan mother who rushed to meet the returning army and asked eagerly who won. She was told that unfortunately her three sons had been killed, but she simply reiterated the question, who won. When told that it was Sparta she went away happy. Rousseau had argued that modern states had no ideal of behaviour in which individual value was so submerged, and Wordsworth followed him. 'The

Spartan and other ancient communities might disregard domestic ties because they had the substitution of country which we cannot have. With us, country is a mere name compared with what it was to the Greeks . . . as that *passion* alone was strong enough then to preserve the individual, his family and the whole State from ever-impending destruction.' In his England infant schools destroyed family unity—and the natural instincts of motherhood:

> We interfere with the maternal instinct before the child is born, by furnishing, in cases where there is no necessity, the mother with baby linen for her unborn child. Now, that in too many instances a lamentable necessity may exist for this, I allow; but why should such charity be obtruded? Why should so many excellent ladies form themselves into committees and rush into an almost indiscriminate benevolence, which precludes the poor mother from the strongest motive human nature can be actuated by for industry, for forethought and for self-denial. When the stream has thus been poisoned at its fountain-head, we proceed, by separating, through infant schools, the mother from the child and from the rest of the family, disburthening them from all care of the little ones for perhaps eight hours of the day. . . .

Wordsworth here in some ways anticipated the Dickens of *Hard Times* and *Bleak House*. In *Hard Times* Dickens satirized the optimistic Utilitarian exaltation of pure knowledge above everything —the useless definition of a horse as a 'graminivorous quadruped', the flattening out of the real boy in the docile student. In *Bleak House* his satire of the philanthropic Victorian do-gooders with their moralizing patronage of the poor reminds one of Wordsworth's excellent ladies forming themselves into committees to *impose* unsuitable ideals and values on communities whose real life they ignore. There is a Dickensian note in the same letter on education where Wordsworth quotes 'Out of the mouths of babes and children . . .' and continues wryly: 'Apparently the infants here contemplated were under a very different course of discipline from that which many in our day are condemned to. In a town of Lancashire, about nine in the morning, the streets resound with the crying of infants, wheeled off in carts and other vehicles (some ladies, I believe, lending their carriages for this purpose) to their schools and prisons.' There is some real wisdom in Wordsworth's objections to this acquiring of unrelated knowledge at the expense of family life, personal freedom, and natural growth of the personality, but his Romantic respect for the whole person, Rousseau's individual consistent with himself, is always tinged by a 'Victorian' middle-class belief that the poor are meant by God to keep to their stations. Economically he was probably quite right that most women had nothing to expect but hard domestic work—but there is a note of lofty patronage in his statements that is not in accord with the passionate concern of *The Prelude* and *The Excursion*. 'A hand full of employment and a head not above it, with such principles and habits as may be acquired without the Madras machinery are the best security for the chastity of wives of the lower rank.'

Coleridge, too, became suspicious of contemporary educational ideals. In his youth he argued vigorously that widespread diffusion of knowledge was socially necessary and listed the ways in which it was being brought about. Methodism, spreading among the middle and lower classes, he saw as a liberalizing and thought-inducing force; large manufactories produced societies where newspapers 'and sometimes larger publications' were regularly read; the growth of book societies in large towns was encouraging. In later life he was enraged by the argument that it was the spread of learning and argument that had caused the recent revolution and wars. The answer was not *less* learning but more. 'The powers that awaken and foster the spirit of curiosity are to be found in every village: books are in every hovel. The infant's cries are hushed with picture-books; and the cottager's child sheds his first bitter tears over pages, which render it impossible for the man to be treated or governed as a child. Here, as in so many other cases, the inconveniences that have arisen from a thing's having become too general, are best removed by making it universal.'

But Coleridge, like Wordsworth, was anxious to emphasize the abstracting and dehumanizing qualities in contemporary education. Reading and writing *in themselves*, he said, were not education

—they were only the means of education. And he was also opposed
to the introduction of infant-schools, at least in the country:

> Is it found that an infant-school child, who has been bawling all
> day a column of the multiplication-table, or a verse from the
> Bible, grows up a more dutiful son or daughter to its parents?
> Are domestic charities on the increase amongst families under this
> system? In a great town, in our present state of society, perhaps
> such schools may be a justifiable expedient—a choice of the lesser
> evil; but as for driving these establishments into the country
> villages and breaking up the cottage home education, I think it one
> of the most miserable mistakes which the well-intentioned people
> of the day have yet made. . . .

Like their political beliefs, their educational theories at their best
sprang from a mistrust of easy optimism and idealism; a desire to
understand what children were *really* capable of and really in a
position to achieve. The virtues of this realism, and the faults of
the cautiousness which went with it both look well beside Lancaster's ingenious systems and Tom Wedgwood's theoretical
approach.

I want to end this chapter with a description of a visit by
Wordsworth to a school in Brixton in 1835, when Wordsworth
was already a poet to be studied in schools. The description is that
of Edward Quillinan who married Wordsworth's daughter, Dora:

> After wine and cake we were *ushered* into the schoolroom. The boys
> rose and bowed, sate and gazed; pencils and slates were brought
> out at word of command; pedagogue gave out, line by line, the
> Sonnet supposed to be written on Westminster Bridge. All the boys
> wrote it, one echoing the Master as the Clerk does the Clergyman.
> When finished several boys in turn read it aloud; very well too.
> They were then called upon to explain the meaning of 'the river
> glideth at his own sweet will'. One boy, the biggest, made a dis-
> sertation on the influence of the moon on the tides, another said
> there was no wind, another that there were no water breaks in the
> Thames to prevent its gliding as it pleased; another that the arches
> of the bridge had no locks to shut the water in and out. One Boy

said there were no boats. Poet explained: was then called on by
Pedagogue to read the Sonnet himself; declined: Ped intreated:
Poet remonstrated: Ped inexorable; Poet submitted. I never heard
him read better. The Boys evidently felt it; thunders of applause;
Poet asked for a half-Holiday for them: granted: thunders on
thunders.

6 *The Literary World*

Observe the march of Milton; his severe application; his laborious
polish; his deep metaphysical researches; his prayer to God before
he began his great work; all that could lift and swell his intellect
became his daily food.

I should not think of devoting less than twenty years to an epic
poem. Ten years to collect materials and warm my mind with
universal science. I would be a tolerable Mathematician. I would
thoroughly understand Mechanics; Hydrostatics; Optics and
Astronomy; Botany; Metallurgy; Fossilism; Chemistry; Geology;
Anatomy; Medicine; then the mind of man; then the minds of
men, in all Travels, Voyages, and Histories. So I would spend ten
years; the next five in the composition of the poem and the five last
in the correction of it. So would I write, haply not unhearing of
that divine and nightly-whispering voice, which speaks to mighty
minds, of predestined garlands, starry and unwithering.

This is an extract from a letter from Coleridge to Joseph Cottle,
the Bristol bookseller who befriended him in youth and published
his early works and the *Lyrical Ballads*. Both Coleridge and Wordsworth had the highest possible respect for the work of literary
genius—both of them saw what they wrote, or meant to write, in
terms of eternity, measured against the great poets—although
Coleridge's diffidence and mental anxieties led him to despair
of his own gifts, and Wordsworth in his old age, closed in and
stolidly pessimistic, said his 'interests in Literature and books in
general seem to be dying away unreasonably fast—nor do I look
or much care for a revival of them'. This chapter is about their
work, not *sub specie aeternitatis* but as part of the contemporary
literary life.

I have already said that neither of them made much money
by their poetic writings. Cottle gave the young Coleridge thirty
guineas in advance for a volume of poems and offered a guinea and
a half per hundred lines of any more verse he might write. The

London publisher, Longman, offered Wordsworth and Coleridge £80 for the second edition of the *Lyrical Ballads*. Longman continued to publish Wordsworth, but Wordsworth felt he was not doing very well out of him and made several attempts to interest John Murray in a new six-volume edition of his poems in 1825. He complained about overheads:

> Southey tells me that Murray can sell more copies of any book that will sell at all than Longman—but it does not follow from that that in the end an Author will profit more, because Murray sells books considerably lower to the Trade and advertises even more expensively than Longman; though that seems scarcely possible. ... my little tract on the Lakes, the first Ed: for which *I* got £9/8/2 was charged £27/2/3 advertising. The 2nd ed. is already charged to me £30.7.2: the immense profits are yet to come. Thus my throat is cut.

The same Murray, Byron's publisher, after an enthusiastic report from Byron on *Kubla Khan*, published this and *Christabel* in 1817 in a volume with *The Pains of Sleep*—for *Christabel* he paid £70 and for *Kubla Khan*, £20.

Both poets had trouble with unsuitable publishing houses—Wordsworth negotiated with a firm called Hurst and Robinson through a poet and journalist called Alaric Watts. Watts stopped negotiations just in time to avoid the firm's failure in the financial crisis in which Constable, Scott's publishers, also failed, leaving the novelist struggling to pay off debts for the rest of his life. Wordsworth at that stage wanted £300 down for an edition of 1,000 copies and no expenses: he finally negotiated an arrangement with Longman's, since Murray simply did not answer his letters. This was for 750 copies, with Wordsworth paying two-thirds of the expense and receiving two-thirds of the profits. Some of the profits he would have made were eroded by a pirated edition produced in Paris in 1828—copyright did not extend abroad.

Coleridge's major publishing troubles were with a publishing firm called Gale and Curtis, who had issued the bound sheets of the periodical *Friend* in 1812. He felt obliged to offer them his

John Murray, Wordsworth's publisher, from an engraving after
a portrait by H. W. Pickersgill

reconstructed *Friend*: he had intended to publish other works
with Murray but found himself contracting to let Gale and Curtis
publish *Sybilline Leaves, Biographia, The Statesman's Manual* and his
unperformed drama, *Zapolya*. Coleridge felt that this firm was
honourable, particularly since Mr Curtis, who called on him, was
a gentleman in clerical orders. He was distressed when it was
pointed out to him that Murray had reasonably expected to have

published the other poems and the drama. His indignation, therefore, when the firm turned out to be neither honest nor stable was extreme. Early in 1817 the firm (now called Rest Fenner) asked him to draw up a plan for an encyclopaedia, of which he was to be general editor on condition that he worked for the encyclopaedia full time and lived in Camberwell, where the press was situated. He dared not leave Highgate because he needed the Gillmans to supervise his opium addiction, but offered to work on it four days a week there and two days, 9–5, in the Paternoster Row office. This was already a parody of all the high hopes he had had for the epic he would write, unifying all knowledge. He wrote despairingly that he felt 'compelled to give up all thought and hope of doing anything of a permanent nature, either as a Poet or a Philosopher' for he had hired himself 'as a Job writer and Compiler' of a work that would consume all his remaining years. In the end it was agreed that he should write the Introduction only— at six guineas a sheet for six sheets. It appeared in the first volume of the *Encyclopaedia Metropolitana*, January 1818, as 'General Introduction; or Preliminary Treatise on Method'. He had agreed that the treatise should be cut, but not that it should be changed. When he received his copy his introduction was 'so bedevilled, so interpolated and topsy-turvied', such a 'compleat Muddle of Paragraphs, without sub—or co-ordination' that he was ashamed of it as a man and a scholar. Worse was to come. Curtis and Fenner spread scandals about him—that they had sent him money to keep him out of jail, that he had cheated Longman, borrowed money from the printer, appeared drunk. Then they went bankrupt. Coleridge had to borrow money to buy back his half-copyrights and the unsold copies of his books. Later he discovered that he had been cheated. Fenner had told him that 1,000 copies of *Zapolya* were to be printed and that Coleridge would receive half the profits. He was *told* that only 100 copies were sold—but the bankruptcy revealed that 2,000 had been printed and 1,100 sold. He believed himself to have lost over £1,200 through the cheating and failure of these publishers.

Not all poets fared so badly. Longman, who offered £80 for the *Lyrical Ballads* paid Tom Moore 3,000 guineas for *Lalla Rookh*.

Murray offered Byron 1,500 guineas for a single canto of *Childe Harold*—Byron cited the amount Longman paid Moore and asked for 2,500 guineas. Cowper's *Task* made £10,000 for Joseph Johnson. But it was not surprising that Coleridge admired the toast Tom Campbell gave at Longman's Saturday public dinner— 'Buonaparte—for having shot a bookseller!' Or even that Wordsworth should declare 'I would a thousand times rather that not a verse of mine should enter the Press again, than to allow any of them to say that I was to the amount of the strength of a hair dependent upon their countenance, consideration, Patronage, or by whatever term they *may* dignify their ostentation and selfish vanity.' He quoted Dr Johnson's dictum 'No, Sir; Authors above Booksellers'.

Another major literary force with which writers had to contend was newspapers, periodicals and journals. The publication of newspapers and periodicals increased enormously at this time. In 1753 7,500,000 stamps for newspapers were sold: by 1821 this had risen to 25 million. In 1818 more than 100,000 people read literary reviews. The Tory newspaper, *The Morning Post*, besides Coleridge's political articles, published much good poetry by Wordsworth, Coleridge, Southey among others. It bought jokes from Lamb at 6*d*. a joke. *The Morning Chronicle* first employed Hazlitt: *The Times* employed Crabb Robinson as the first foreign correspondent during the Napoleonic Wars. Southey was offered the editorship of *The Times* but refused it—at that time the newspapers were often corrupt and their proprietors not above collecting money to suppress news. But it was the big reviews which were influential. *The Edinburgh Review* was founded in 1802 by Brougham, Jeffrey, Horner and Sydney Smith—its views were Whig and liberal. Its great rival, *The Quarterly*, founded in 1809, was a Tory publication. The two together at the time of Waterloo had a circulation of over 20,000. *The Westminster Review* was utilitarian and supported Reform. *Blackwood's Magazine* published poetry, essays, tales and novels, including, later, those of George Eliot—but in its early days it was characterized by a strong political bias in favour of the Tories, and a style of wild personal abuse, and invective, particularly against the so-called 'Cockney' school which included

A breakfast party given by the poet and banker, Samuel Rogers, in 1815; from an engraving by Charles Mottram. *Seated, l. to r.*, R.B.Sheridan, Thomas Moore, Wordsworth, Robert Southey, Coleridge, Samuel Rogers, Lord Byron, G.S.Kemble, *Standing, l. to r.*, John Flaxman, Sir Walter Scott, James Mackintosh, Lord Landsdowne, Sydney Smith, Washington Irving, Francis Jeffrey, Thomas Stothard, Thomas Lawrence, J.M.W.Turner, T. Campbell.

Keats as well as Leigh Hunt. Leigh Hunt himself ran various short-lived periodicals: *The Liberal*, for which Byron and Shelley wrote; *The Reflector*; *The Examiner*, for which Hazlitt wrote great theatre criticism and essays and in which Keats was first published. *The Examiner* ran from 1808 to 1825. *The London Magazine* (1820–9) was edited by John Scott as a deliberately *London* magazine to a very high standard. It published De Quincey's *Confessions of an English Opium Eater*, the essays of Elia, work by Keats, Hazlitt, Clare, Landor, and Carlyle. *The Gentleman's Magazine* was a true miscellany ranging from information about sheep dips to religious poems—and the fashionable magazines of the period too, *The Beau Monde* for instance, had political, literary and artistic sections amongst reports on clothes and high life.

The poets' encounters with these periodicals were not always happy. *The Edinburgh Review* was edited by Francis Jeffrey, whose standards were neo-classical, conservative and conventional—he claimed that he knew most of the *Lyrical Ballads* by heart, but was critical of the Romantic poets in public. Coleridge in the *Biographia* wrote an excellent passage on *The Edinburgh Review*: he recommended it for its services in the diffusion of knowledge and for its avowed intention only to review selected books of merit, but pointed out that it frequently reviewed 'works neither indecent or immoral, yet of such trifling importance even in point of size and, according to the critic's own verdict, so devoid of all merit as must excite in the most candid mind the suspicion either that dislike or vindictive feelings were at work; or that there was a cold prudential pre-determination to increase the sales of the review by flattering the malignant passions of human nature'. This vindictiveness, he considered, was bad—not because of the 'damnatory style' itself—but because it was often *personal*, dragging in an author's cast-off youthful work, making wild unillustrated assertions about books.

Coleridge himself wrote a review for the *Edinburgh* of Clarkson's *History of the Abolition of the Slave Trade*, and was distressed because two paragraphs were added to it, in which he was '(In a vulgar style of rancid commonplace metaphors) made to contradict myself—first, in a nauseous and most false ascription of the

Supremacy of Merit to Mr Wilberforce, and secondly, in an attack on Mr Pitt's Sincerity substituted for a Paragraph, in which I had both defended it and him; and proved that of all the parliamentary Friends of the Africans he was the most effective.' The distortion of his views about Wilberforce was particularly galling as there was much unpleasant controversy at the time as to the respective parts played in the abolition of slavery by Wilberforce and Clarkson, and Clarkson was a personal friend of the Wordsworths and of Coleridge himself.

Jeffrey is now probably best remembered for his ferocious review of Wordsworth's *Excursion* in 1814 which began 'This will never do', and continued to berate Wordsworth for 'rapturous mysticism' and for placing unsuitable intellectual harangues in the mouths of low characters—Wordsworth said he had refused to 'pollute my fingers with touching his book', but had probably read and was clearly deeply hurt by the review, which he quoted as 'This will not do' in a letter to Mrs Clarkson. Coleridge was enraged by the 'infamous' review, and it was partly to correct its imperceptive views that he wrote his famous critique of Wordsworth's characteristic merits and defects in the *Biographia*. He also claimed in the *Biographia* that Jeffrey had visited Keswick, paid innumerable 'high coloured compliments' to Coleridge, and been told that there was no Lake School of poets since their styles and dates of composition did not agree—but Jeffrey had immediately gone home and written an attack on 'the School of whining and hypochondriacal poets that haunt the Lakes'. Jeffrey denied this charge in a review of *Biographia* in 1817. But his hostility to the 'Lake School' was persistent.

Hazlitt's review of *The Excursion* in *The Examiner* was, by contrast, highly percipient. It was true that he made a wild attack on country people—'All country people hate each other'—dictated more by metropolitan loyalty than relevance, but his understanding of Wordsworth's greatness and defects was excellent. He praised Wordsworth's quality of imagination in a landscape metaphor* both poets might have used. 'Every object is seen through the medium of innumerable recollections, is

* See below, Chapter 7, *passim*.

clothed with the haze of imagination like a glittering vapour; is
obscured with the excess of glory, has the shadowy brightness of
a waking dream.' He criticized Wordsworth, percipiently, for 'an
intense intellectual egotism' which swallowed up everything and
made Wordsworth incapable of writing dramatically—all three
protagonists of the poem, the recluse, the pastor and the peddler,
were really the one poet, a trinity speaking with one voice. But
he quoted a magnificent sentence from Sir Thomas Browne which
he felt illustrated Wordsworth's interest in the elements and early
formation of the human personality: 'God knew Adam in the
elements of his chaos, and saw him in the great obscurity of nothing.'

It is perhaps worth pointing out that Coleridge's summing up—
in a letter to Lady Beaumont—of what he believed to be the causes
of the apparent stiffness, banality and egocentricity of parts of
The Excursion covers the same area as both Hazlitt's praise and
blame. He believed that Wordsworth was so absorbed in the
examination of the mental processes by which he personally had
arrived at certain aspects of knowledge of the elements of his
chaos that he forgot that many of his discoveries might seem
obvious to someone who had not shared the working through:

> As proofs meet me in every part of the *Excursion*, that the Poet's
> genius has not flagged, I have sometimes fancied, that having by
> the conjoint operation of his own experiences, feelings and reason
> *himself* convinced *himself* of Truths, which the generality of persons
> have either taken for granted from their Infancy, or at least
> adopted in early life, he has attached all their own depth and
> weight to doctrines and words, which come almost as Truisms or
> Common-places to others.

Lady Beaumont unwisely showed this letter to Wordsworth,
who wrote Coleridge an agitated letter of self-defence—he had
meant to be commonplace—demanding why Coleridge thought
the unpublished Poem on his own Life better. Coleridge answered
the letter, but his full explanation was left to *Biographia*, which the
sensitive Wordsworth rejected. Charles Lamb, too, became em-
broiled in the critical reception of the poem—he wrote a long and
laudatory review for *The Quarterly*, which the editor altered out of

recognition, and Lamb, too, was writing agitated letters—of apology to Wordsworth.

Coleridge's relationship with reviewers was even stormier than Wordsworth's. From *The Quarterly* he might have expected encouragement, since Southey wrote regularly and prominently for it—indeed, Coleridge in 1819 was proposing to William Blackwood of *Blackwood's Magazine* that he should write their *leading* articles— 'by *leading* I mean that one article which is expected to be most talked of, as for instance several of Mr Southey's in the *Quarterly*.' (This is possibly the first use of the term 'leading article'.) But Southey had already, anonymously, in *The Critical Review* dismissed *The Ancient Mariner* as 'a poem of little merit', 'a Dutch attempt at German sublimity'. In 1816 Coleridge was saying that his reputation suffered more from the 'studied silence' of *The Quarterly* than from the attacks of *The Edinburgh*, and in 1817 he was reporting the gossip of 'a very eminent bookseller' who, he said, had been told by Byron, Scott and other great men that 'taking him all in all Mr C. is the greatest man, we have; but *I* would not have a work of his, if it were given me ready printed— for the Quarterly Review takes no notice of his works, or but in a half way that damns a man worse than anything; and *our* Review (the Edinburgh) is *decided* to write him down.'

The history of Hazlitt's periodical attacks on Coleridge makes frightening reading. He tried to annihilate the *Christabel* volume in *The Examiner* in June 1816: in September of that year he attacked *The Statesman's Manual* before it had appeared and after publication wrote two more attacks on it. On 2 August 1817 he reprinted in *The Morning Chronicle* a passage from *Fears in Solitude* to show up the contrast between Coleridge's early and late views on the war. He attacked *The Statesman's Manual* again in *The Edinburgh Review* and reviewed the *Biographia* savagely in its August 1817 issue. He also wrote two tirades in *The Yellow Dwarf*. Other well-known figures joined in: the popular poet Tom Moore berated *Christabel* in *The Edinburgh* and John Wilson ('Christopher North') was savage in *Blackwood's*.

Blackwood's was run by John Gibson Lockhart and John Wilson, who was so assiduously and charmingly attentive to the Wordsworths at Rydal, but wrote anonymous and virulent abuse under the pen name of Christopher North. Lockhart was Walter Scott's son-in-law and biographer, and was probably the author of *Peter's Letters to His Kinsfolk*, full of literary and personal gossip. This distressed Wordsworth and his family and even Mrs Coleridge, who wrote of it 'What a rage for personality in the present day! not a periodical publication comes out but something is said upon living characters; 'tis not the thing I think, at all, to speak so much of people while they are living; in the literary gazette there was a full account of our juvenile american Scheme, and that *Mrs Fricker* and *Mrs Southey* had consented to go with the young people in their wild Scheme of colonization.' Wordsworth was more severe still on *Blackwood's* in 1819.

> I know little of Blackwood's Magazine, and wish to know less. I have seen in it articles so infamous that I do not chuse to let it enter my doors. The Publisher sent it to me some time ago and I begged (civilly you will take for granted) not to be troubled with it any longer. ... Perhaps I ought to have mentioned that the articles that disgusted me so were personal—referring to myself and friends and acquaintance, especially Coleridge.

This literary vituperation overflowed into tragedy. John Scott, the brilliant editor of *The London Magazine*, after his magazine had attacked Lockhart's work in *Blackwood's* was called out to fight a duel at Chalk Farm with one of Lockhart's henchmen, in which he was fatally wounded within a year of founding the *London*. Lamb's biographer, Serjeant Talfourd, describes this incident of black comedy most movingly. Scott, he said, 'at last met his death almost by lamentable accident, in the uncertain glimmer of moonlight, from the hand of one who went out resolved not to harm him. ... Such was the melancholy result— first of a controversy too envenomed—and afterwards of enthralment in usages, absurd in all, but most absurd when applied by a literary man to a literary quarrel.'

Wordsworth particularly attracted, as well as critical hostility and personal spite, a great deal of comment by parody. *Peter Bell's* publication in 1819 aroused a spate of these. Keats's friend Reynolds wrote one before publication—with a Wordsworthian preface, supplementary essay and footnotes; there was 'The Dead Asses, a Lyrical Ballad' as well as Shelley's savage *Peter Bell the Third*, which attacked in general complacency about poverty and Peterloo. Coleridge asked to see Reynolds's parody before publication and found it funny and inoffensive (it was designed with 'Peter Bell' as the Leech-gatherer 'poring and prosing' over the graves of all Wordsworth's characters and Wordsworth himself). Coleridge's judgment on parodies seems sane and, in Wordsworth's case, prophetic:

> Parodies on new poems are read as satires; on old ones—the soliloquy of Hamlet for instance—as compliments. A man of genius may securely laugh at a mode of attack by which his reviler, in half a century or less, becomes his encomiast.

Coleridge himself made two attempts to run periodicals singlehanded. In 1796 he launched *The Watchman*, a largely political paper, anti-Pitt, advocating general suffrage—it was to be published every eight days in order to avoid the newspaper tax. It folded at a considerable loss after ten issues had appeared; Coleridge's description in *Biographia* of his tour through the Midlands (where the wealthy dissenting Liberals were most in evidence), to gain subscribers is still fascinating. He describes himself lecturing a Calvinist tallow-chandler for half-an-hour:

> I argued, I described, I promised, I prophesied, and beginning with the captivity of nations I ended with the near approach of the millennium, finishing the whole with some of my own verses describing that glorious state out of the *Religious Musings*. . . . My taper man of lights listened with perseverent and praiseworthy patience. . . . 'And what, Sir,' he said, after a short pause, 'might the cost be?' 'Only four-pence,' (O! how I felt the anti-climax, the abysmal bathos of that *four-pence*)! 'Only four-pence, Sir, each number, to be published on every eighth day.' 'That comes to a deal of money at the end of a year. And how much did you say there was to be for the money?' 'Thirty-two pages, Sir! large

THE

WATCHMAN.

Nº II.

WEDNESDAY, MARCH 9, 1796.

Published by the Author, S. T. COLERIDGE,
Bristol:

And by PARSONS, Paternoster-Row, London.

THAT ALL MAY KNOW THE TRUTH;
AND THAT THE TRUTH MAY MAKE US FREE!

ESSAY ON FASTS.

Wherefore my Bowels shall sound like an Harp.

ISAIAH, XVI. 11.

FASTING has been commanded by every religion
except the Christian.——It was practised with extreme
rigour by the ancient Priests; a fact which disproves the
common opinion, that Priests are the same in all ages.——
We collect from Herodotus and Porphyry, that before
their annual sacrifice of a cow to Isis, the Ægyptians
fasted forty days: and Pythagoras, in addition to the perpetual and fishless Lent which he observed, is reported
to have abstained from all food whatsoever, forty days:
and so did Elijah, but with this advantage over Pythagoras, that he had double-dined on viands angelically
prepared. This coincidence of number in the days seems
to cast a shade of doubt on the genuineness of the beginning of the fourth chapter of Matthew and of Luke:
in which the same miraculous circumstance is related of
our Saviour. It was the policy of the early Christians
to assimilate their religion to that of the Heathens in all

D   possible

octavo, closely printed.' 'Thirty and two pages? Bless me, why except what I does in a family way on the Sabbath, that's more than I ever reads, Sir! all the year round. I am as great a one as any man in Brummagem, sir! for liberty and truth and all them sort of things, but as to this (no offence, I hope, Sir) I must beg to be excused.'

The Friend appeared much later in 1809–10. It is difficult not to see *The Friend; a Literary, Moral and Political Weekly Paper* as a tragedy. It meant so much to its author, on all sorts of fronts. Sara Hutchinson worked with him on it, as his amanuensis: it was to prove that he had the tenacity and courage to produce regular work. It was also to be a vindication of his literary beliefs and his beliefs about the way the language used affected moral and political thought. He saw it as a serious writer's attempt to counteract the debasing influences of slick and vituperative or partisan journalism. He saw it in opposition both to Cobbett's *Political Register* and to Addison and Steele's *Spectator*. Cobbett 'applies to the Passions that are gratified by Curiosity, sharp and often calumnious Personality, the Politics and the Events of the Day and the names and characters of notorious Contemporaries. From all these Topics I not only abstain as from Guilt; but to strangle these Passions by the awakening of the nobler Germ in human nature is my express and paramount *Object*.' Addison's easy prose, he considered, had 'innocently contributed to the general taste for unconnected writing'—people now disliked long words, long sentences and complex thoughts. *His* periodical was to restore all these and was addressed only to men who made an effort to think. It was to be produced one sheet at a time on stamped paper like a newspaper, but sent through the post to avoid paying news-vendors (like Cobbett's work). It is usually claimed that he was hopelessly idealistic and incompetent about *The Friend*, but the truth is that on many fronts he was both pertinacious and competent. He organized the paper, printing and distribution well, and produced twenty-eight numbers. Readers were annoyed by his ponderous style and his habit of breaking off in mid-thought or even mid-sentence 'to be concluded in next number'—but some of the delays were caused by Wordsworth's and Southey's views, retailed to Daniel Stuart in London who was organizing Coleridge's supply of stamped paper, that he was quite incapable of going on with it. He was admittedly hopelessly over-confident about his subscribers, too many of whom were agreeable 'friends of friends' who never paid up, and he organized his payments badly, hoping vaguely that subscribers would *send* him the money, post-paid, and then requesting subscribers to send money, to a certain George Ward, a bookseller in London, without warning Ward— who was understandably irritated when he received letters from subscribers asking him to call and collect the money—the letters often not post-paid. *The Friend* is hard reading, intricate, Jacobean in style, and spends several issues defining the nature of communication between writer and reader before it communicates. But there are moments when Coleridge succeeds in his primary aim—that of communicating the kind of 'delight' that comes from true understanding—'the distinct perception of a fundamental truth'—things taught in childhood about the nature of language or morals and suddenly truly *grasped*. It was like him to try and do this in an intermittent journal, combining as always, an inevitable element of failure with any achievement.

Wordsworth wrote for *The Friend*, and published poems in newspapers: he never made great efforts to reach a large audience. He had the desire, often found in great and original writers, for a popular, uneducated audience. He remarked the influence: amongst the poor of 'half-penny Ballads and penny and two penny histories'—some of which were good, though others were 'superstitious' or 'indelicate'. He felt the power of these 'struggling papers' to be so strong 'that I have many a time wished I had talents to produce songs, poems and little histories that might circulate among other good things in this way, supplanting partly the bad; flowers and useful herbs to take the place of weeds. Indeed some of the Poems which I have published were composed, not without a hope that at some time they might answer this purpose.'

But, unlike Burns, Wordsworth, although he wrote about the poor, did not write close to any vernacular tradition that might appeal to them. His brush with popular methods of disseminating literature came with the modish Annuals—designed, as he told

However this may be, the Understanding or regulative
faculty is manifestly distinct from Life and Sensation, its'
function being to take up the *passive affections* into distinct
Thought of the Sense both according to its' own essential forms.* These Forms however, as they are first a-
wakened by impressions from the Senses, so have they no
Substance or Meaning unless in their application to Objects of the Senses ; and if we would remove from them
by careful Abstraction, all the influences and intermix-
tures of a yet far higher Faculty (Self consciousness for instance), it would be difficult, if at all possible, to distinguish its' Functions from those of Instinct, of which it
would be no inapt Definition that it is a more or less limited Understanding without Self-consciousness, or spon-
taneous Origination. Besides : the Understanding with
all its axioms of sense, its Anticipations of Apperception,
and its' Analogies of Experience, has no appropriate Object, but the material World in Relation to our worldly Interests. The far-sighted Prudence of Man, and the more
narrow, but at the same time far more certain and effec-
tual, Cunning of the Fox, are both no other than a nobler
Substitute " *for Salt, in order that the Hog may not putri-
fy before its destined hour.*"

But God created Man in his own Image : to be the
Image of his own Eternity and Infinity created he Man.
He gave us Reason and with Reason Ideas of its own formation and underived from material Nature, self-consciousness, Principles, and above all, the Law of Conscience,
which in the power of an holy and omnipotent Being *com-
mands* us to attribute Reality—among the numerous Ideas

---

* Aristotle, the first systematic Anatomist of the Mind, constructed the
first Numeration Table of these innate Forms or Faculties (N. B. not innate
Ideas or *Notions*) under the name of Categories : which Table though both
incomplete and erroneous, remains an unequivocal Proof of his Penetration
and philosophical Genius. The best and most orderly arrangement of the
original forms of the Understanding (the *Moulds* as it were both of our Notions and judgements concerning the Notices of the Senses) is that of Quantity, Quality, Relation, and Mode, each consisting of three Kinds. There is
but one possible way of making an enumeration of them *interesting*, or even
endurable to the general Reader : the history of the *origin* of certain useful
Inventions in machinery, in the minds of the Inventors.

(To be continued.)

PENRITH : PRINTED AND PUBLISHED BY J. BROWN ; AND SOLD BY
MESSRS. LONGMAN AND CO. PATERNOSTER ROW, LONDON.

The last page from an issue of Coleridge's second magazine, *The
Friend*. Several numbers were allowed to finish in mid-sentence

the editor of *The Friendship's Offering*, 'principally for the sofa table'. These precursors of the coffee-table book were embellished with pretty pictures. Wordsworth said that he would have liked this one better if it were less about the fine world and 'pressed closer upon common life'—but he saw that 'would not suit the market'. However, these annuals paid well, and Wordsworth, after refusing several invitations to write for them, accepted an offer from *The Keepsake* in 1828—100 guineas for 12 pages of verse. He was very short of money; as his daughter Dora said, the commission was 'degrading enough I must confess but necessity has no law'. It is interesting to note that George Eliot uses *The Keepsake* in *Middlemarch* as an example of provincial vulgarity, which the sophisticated Dr Lydgate can afford to sneer at. She describes it as 'the gorgeous watered-silk publication which marked modern progress at that time', with silly engravings of 'ladies and gentlemen with shiny copper-plate cheeks and copper-plate smiles'. Wordsworth sent six sonnets to the Christmas 1828 *Keepsake*, which contained several full-page steel engravings and contributions by Walter Scott, Tom Moore, Southey, Coleridge, Mrs Hemans and Shelley. He wrote a poem to go with a picture by James Holmes of a girl with a sheaf of corn simpering coyly from under a shady hat. He was inclined to be belligerent about this popularizing and wrote to the poetess Maria Jane Jewsbury: 'I think you do quite right in connecting yourself with these light things. An Author has not fair play who has no share in their Profits. . . . Therefore let the Annuals pay—and with whomseoever you deal make hard bargains. Humility with these gentry is downright simpleness.'

But he was angered to find that of the six sonnets he sent in only two were printed—and the editor had the impudence to write to Wordsworth complaining that he had not filled the agreed number of pages, and asking for more poems. As Wordsworth indignantly pointed out, this meant in principle that he could go on writing *forever* and being rejected without his contract being fulfilled. He became highly disillusioned and commented ruefully: 'I am properly served for having had any connection with such things. My only excuse is, that they offered me a very liberal sum, and that I have laboured hard through a long life without more pecuniary emolument than a lawyer gets for two special retainers or a public performer sometimes for two or three songs.'

The financial uncertainties of authorship led Wordsworth to an eloquent and sustained campaign in the cause of the extension of copyright. A Copyright Act in 1814 had increased the term of protection for an author's work from fourteen to twenty-eight years after the date of publication—or for the rest of the author's life, if that was longer. At his death, a writer's works became public property, except for posthumous works, which were protected for a further twenty-eight years. Thomas Noon Talfourd, Lamb's biographer, introduced a bill to extend the period to sixty years in 1837 and again in 1838 with Wordsworth's whole-hearted support, but it failed to become law. Talfourd tried again in 1839 and again in 1841 when the Bill was opposed by Macaulay and defeated by 7 votes despite Talfourd's sincere eloquence. Talfourd said that he hoped that 'the voices of Wordsworth and Southey, of Moore and Rogers, of Coleridge speaking as it were from the grave and the son of Sir Walter Scott would weigh against all the powers and genius of my right honourable friend's address'. In 1842 a Bill was made law allowing a period of forty-two years from publication, or the length of the author's life, whichever was longer. Wordsworth was energetic, writing to Peel, Gladstone, the Chancellor of the Exchequer, and persuading Lockhart to publish an article in *The Quarterly* for which he furnished information. He was chiefly concerned with the heirs of the author, and gave the copyright law as one reason for delaying the publication of the poem on the formation of his own mind:

Its publication has been prevented merely by the personal character of the subject. Had it been published as soon as it was finished, the copyright would long ago have expired in case of my decease. Now I do honestly believe that that poem, if given to the world before 28 years had elapsed after the composition, would scarcely have paid its own expenses. If published now, with the aid of such reputation as I have acquired, I have reason to believe that the profit from it would be respectable; and my heirs, even as the law now is, would benefit by the delay: but in the other case neither they nor I would have got a farthing from it, if my life had not been prolonged; the profit, such as it might be, would all have gone to printers and publishers and would, of course, continue to do so.

In the summer of 1840 when he was asked to subscribe to a memorial to Shakespeare at Stratford, he refused:

Literature stands much less in need of monuments to the dead than of justice to the living. And while so little attention is paid by the Legislature and by the public also to the principles set forth in Sergeant Talfourd's Copyright Bill, I cannot do more, upon the present occasion, than offer respectfully to the Committee my good wishes.

What was the poets' relationship with the other writers of the time? They were contemporaries after all of Blake, Byron, Jane Austen, Keats, Mrs Radcliffe and Tennyson. Coleridge in his early days was much influenced by the eighteenth-century poems of sensibility as opposed to the neo-classical polished verse of Pope: he wrote several 'effusions' and several casual conversation poems with a deliberately informal structure. An interesting example of his early poetry of sensibility is a poem addressed to the Reverend W. J. Hort while teaching a young lady some song-tunes on his flute. The exclamations and emotionalism are typical of the slighter verse of the time:

> O skill'd with magic spell to roll
> The thrilling tones that concentrate the soul!
> Breathe through thy flute those tender notes again,
> While near thee sits the chaste-eyed maiden mild;
> And bid her raise the poet's kindred strain
> In soft empassioned voice, correctly wild.

'Correctly wild' seems at first glance an anomaly—an eighteenth-century propriety yoked by violence to a romantic virtue—but in fact may well be an indication that Coleridge had learned what Boyer taught him, that poetry, even of the 'wildest odes', had a logic of its own, as severe as that of science. But the tone of the whole poem suggests not passion but a poetic convention of emotion, and the 'correctly' suggests in context propriety rather than strict logic.

The poem of sensibility was part of the tradition of the conversation poem, and Coleridge, sending his long and beautiful meditation on *The Nightingale* to Wordsworth in 1798, accompanied it with a much more vulgar conversational letter-poem, half-mocking the whole convention he was using:

> In stale blank verse a subject stale
> I send *per post* my *Nightingale*;
> And like an honest bard, dear Wordsworth,
> You'll tell me what you think, my Bird's worth.
> My opinion's briefly this—
> His bill he opens not amiss;
> And when he has sung a stave or so,
> His breast, and some small space below,
> So throbs and swells, that you might swear
> No vulgar music's working there.
> So far, so good; but then 'od rot him!
> There's something falls off at his bottom.
> Yet sure, no wonder it should breed
> That my Bird's Tail's a tail indeed
> And makes its own inglorious harmony
> Aeolio crepitu, non carmine.

A hero of the Romantic movement both in France and England was Chatterton, the young poet who wrote works of an imaginary fifteenth-century monk, Thomas Rowley, and poisoned himself with arsenic at the age of seventeen in despairing poverty. Chatterton's poems showed great talent, forgeries or not, and he became an archetypal symbol of genius crushed by indifference. Coleridge's *Monody* on his death is another early effusion—and Coleridge's own later criticism of it (1797) shows his appreciation of the faults of its style:

The Monody *must not* be reprinted . . . on a life and death so full of heart-giving *realities* as poor Chatterton's to find such shadowy nobodies, as cherub-winged DEATH, Trees of HOPE, bare-bosom'd AFFECTION, and simpering PEACE—makes one's blood circulate like ipecacacuanha [sic]—But so it is. A young man by strong feelings is impelled to write on a particular subject—and this is all, his feelings do for him. They set him upon the business and then they leave him.—He has such a high idea, of what Poetry ought to be, that he cannot conceive that such things as his natural emotions may be allowed to find a place in it—his learning therefore, his fancy, or rather conceit, and all his powers of buckram are put on the stretch—It appears to me, that strong feeling is not *so* requisite to an Author's being profoundly pathetic, as taste and good sense.

This passage introduces at an early point in Coleridge's life the insistence on the concrete as opposed to the abstract, reality as opposed to fancy and dramatics, which recurred in his political and educational thinking. The eighteenth-century models are rejected partly because of their lack of immediacy and their abstraction, powerful enough in the forms in which it was first used.

Coleridge published three sonnets under the name of Nehemiah Higginbottom, parodying his own (and Charles Lamb's) early style, one mocking 'the spirit of doleful egotism', the second 'low creeping language and thought under the pretence of simplicity', and the third, a burlesque lament for the house that Jack built, composed of over-elaborate and 'swelling' phrases from his own work. He said later that what he had early learned from Cowper and Bowles whom he early admired was the combination of natural thoughts with natural diction—the reconciliation of head and heart. The ballads collected by Bishop Percy seemed in some ways to have the same qualities of naturalness and immediacy—and since Wordsworth and Coleridge's medievalizing sprang from a desire for the direct and non-ornamental they did not approve of the excesses of the Gothic school of the time, the novels of Mrs Radcliffe and Monk Lewis, with their spectres, mouldering skeletons, dungeons and delightful horrors. Coleridge indeed wrote a letter with a high moral tone to the daughter of the poetess Mrs Robinson, refusing to contribute a poem to a memorial collection for Mrs Robinson on the grounds that Monk Lewis and Tom Moore were contributing. He begged Mrs Robinson not to be wounded 'but I have a wife, I have sons, I have an infant Daughter—what excuse could I offer to my own conscience if by suffering my name to be connected with those of Mr Lewis or Mr Moore I was the *occasion* of their reading the Monk or the wanton poems of Thomas Little Esqre?'

In 1798 he was criticizing Monk Lewis's drama *Castle Spectre* on more literary grounds. There was, he said, no character at all in the play. The author had written a postscript claiming originality in one character—'a negro who *had* a warm and benevolent heart but having been kidnapped from his country and barbarously used by the Christians becomes a Misanthrope—This is all! Passion—horror! agonizing pangs of Conscience! Dreams full of hell, serpents and skeletons! starts and attempted murders etc. etc. etc.; but positively not *one* line that marks even a superficial knowledge of human feelings, could I discover. . .'.

The benevolent bookseller Cottle, whom Coleridge dismissed as 'a well-meaning Creature; but a great Fool' (because he told Coleridge it was not opium that had injured him but the Devil), had epic ambitions and wrote a twenty-four volume *Alfred* clearly in the Gothic tradition. Lamb describes it magnificently:

> I got as far as the Mad Monk the first day and fainted . . . Mr Cottle soars a high pitch: and when he *is* original it is in a most original way indeed. His terrific scenes are indefatigable. Serpents, asps, spiders, ghosts, dead bodies, staircases made of nothing, with adder's tongues for bannisters. What a brain he must have! He puts as many plums in his pudding as my grandmother used to do; —and then his emerging from Hell's horrors into light, and treading on pure flats of this earth—for 23 books together!

William Combe, in his *Tour of Dr. Syntax in Search of the Picturesque*, a remarkably sustained parodical commentary on the aesthetic tastes and social life of the time, has the learned and impoverished doctor musing in a graveyard:

What golden gains my book would boast
If I could meet a chatty ghost
Who would some news communicate
Of its unknown and present state:
Some pallid figure in a shroud
Or sitting in a murky cloud
Or kicking up a new-made grave
Or screaming forth some horrid stave. . . .
Something to make the misses stare
And force upright their curly hair. . . .
And thus to tonish folks present
The Picturesque of Sentiment.

Walter Scott was an early admirer of Monk Lewis. He was a friend of Wordsworth, who admired his stoicism in illness and his moral rectitude, and wrote *Yarrow Revisited* and his sonnet on Scott's hopeless departure for Naples in search of health, moved by the great man nearing his end when he visited him at Abbotsford. But both poets were stringently critical of Scott as a poet. Coleridge wrote a long letter to Wordsworth on the publication of *The Lady of the Lake* in 1810, complaining that the poem was prosaic and verbose with a movement 'between a sleeping Canter and a Marketwoman's trot—but it is endless—' He went on:

In short, my dear William!—it is time to write a Recipe for Poems of this sort—I amused myself a day or two ago on reading a Romance in Mrs Radcliffe's style with making out a scheme, which was to serve for all romances a priori—only varying the proportions—A Baron or Baroness ignorant of their Birth and in some dependent situation—Castle—on a Rock—a Sepulchre—at some distance from the Rock—deserted Rooms—Underground Passages—Pictures—A ghost so believed—or—a written record—blood on it—A wonderful Cut Throat etc. etc. etc.—Now I say it is time to make out the component parts of the Scottish Minstrelsy—The first Business must be, a vast string of patronymics and names of Mountains, Rivers, etc.—the most commonplace imagery the Bard gars look almaist as well as new by the introduction of Benvoirlich, Vam Var. . . .

Coleridge produced his own cogent parody:

> How should the poet e'er give o'er
> With his eye fix'd on Cambus-More—
> Need reins be tightened in Despair
> When rose Benledi's ridge *in air*
> Tho' not one image grace the Heath,
> It gains such charm from flooded Teith—
> Besides you need not travel far
> To reach the Lake of Vennachar—
> Or *ponder refuge* from your Toil
> By far Lochard or Aberfoil.

He ended his 'recipe' with 'Item—the Poet not only may but must mix all dialects *of all ages* and all styles'.

There was perhaps something of envy in Coleridge's reaction to Scott's immense popularity, which he saw as another instance of the desire for facility and refusal to *think* which affected periodical literature, and induced him to make the style of *The Friend* so perversely complex: in places Scott's poems and novels, he said, 'supply both instance and solution of the present conditions and components of popularity, viz., to amuse without requiring any effort of thought, and without exciting any deep emotion'. This was not just: Scott was a voluminous writer and wrote many meretricious and ephemeral tales, but his great novels show a sense of history which is both profound and as *practical* and particular as Coleridge could have desired.

Wordsworth himself was capable of banal medievalizing and romantic rubbish; although, as with the simpler lyrical ballads, one has the sense that he envisaged some more basic human drama even where he drops off into apparent overdone sentiment. He was quite shrewd about Scott's novels, predicting accurately that they were 'likely to be much overrated on their first appearance and will afterwards be as much undervalued'. He also neatly picked out a real fault in Scott's presentation—the fact that his pictures of life did not rise and fade unostentatiously but were 'fixed upon an easel for the express purpose of being admired'. He liked Scott's accurate delineation of Highland manners but felt he had not enough humour to do creditable caricatures, and merely made his characters 'too peculiar and *outré*'. Dorothy was a careful reader of novels and a severe critic of them. She admired Richardson's masterpiece the voluminous *Clarissa,* and complimented Mrs Clarkson on one of her husband's books by saying 'Clarissa Harlowe was not more interesting when I first read it at 14 years of age'. She describes Mary reading the second volume of a novel *The Recluse of Norway* by one of the celebrated lady novelists, the sisters Anna Maria and Jane Porter, in which she found 'a wonderful cleverness . . . notwithstanding the badness of the style'. But Dorothy objected to love in novels: 'When love begins almost all novels grow tiresome. The first volume has not a word of it.' She condemned Scott for the same reasons. In *Waverley* she found the hero completely unsympathetic and 'all the Scotch Characters outrageously masked by peculiarities . . . and as usual the love is sickening'. This is not just Dorothy being spinsterish: in Scott's novels the romantic passion often is sickening, whatever the political tensions.

Coleridge was observant enough to notice the qualities of William Blake's work, about which he wrote with enthusiasm and wit:

> I have this morning been reading a strange publication—viz. Poems with very wild and interesting pictures, as the swathing, etched (I suppose) but it is said—printed and painted by the Author, W. Blake. He is a man of Genius—and I apprehend, a Swedenborgian—certainly, a mystic *emphatically.* You perhaps smile at *my* calling another Poet, a *Mystic*; but verily I am in the very mire of commonplace common-sense compared with Mr Blake. . . .

He was also a decisive critic of Blake's pictures, disliking the 'title page and following emblem' of *Songs of Innocence* which had 'as few beauties as could be in the compositions of a man who was capable of such faults and such beauties'. He referred perceptively to Blake's 'despotism in symbols' and criticized his

> irregular unmodified Lines of the Inanimate, sometimes as the effect of rigidity and sometimes of exossation—like a wet tendon. So likewise the ambiguity of the Drapery. Is it a garment—or the

body incised and scored out? The *Limpness* (c the effect of Venigar on an egg) in the upper one of the two prostrate figures in the Title page, and the *eye*-likeness of the twig posteriorly on the second—and the strait line down the waistcoat of pinky gold-beater's skin in the next drawing, with the I don't know whatness of the countenance, as if the mouth had been formed by the habit of placing the tongue, not contemptuously, but stupidly between the lower gums and the lower jaw—these are the only *repulsive* faults I have noticed.

The poets' friendship with Southey has already been described. He wrote on Coleridge's death: 'Forty years have elapsed since our first meeting—and one consequence of that meeting has been that I have resided during the last thirty in this place, whither I first came with no other intention than that of visiting him'. Southey seems to have been in many ways an admirable man—industrious both as a writer and in his attempts to move public opinion on behalf of the poor. He was a bibliophile with a vast collection of books, and wrote on an immense variety of subjects. He wrote several large epics, and excellent *Lives* of Nelson, Wesley and Cowper, an erudite *History of Brazil* and a *History of the Peninsular War* as well as editing various medieval works, including Malory, and translating from the Spanish. He became Poet Laureate in 1813 after Scott had refused an offer of the post, and was succeeded by Wordsworth, who would not accept it until Sir Robert Peel assured him that it carried with it no obligation to write poems in celebration of public events—Southey was distressed at failing to produce a poem for Queen Victoria's coronation. Southey died of brain damage from overwork, having had no capacity to recognize or remember people for some time before his death. Coleridge, writing to Godwin to comfort him for Southey's unfavourable review of Godwin's *Life of Chaucer* in 1803, summed up his views of the man—and the reviewer—after his own period of hero-worship was over. Personal distress dictated some of his later judgments of Southey, who supported his own wife and children when he could not, but (besides the initial fatal encouragement of Coleridge's marriage) had the coldness of heart

Robert Southey (1774–1843), from a portrait by H. Eldridge, 1804

to write his contemptuous review of *The Ancient Mariner* 'with Hartley playing in the same room with him'. Coleridge disliked Southey's reviewing. Reviewing, he said, brought out even in the best minds 'presumption, petulance, and callousness to personal feelings, and a disposition to treat the reputations of their Contemporaries as playthings placed at their own disposal'. Reviewing, he said flatly, was immoral, 'injurious in its effects on the public Taste and Morality, and still more injurious in its influences on the Head and Heart of the Reviewer himself'. But his summing-up of the high-handed disregard for feelings that Southey's undoubted rectitude could take is a masterly piece of psychology. 'I have learnt,' he told Godwin, 'how difficult it is for a man who has from earliest Childhood preserved himself immaculate from all the common faults and weaknesses of human nature, and who never creating any small disquietudes has lived in constant and general esteem and honor, to feel remorse or admit that he has done wrong. Believe me, there is a bluntness of Conscience superinduced by a very unusual Infrequency as well as by the Habit and Frequency, of wrong Actions.'

There seems to have been something protective and irritated together in the feelings of the Wordsworths, Coleridge and Lamb about Godwin, once the first flush of wild enthusiasm had left them. Godwin was in some ways a tragic figure. He did not believe in marriage but married Mary Wollstonecraft in 1797 for the birth of their child Mary, who later became Shelley's second wife. He seems to have been made happy and humanized by this relationship, but Mary Wollstonecraft died at the birth of her daughter and his second wife, Mrs Clairmont (whose daughter by a former marriage bore a daughter to Byron), was not nearly so congenial. Wordsworth and Coleridge's letters suggest he was prickly-tempered: both apologize more than once for not calling on him as immediately as he expected, and Coleridge once got drunk and attacked Godwin in front of his wife, for which he suffered agonies of slightly comic remorse for days afterwards. Lamb's biographer, Serjeant Talfourd of the Copyright Bill, described Godwin as monumentally calm and unshockable: he sat at the performance of his tragedy, *Antonio or the Soldier's Return*, which failed hopelessly, applauding the sense of the audience who would applaud when the proper season arrived—at last he admitted 'that the audience seemed rather patient than interested, but did not lose his confidence till the tumult arose, and then he submitted with quiet dignity to the fate of genius'. In later life, in desperate financial straits, the Godwins ran a shop in Skinner Street which sold 'the prettiest and wisest books for children issued' and had a reputation for shamelessly and calmly borrowing money from friends to keep the business going. Talfourd wrote of his usual appearance:

> No one would have expected the author of these wild theories which startled the wise and shocked the prudent, in the calm, gentlemanly person who rarely said anything above the most gentle common-place, and took interest in little beyond the whist-table. His peculiar opinions were entirely subservient to his love of letters. He thought any man who had written a book had attained a superiority over his fellows which placed him in another class, and could scarcely understand other distinctions.

He seems, perhaps for this reason, a curiously remote and un-finished human being, whose major quality is an engaging innocence, accompanied, as it so often is, by general benevolence and mild private egotism.

   Much the most attractive of their friends was Charles Lamb, who objected to being described as 'my gentle-hearted Charles' in Coleridge's *This Lime-Tree Bower My Prison*. He does seem to have been almost entirely without malice, and the circumstances of his life forced him into a persistent goodness of heart which was very nearly saintly. He was at Christ's Hospital with Coleridge and in early youth clearly worshipped him. In 1796 he had an attack of insanity and was confined to a madhouse for six weeks, and wrote to Coleridge after the event in a vein that suggested it was Coleridge's letters which 'roused me from my lethargy and made me conscious of existence'. His madness he said gave him 'many, many hours of pure happiness. Dream not, Coleridge, of having tasted all the grandeur and wildness of fancy till you have gone mad! All now seems to me vapid, comparatively so.' His

Jowis ratherish unwell

Chs Lamb

Charles Lamb (1775–1834), from an engraving

respectable brother clearly felt Coleridge to be in some way responsible for this fit of mania, deprecated 'you and your damned foolish sensibility and melancholy', and Lamb guiltily burned most of his dangerous 'literature' and his own poems, his book of extracts from Beaumont and Fletcher and, almost, all Coleridge's letters.

It was not, however, Lamb's insanity which finally caused the trouble. In 1796 his sister Mary, in an attack of madness, knifed and killed her mother. At the inquest the jury, of course, brought in the verdict—'*Lunacy*'.

Mary was confined in an asylum but released on Charles's assurance that he would personally be responsible for her safe-keeping. Throughout the rest of his life he cared for her devotedly, taking her back at intervals to the asylum when she told him she could feel the madness returning—they kept a strait-jacket with them. Together they wrote the famous *Tales from Shakespeare* which, with Lamb's *Adventures of Ulysses*, made available to children the great imaginative stories they believed so strongly should be part of their education. This meant that he was unable to marry, though he did once propose to a beautiful actress. He took to drink and smoking, and described his excesses with rueful charm. In 1798 he refused an invitation to stay with Coleridge because 'you have a power of exciting interest, of leading all hearts captive, too forcible to admit of Mary's being with you. I consider her as perpetually on the brink of madness. I think you would almost make her dance within an inch of the precipice: she must be with duller fancies, and cooler intellects.' Indeed, Coleridge's distress over the quarrel with Wordsworth—over which Lamb behaved with generosity and tact—did bring on an attack of Mary's madness.

In 1800 Lamb was again appealing to Coleridge as a close and understanding friend when his old servant died and Mary was made ill again. The simplicity of his pain is a powerful contrast to his jocular, self-deprecating public style:

My dear Coleridge—I don't know why I write, except from the propensity misery has to tell her griefs. . . . I am left alone in a house with nothing but Hetty's dead body to keep me company. To-morrow I bury her, and then I shall be quite alone, with nothing but a cat, to remind me that the house has been full of living beings like myself. My heart is quite sunk, and I don't know where to look for relief. Mary will get better again, but her constantly being liable to such relapses is dreadful; nor is it the least of our evils that her case and all our story is so well known around us. We are in a manner *marked*. Excuse my troubling you but I have nobody by me to speak to me. I slept out last night, not being able to endure the change and the stillness; but I did not sleep well and I must come back to my own bed. I am going to try and get a friend to come and be with me tomorrow. I am completely ship-wrecked. My head is quite bad. I almost wish that Mary were dead.

This is another side of the man who wrote, more in the style of Elia, to Southey:

I am going to stand godfather; I don't like the business; I cannot muster up decorum for these occasions; I shall certainly disgrace the font. I was at Hazlitt's marriage, and had like to have been turned out several times during the ceremony. Anything awful makes me laugh. I misbehaved once at a funeral. Yet I cannot read about these ceremonies with pious and proper feelings. The realities of life only seem the mockeries.

It was the serious side of Lamb which objected to the 'gentle-hearted' in *This Lime-Tree Bower*: because he admired Coleridge so much, it was necessary for him to keep a proper distance and preserve his own identity. He was one of the shrewdest and best critics of Coleridge's work in his life-time, and understood the import of *The Ancient Mariner* and the wrong-headedness of Wordsworth's apology for it. On receiving the volume containing *This Lime-Tree Bower* he wrote:

For God's sake (I never was more serious) don't make me ridiculous any more by terming me gentle-hearted in print, or do it in better verses. It did well enough five years ago when I came to see you and was moral cox-comb enough at the time you wrote the lines, to feed upon such epithets; but besides that the meaning of 'gentle' is equivocal at best, and almost always means poor-spirited; the very quality of gentleness is abhorent to such vile trumpetings. My *sentiment* is long since vanished. I hope my *virtues* have done *sucking.* I can scarce think but you meant it in joke.

It seems likely that Lamb, whose public *persona was* mildly gentle-hearted, resented Coleridge seeing him in that way with all the ferocity with which one does resent imperceptive *half*-truths from friends. He himself liked to mock Coleridge in public, and in one of Elia's essays on borrowing he castigated 'Comberbatch, match-less in his depredations' for taking people's books on the theory that they should be the property of the people who could best understand and appreciate them. 'Should he go on acting upon this theory, which of our shelves is safe?' Coleridge, sensitive about his book-borrowing, was indignant about this. It is difficult not to see Lamb's relationship with Coleridge, too, in the passage where he declared 'I would not be domesticated all my days with a person of very superior capacity to my own' not out of jealousy, but because 'too frequent doses of original thinking from others restrain what lesser portion of that faculty you may possess of your own. You get entangled in another man's mind even as you lose yourself in another man's grounds. . . . The constant operation of such potent agency would reduce me, I am convinced, to imbecility. You may derive thoughts from others; your way of thinking, the mold in which your thoughts are cast, must be your own.'

And Lamb kept his independence and his lifelong friendship with both Wordsworth and Coleridge. Wordsworth dedicated *The Waggoner* to him, but there was a bad time when Lamb criticized *The White Doe* before publication, on the grounds that 'the principal characters do nothing'. Wordsworth, who had intended to present a spiritual state, not a drama, was infuriated by this, although it is arguable that in fact the poem does fail because as a tale it is not fully realized, and therefore the response to the spiritual truths is confused. Wordsworth wrote most un-pleasantly to Coleridge 'Let Lamb learn to be ashamed of himself in not taking some pleasure in the contemplation of this picture, which supposing it to be even but a sketch, is yet sufficiently made out for any man of true power to finish it for himself. . . . Of one thing be assured, that Lamb has not a reasoning mind, therefore cannot have a comprehensive mind, and, least of all, has he an imaginative one.'

Lamb died in the same year as Coleridge, by whose death he was deeply affected. Wordsworth wrote an epitaph for him of which only three lines appeared on his tombstone—Mary Lamb disliked Wordsworth's veiled references to the family troubles and to Lamb's employment as a clerk in the India Office—but Wordsworth published a much longer version elaborating on Lamb's care for this sister, a subject that moved him in Dorothy's state of collapse, despite Crabb Robinson's belief that it should not be published in Mary Lamb's life-time.

Hazlitt was a friend of Lamb's and in the early days of the other poets: his essay *My First Acquaintance with Poets*, in which he described his first meeting with Coleridge and subsequently with Wordsworth, is amusing and illuminating. His physical descriptions of the poets were good: Wordsworth 'gaunt and Don Quixote-like' with 'an intense high narrow forehead, a Roman nose, cheeks furrowed by strong purpose and feeling and a convulsive inclination to laughter about the mouth a good deal at variance with the solemn stately expression of the rest of his face'. He described their intonation when reading as 'a chaunt which acts as a spell upon the hearer and disarms the judgement'. His descriptions of Coleridge show signs of a mixture of malice and disappointed hero-worship. Coleridge's walk, shifting from one side of the footpath to the other 'struck me as an odd movement; but I did not at that time connect it with any instability of purpose or involuntary change of principle as I have done since.' His comments on Coleridge's *nose* were ruder: 'The rudder of the face, the index of the will, was small, feeble, nothing—like what he has done.' But his tribute to Coleridge's effect on his life says much of him as well as of Coleridge:

I was at that time dumb, inarticulate, helpless, like a worm by the wayside, crushed, bleeding, lifeless. . . . My soul has indeed remained in its original bondage, dark, obscure, with longings infinite and unsatisfied; my heart, shut up in the prison house of this rude clay, has never found nor will it ever find, a heart to speak to; but that my understanding also did not remain dumb and brutish, or at length found a language to express itself, I owe to Coleridge.

Hazlitt meant to be a genius and for a long time tried to be a genius at painting, in the manner of Titian. His earliest published work, an *Essay on the Principles of Human Action*, was a philosophical refutation of Hobbes's contention that the spring of all our actions is self-love. He believed that sympathetic identification with others—imagination—was a necessary and inevitable function of the human mi ..d. But h was driven to rapid journalism as a means of subsistence, and this, some kind of personal incapacity for friendship, and sexual troubles soured him. His marriages were not happy; the first ended in divorce, and his *Liber Amoris*, published in 1823, is the record of a desperate and miserable love affair with a young girl at an inn. When he was visiting Southey and Coleridge at Grasmere in 1804 he had to leave secretly at night, in Coleridge's shoes, over the mountains because the farmers of the neighbourhood were chasing him on horseback for 'some gross attacks on women', one of which, Wordsworth reported, included his spanking a girl who 'refused to gratify his abominable and devilish propensities'. Coleridge later believed that shame over his indebtedness to them over this episode prompted his viciousness as a reviewer, which is in part likely. Lamb describes him plunged in some private gloom when taken to see two very pretty girls: 'They neither laughed nor sneered, nor giggled, nor whispered—but they were young girls—and he sat and frowned blacker and blacker, indignant that there should be such a thing as youth and beauty, till he tore me away before supper, in perfect misery, and owned he could not bear young girls; they drove him mad.'

The sourness was very real. His review of *The Statesman's Manual* published *before* the book asserted that Coleridge only believed things against reason. 'Truth is to him a ceaseless round of contradictions: he lives in the belief of a perpetual lie, and in affecting to think what he pretends to say . . . He would have done better if he had known less. His imagination thus becomes metaphysical, his metaphysics fantastical, his wit heavy, his arguments light, his poetry prose, his prose poetry, his politics turned—but not to account.' Exaggerated partial truths are always the most damaging abuse. Wordsworth declared grandly that Hazlitt was 'not a proper person to be admitted into respectable society, being the most perverse and malevolent Creature that ill luck has ever thrown in my way'.

But to the young Keats, who possessed his *Essay on the Principles of Human Action* and attended his lectures on the English Poets, Hazlitt's mind was one of the three great things to be thankful for in his time. It was from Hazlitt, Walter Jackson Bate argues, that Keats learned about Shakespeare's 'Negative Capability': Hazlitt who said that Shakespeare was 'the least of an egotist that it was possible to be. He was nothing in himself; but he was all that others were, or that they could become.' It was this ideal of the poet that Keats set so magnificently against 'the wordsworthian or egotistical sublime', and Walter Jackson Bate points out with great insight that Hazlitt was more perceptive than any other English critic about the growing subjective and personal emphasis in the arts which was alienating the arts from society. Some of his strictures on Wordsworth were of 'what he feels to be an obtrusion of the poet's personal feelings, interests, defenses, and the danger of losing that "high and permanent interest beyond ourselves" to which arts should aim'.

Thomas De Quincey was another who began by passionate admiration and ended by attacking. As a young man he made an anonymous gift of money to Coleridge. He made friends with the Wordsworths and rented the Town End cottage to be near them: he was helpful with Wordsworth's proofs and charming to the children. He was estranged from the Wordsworths when he took to opium in heavy doses and took a local 'statesman's' daughter, Margaret Sympson, as his mistress, whom he married after she bore him a child. The Wordsworths were unpleasant as much because of Margaret's low social standing as because of the illicit affair, and De Quincey did not forgive them. He was a strange, brilliant, dilatory man, a loved and loving husband and father, now chiefly remembered for his glamorous and horrific descriptions of the effects of opium and opium dreams. His interest in the effect of his own childhood experiences—'the deep, deep tragedies of infancy that lurk to the last'—on his creative powers and adult admiration illuminates, in another luridly lit world,

Thomas De Quincey (1785–1859), from an engraving

that of Wordsworth. His interest in the creative power and the insights of opium dreams illuminates Coleridge and *Kubla Khan*, that 'involute' of dream imagery (De Quincey's word). His oriental dreams of unimaginable horror and mythological torture relate to *The Ancient Mariner*. His descriptions of his opium indolence are very much akin to Coleridge's:

> The opium eater loses none of his moral sensibilities or aspirations; he wishes and longs as earnestly as ever to realize what he believes to be possible and feels to be exacted by duty; but his intellectual apprehension of what is possible infinitely outruns his power, not

of execution only, but even of power to attempt. He lies under the weight of incubus and nightmare; he lies in sight of all that he would fain perform, just as a man forcibly confined to his bed by the mortal languor of a relaxing disease who is compelled to witness injury or outrage offered to some object of his tenderest love. . . .

His essays on Coleridge and Opium and Coleridge's plagiarisms, and his *Recollections of the Lake Poets* are lively and fascinating but, as mentioned earlier, bear traces of malice and exaggeration: critics, particularly of Coleridge, have shown a strange propensity to believe De Quincey's opium-laden fantastic reports about Coleridge's fantasies and evasions rather than Coleridge himself.

Wordsworth could find few good words for the glamorous and successful Lord Byron. 'Let me only say one word upon Lord B. The man is insane; and will probably end his career in a mad-house. I never thought him anything else since his first appearance in public. The verses on his private affairs excite in me less indignation than pity. The latter copy is the Billingsgate of Bedlam,' he wrote to John Scott, the ill-fated editor of *The London Magazine* in 1816, and went on in the same vein for another paragraph. And later he was suggesting to Gifford, the editor of *The Quarterly*

that every true Englishman disallows the pretensions of *The Review* to the character of a faithful defender of the institutions of the country while it leaves that infamous publication, *Don Juan*, unbranded. I do not mean by a formal critique, for it is not worth it—it would also tend to keep it in memory—but by some decisive words of reprobation, both as to the damnable tendency of such works, and as to the despicable quality of the powers requisite for their production. . . .

What avails it to hunt down Shelley and leave Byron untouched?

He did once meet Byron at a London dinner party, where he is said to have 'tried to talk his best and talked too much'. And Byron, though on that occasion he said Wordsworth inspired him with '*reverence*', attacked him violently for his 'drowsy, frowzy poem called the Excursion', and for his politics, in *Don Juan*.

Byron's relationship with Coleridge was happier. He helped

Haydon's painting, *Christ's Triumphal Entry into Jerusalem*, painted during the years 1816–20. The third figure from the right, with bowed head and hand on heart, represents Wordsworth

Coleridge to find a publisher for his poems, and encouraged him to write another tragedy for Drury Lane. He was also an enthusiastic supporter of Coleridge in the matter of the unpublished *Christabel*, whose metre had been plagiarized by Scott in the *Lay of the Last Minstrel* and used by Wordsworth in *The White Doe*, which was printed originally with an acknowledgment to *Christabel*, later omitted, to Coleridge's distress. It was after Byron's publication of the priority of *Christabel* that Scott belatedly acknowledged his indebtedness: Byron spoke of it as 'that wild and singularly original and beautiful poem', and his enthusiasm was a great encouragement to Coleridge at that time. Byron also sent Coleridge £100, although, he said, he himself 'could not command 150 in the world' when he heard that Coleridge 'in great distress' had applied to the Literary Fund for help. The two poets met once only—when Coleridge recited *Kubla Khan* and said of Byron that 'He has the sweetest Countenance that I ever beheld—his eyes are really Portals of the Sun, things for Light to go in and out of'. He asked Byron for a signed copy of his poems, to be left to his children.

Both poets met the young Keats, and both outlived him. Keats records his walk with Coleridge across Hampstead Heath for two miles—which Coleridge, since he clearly did most of the talking, remembered as lasting 'a minute or so'—the conversation covering 'Nightingales, Poetry—on Poetical sensation—Metaphysics—different genera and species of Dreams—Nightmare—a dream accompanied by a sense of touch—single and double touch—A dream related—First and second consciousness—the difference explained between will and Volition. . . . Monsters—the Kraken —Mermaids—southey believes in them—southey's belief too much diluted—A Ghost story—Good morning—I heard his voice as he came towards me—I heard it as he moved away—I had heard it all the interval—if it may be called so.' The subjects are deeply part of the poetry of both poets, and Coleridge is seen for an immortal moment almost like the nightingale itself talking in a timeless interval to the perfectly receptive audience.

Wordsworth's impression on Keats was less fortunate: Keats was amused and annoyed at being told by Mrs Wordsworth 'Mr Wordsworth is never interrupted'. But one of their meetings, too, achieved immortality of a different kind—at Haydon's 'immortal dinner' in his painting room with his huge painting 'Christ's entry into Jerusalem' (in which Wordsworth appears) 'towering up behind us as a background'. Lamb got drunk and merry, and mocked the Comptroller of Stamps—but Haydon's description of the party is marvellously memorable:

Wordsworth's fine intonation as he quoted Milton and Virgil, Keat's eager inspired look, Lamb's quaint sparkle of lambent humour, so speeded the stream of conversation that in my life I never passed a more delightful time. All our fun was within bounds. Not a word passed that an apostle might not have listened to. It was a night worthy of the Elizabethan age, and my solemn

'Jerusalem' flashing up by the flame of the fire, with Christ hanging over us like a vision, all made a picture which will long glow up on

> that inward eye
> Which is the bliss of solitude

Keats made Ritchie promise he would carry his 'Endymion' to the great desert Sahara and fling it in the midst. Poor Ritchie went to Africa and died, as Lamb foresaw, in 1819. Keats died in 1821, at Rome. C. Lamb is gone, joking to the last. Monkhouse is dead, and Wordsworth and I are the only two now living [1841] of that glorious party.

7 Landscape

This chapter concerns certain aspects of man's relationship to the earth and his natural surroundings in the poets' life-times. The subject is a highly complicated one and I mean to concentrate largely on one part of it, the theories of natural beauty that became ideals for poets and for painters in the period.

Interest in natural surroundings increased at the time for a variety of sometimes conflicting reasons. There was the reaction against the eighteenth-century ideals of order in civilization— neo-classical harmony, hierarchic society, the rule of Man over Nature which some saw symbolized in the highly formal gardens of Le Nôtre. This produced an interest in the uncontrolled, from forest and mountain scenery to deliberately irregular gardens. Châteaubriand's noble savages in the American forests were natural man in natural surroundings. Rousseau, whose Child of Nature had certain social qualities, praised the irregular English garden as opposed to the French ordered one—it represented constitutionalism and man's alliance with Nature. There was also a concurrent reaction against the anxiety about the later versions of Man's Control over Nature which appeared in industrial defilement of the landscape and what Wordsworth called 'the increasing accumulation of men in cities': these men's minds were being blunted to 'a state of almost savage torpor'; Wordsworth hoped to rescue them through the use of the power of the human mind combined with 'certain powers in the great and permanent objects that act upon it', which in *The Prelude*, became the presence of mountains and sky and rivers, darkness and light. The desire for the unlimited and uncontrolled produced an interest in cataracts and mountains and winds and avalanches, and the kind of men that went with them—Salvator Rosa's *banditti* summed up for ever in Horace Walpole's immortal letter on his tour of the Alps with Gray in 1739: 'Precipices, mountains, torrents, wolves, rumblings, Salvator Rosa!' It worked on men's minds with the

accounts of explorations into the dangerous and the unknown—
James Bruce's *Travels to discover the Source of the Nile* (1790),
Mungo Park's *Travels in the Interior of Africa* (1799)—Park was a
friend of Scott—or the Quaker William Bartram's *Travels through
North and South Carolina* (1791), which both poets eagerly read.
The reaction against industrialism produced a different pre-
occupation: the feudal nostalgia for agricultural man, living and
working in harmony with Nature, the vision of Cobbett's *Rural
Rides* and of Wordsworth's Cumberland statesmen, and of
Constable's *Hay-Wain*—a vision even then containing an element
of the pure nostalgia which has become an increasingly important
component of English artistic emotion about landscape ever since.
The changes brought about by enclosures produced a regret for
lost beauties which led to the careful preserving topographies
and Bewick's engravings and some of Clare's best writing. These
preoccupations were not necessarily separate. At the highest level
Sir Walter Scott can describe the clash and change of cultures by
placing the Scottish robber barons—Rob Roy—in proper
Romantic wild scenery, and yet treating careful agricultural
workers and town dwellers with equally affectionate skill. And as
preoccupation with the earth produced tourists and travellers and
guides and drawings, so the interest in the peasantry and the
cataracts became amalgamated in the search for the picturesque.
By 1788 Wilberforce was already writing that 'the banks of the
Thames are scarcely more public than those of Windermere'.
Wordsworth and Coleridge were involved in all this at many
levels. Wordsworth wrote a *Guide to the Lakes,* and was full of precise
ideas about the advisability and impropriety of man-made improvements to landscape; both were close friends of Sir George
Beaumont, patron of Constable and many other artists, painter
and founder of the National Gallery; both were passionate walkers
and tourists. Both, too, used images of the movement of light on
landscape to convey their most deeply felt ideas about the nature
of imagination, the relationship between the natural world and the
mind of man.

A book which had a profound influence on the aesthetic thought
of the next hundred years was Edmund Burke's treatise *On the*

Sublime and the Beautiful, published in 1756. In this Burke argued that man had two fundamental 'instincts' which lay behind all his passions and emotions—self-propagation and self-preservation. Objects perceived by the senses (which communicated with these subconscious instincts, not with the mind) appealed to one or the other. Pleasing things which were sensually desirable, with qualities of softness or smoothness or harmony, appealed to the instinct of self-propagation and were called Beautiful. Those which appealed to the human apprehension of fear, pain, thwarting forces, or infinity were concerned with the instinct of self-preservation, and were Sublime. One of Burke's most important contributions to the discussion of aesthetic emotion was his analysis of *why* terrifying, infinite, or empty things were attractive to the human mind. He ascribed some of the sense of the sublime to a sense of a real power or danger faced without damage: 'Whatever leads to raise man in his own opinion produces a sort of swelling and triumph that is extremely grateful to the human mind. And this swelling is never more perceived, nor operates with more force, than when without danger we are conversant with terrible objects—the mind always claiming to itself some of the dignity or importance of the things which it contemplates.' He listed the attributes of the sublime, which were

(1) *Obscurity* (which induced Terror)—as seen in Milton's darknesses

(2) *Power*

(3) *Privations*—Vacuity, Darkness, Solitude, Silence

(4) *Vastness*—height and depth

(5) *Infinity*—a 'tendency to fill the mind with that sort of delightful Horror' and artificial infinity which included

(6) *Succession*—an endless progress beyond limits and

(7) *Uniformity*—a round and therefore artificially endless church, the Pantheon, as opposed to the cruciform cathedrals.

Several of these later qualities—architectural infinity, as well as the senses of obscurity, privation and vastness—can be seen in De Quincey's artistic reconstructions of the endless seas and palaces of his opium dreams, or in John Martin's engravings of Milton's

Pandemonium or the *Fall of Nineveh*. The same qualities are present, combined into great poetry, in Wordsworth's description of his undergraduate walking tour in the Alps, where he saw

> the immeasurable height
> Of woods decaying, never to be decayed,
> The stationary blasts of waterfalls,
> And in the narrow rent at every turn
> Winds thwarting winds, bewildered and forlorn,
> The torrents shooting from the clear blue sky,
> The rocks that muttered close upon our ears,
> Black drizzling crags that spake by the way-side
> As if a voice were in them, the sick sight
> And giddy prospect of the raving stream,
> The unfettered clouds and region of the Heavens,
> Tumult and peace, the darkness and the light—
> Were all like workings of one mind, the features
> Of the same face, blossoms upon one tree;
> Characters of the great Apocalypse,
> The types and symbols of Eternity,
> Of first and last and midst and without end.

Pandemonium, an illustration by John Martin for Milton's *Paradise Lost*. 'Anon out of the earth, a fabric huge / Rose like an exhalation . . .'

The picturesque: frontispiece from *Sir Uvedale Price on the Picturesque*,
edition of 1842

To Burke's categories of the Sublime and the Beautiful later
writers and painters added the category of the 'picturesque', which
was neither smoothly pleasing nor imposing and horrifying but
consisted of certain qualities which produced—initially—attractive non-classical paintings. Uvedale Price, an early proponent of
the theory, wrote 'the two opposite qualities of roughness and of
sudden variation, joined to that of irregularity, are the most efficient
causes of the picturesque'. Controversy raged as to whether this
really was a *new* category, but popular taste confirmed it. A pioneer
was the Reverend William Gilpin, whose descriptions of his sketching tours round the English counties introduced the concept of
picturesque travel. In his *Tour of the Lakes* Gilpin made an *Analysis
of Romantic Scenery*, dividing every view into three parts: *Background*,
containing Mountains and Lakes; *Off-skip*, comprising Valleys,
Woods, Rivers; *Foreground*, comprising Rocks, Cascades, Broken

Tintern Abbey, from William Gilpin's *Observations on the River Wye*,
edition of 1799

Ground and Ruins. Only certain objects were picturesque—they
had to have the required roughness or oddity but not be positively
ugly. Mountains were picturesque in 'the pyramidical shape and
easy flow of an irregular line' but saddlebacks, alps, and indeed
most mountains were suggestive of 'lumpishness, heaviness' and
were thus disgusting. Gilpin still has an idealizing eye but can
only use it on certain subjects. The Thames at Twickenham in his
view 'in spite of its beauty and even grandeur . . . still falls short,
in a picturesque light, of a Scottish river with its rough accompani-
ments'. He admired at Tintern Abbey the ruins in the Foreground
where, to the beauty of the architecture 'are superadded the
ornaments of Time. Ivy, in masses uncommonly large, has taken
possession of many parts of the walls; and gives a happy contrast
to the grey-coloured stone. . . . Nor is this undecorated. Mosses
of various hues, with lychens, maiden hair, penny-leaf and other
humble plants, overspread the surface . . . all together they give
those full-blown tints which add the richest finishing to a ruin.'
He believed that trees should have 'form, lightness and proper

balance' to be truly beautiful, yet he showed an enthusiasm for decayed or damaged trees akin to the literary interest in Gothic and grotesque figures. 'How many forests have we wherein you shall have for one living tree, twenty-four evil-thriving; rotten and dying trees; what rottenness! what hollowness! what dead arms! withered tops! curtailed trunks! What loads of mosses! dropping boughs and dying branches shall you see everywhere! . . . Yet these are often the very capital sources of picturesque beauty.' Uvedale Price, in *A Dialogue on the Distinct Characters of the Picturesque and Beautiful*, has three characters who go on a walk past various scenes, typically picturesque: a hovel beneath a gnarled oak with an aged gipsy, a rusty donkey, mellow tints and dark shadows, a hollow lane with crumbling banks under the roots of 'junipers, heath and furze which with some thorns and a few knotty old pollard oaks and yews clothed the sides'. The parsonage, 'a singular mixture of neatness and irregularity', was a picturesque building, and the parson's daughter who had a squint and uneven teeth but was 'clear and clean and upright' was a picturesque human being. Price was criticized by his opponent in the argument, William Payne Knight, for not making her hobble and giving her irregular hips and shoulders whilst he was at it.

Coleridge's note-book entry in 1803 is recognizably looking for the same visual stimuli:

> That sweet delicate birch with its tri-prong Root—and the other twisty little creature near it. O Christ, it maddens me that I am not a painter or that Painters are not I! The *chapped Bark* of the lower part of the Trunk, the Bark like a Rhinoceros rolled in mud and exposed to the tropic Heat/the second Fall to Sheep forced through water and vaulting over each other throwing off the pearly streams from their heavy fleeces.

Picturesque travel and literature produced a kind of strange language of description. Thomas West's *Guide* to the Lakes is typical, both in the way in which the 'views' were presented from recommended 'stations' as *pictures* created by and for the tourists, and the language used to recommend these views. The 'next grand view' of Coniston, for instance, 'is had in the boat and from the centre of the lake' and shows 'verdant meadows, inclosed with a variety of grounds rising in an exceedingly bold manner. These objects are beautifully diversified amongst themselves, and contrasted by the finest exhibition of rural elegance (cultivation and pasturage, waving woods and sloping inclosures, adorned by nature and improved by art) under the bold sides of stupendous mountains. . . .' Later he writes: 'To the north is a most awful scene of mountains heaped upon mountains, in every variety of horrid shape. Amongst them sweeps to the north a deep winding chasm, darkened by overhanging rocks, that the eye cannot pierce, nor the imagination fathom—.'

Coleridge, a linguistic precisian who knew his Burke, had an amusing encounter with some tourists in Scotland in 1803, well described by Dorothy Wordsworth. They were near a waterfall:

> C., who is always good-natured enough to enter into conversation with anybody whom he meets in his way began to talk with the gentleman, who observed that it was a '*majestic* waterfall'. Coleridge was delighted with the epithet, particularly as he had been settling in his own mind the precise meaning of the words grand, majestic, sublime, etc. and had discussed the subject with Wm. at some length the day before. 'Yes, sir,' says Coleridge, 'it is a majestic waterfall.' 'Sublime and beautiful' replied his friend. Poor C. could make no answer, and, not very desirous to continue the conversation, came to us and related the story, laughing heartily.

The description of Dunald-Mill-Hole by a Mr A. W. in 1760 begins enthusiastically 'The entrance of this subterraneous channel has something most pleasingly horrible in it', which reminds one of the Gothic enthusiasms of the girls in Jane Austen's *Northanger Abbey*. Jane Austen could mock the picturesque too, as in *Sense and Sensibility*, when the sensible Edward says 'I like a fine prospect but not on picturesque principles. I do not like crooked, twisted, blasted trees—', but the memoir prefixed to *Northanger Abbey* records that 'At a very early age she was enamoured of Gilpin on the Picturesque; and she seldom changed her opinion on books or men'. She used Gilpin to help with the setting of Pemberley in *Pride and Prejudice*, and Henry Tilney in *Northanger Abbey* itself gives Catherine a lecture on the picturesque: 'Foregrounds, distances and second distances; side screens and perspectives; light and shades; and Catherine was so hopeful a scholar . . . that she voluntarily rejected the whole city of Bath as unworthy to make part of a landscape.'

Another writer who was interested in picturesque landscape—and made extensive use of it—was Mrs Radcliffe, also satirized in *Northanger Abbey*. In *The Romance of the Forest* (1792) she composed, not unskilfully, a picturesque scene of a chateau over a lake 'environed by mountains of stupendous height, which, shooting into a variety of grotesque forms, composed a scenery singularly solemn and sublime'. But her travel diaries—and in particular her account of a ride over Skiddaw in 1794—have an actuality, an accuracy of pace and structure closer to Wordsworth's than to the guidebooks. She is good on the thinning air and effective with height. 'At length as we ascended, Derwent-water dwindled on the eye to the smallness of a pond, while the grandeur of its ampitheatre was increased by new ranges of dark mountains, no longer individually great but so from accumulation—a scenery to give ideas of the breaking-up of a world.'

Before considering Wordsworth's own *Guide to the Lakes* it is interesting to consider a little more thoroughly the various effects on tourists and art of seeing landscape very much in terms of paintings, already composed, or about to be composed. The painters of landscape whom the enthusiastic British travellers on the Grand Tour had discovered in the eighteenth century and had used in their creation of the new vision of landscape were Claude, Nicolas and Gaspar Poussin, and Salvator Rosa. Sir George Beaumont had a collection of Claudes which he left to form part of the National Gallery's initial collection, one of which he took everywhere with him in his travelling carriage. Claude appealed because of the delicacy and poetry of his ideal landscapes, his creation of luminous distances, representative of the infinity for which the Romantics longed, but seen in terms not of awe but of a harmony between man and Nature, vision and object which even in his work has an element of nostalgia, and to them seemed much more part of a vanished past. Claude apparently painted his great landscapes not in the studio but from Nature, and the quality in them which appealed both to English painters such as Richard Wilson and, I think, to the poets, was their treatment of light— light creating and transforming foliage, water and distances, light as an object of contemplation. Lord Clark says that one of the chief lessons of Claude is 'that the centre of landscape is an area of light'. Nicolas Poussin painted highly complex and allusive studies of mythological figures in landscapes, which, along with the calmer, milder processions and temples of Claude, had a profound effect on Keats: they were intellectually and geometrically subtle, but Hazlitt, who noted that Poussin's landscapes were subdued to his ruling idea, wrote that his scenery had 'the unimpaired look of original nature, full, solid, large, luxuriant, teeming with life and power'. Lord Clark compares Poussin to Milton, and his sense of order and energy in Nature may have affected Wordsworth and Coleridge as Milton's did. Salvator Rosa was a Byronic figure himself, a friend of bandits and outlaws, and his scenes with bandits, wild trees and precipices provided the inspiration for much wilder romanticizing. These painters also had a great influence on the nineteenth-century English masters of landscape, Constable and Turner. Constable was shown Sir George Beaumont's Claude—*Hagar and the Angel*— as a boy and 'looked back on this exquisite work as an important epoch in his life'. He made detailed copies of both Claude and Poussin for much of his life, and Turner, who was influenced by Claude in his early classical work and fascination with light on the sea, left instructions that one of his paintings should always be hung next to a Claude. He was also influenced indirectly by Salvator Rosa's alpine scenery and the tradition of British art inspired by it.

Again, the popular picturesque tradition suggests how persuasive was this aesthetic tradition in the world in which Wordsworth, Coleridge and Constable moved. In 1778 *The Monthly Magazine* wrote that 'To *make the Tour* of the Lakes, to speak in

Hagar and the Angel, by Claude Lorrain

Landscape with a waterfall, by Salvator Rosa

fashionable terms, is the *ton* of the present hour'. Thomas West's guide presented the fashionable tourist's journey, in pictorial terms, 'from the delicate touches of *Claude*, verified on *Coniston* Lake, to the noble scenes of *Poussin*, exhibited on *Windermere* water, and from there to the stupendous romantic ideas of *Salvator Rosa*, realized in the Lake of *Derwent*'. In Uvedàle Price's *Dialogue*, mentioned above, the three travellers end their picturesque tour in a picture gallery, where they compare a Salvator Rosa with a Claude, as typical examples of the sublime and the beautiful. In the Claude 'everything seems formed to delight the eye and the mind of man': in the Salvator 'to alarm and terrify the imagination'.

The insistence on painting as an inspiration caused certain emphases to be made in landscape description, and inspired the use of certain mechanical viewing devices. Colour and shape in landscape were emphasized and even changed to suit preconceived ideals. Sublimity required darkness, with occasional violent contrasts of light or livid light. Claudian beauty, and the picturesque tradition deriving from it created a great interest in surfaces and textures but tended to restrict colours to Claude's golds and browns. Brown was particularly evocative: Sir George Beaumont painted from Nature, but included a fiddle in his sketching apparatus, since 'a good picture, like a good fiddle, should be brown', and said that every landscape should contain one brown tree. He asked Constable once 'Do you not find it very difficult to determine where to place your *brown tree*?' to which Constable replied 'Not in the least for I never put such a thing into a picture'. And when Sir George 'recommended the colour of an old Cremona fiddle for everything' Constable retaliated by placing one on the green lawn outside the house. But the colour had deep poetic associations and meaning beyond the effect of varnish on paintings or fiddles. Milton used it to suggest mysterious shade,

> and where the unpierced shade
> Imbrowned the noon-tide bowers,

Thomson in *The Seasons* talked of 'brown night' and the end of Coleridge's *Dejection* ode describing a wind-torn scene typical of the picturesque tradition crossed with Salvator's sublime, in my opinion greatly inferior to the rest of the poem, achieves a sudden moment of concrete vision when it addresses the Mad Lutanist, 'in this month of showers, Of dark-brown gardens . . .' where the word is accurate and traditionally powerful together.

Gilpin was cautious about colour. What he could see, he did not consider always suitable for inclusion in pictures which although they 'should avoid such images as are trite and vulgar' should seize only those which are easy and intelligible.

Thus he could *see* that trees appeared blue and purple, as well as brown, but feared they might displease the traditionally-minded spectator:

> The appearance of blue and purple trees, unless in the remote distance, offends, and though the artist may have authority from nature for his practice, yet the spectator, not versed in such effects, may be displeased.

He was equally cautious about form, remarking that nature worked on 'a *vast scale*, and, no doubt, harmoniously, if her scheme could be comprehended'. But since 'the immensity of nature is beyond human comprehension' the artist devised 'little rules which he he calls *the principles of picturesque beauty* to adapt such diminutive parts of nature's surfaces to his own eye, as come within its scope'. Thus an artist was free, within limits, to use his imagination to alter the scenery, or amalgamate various scenes, to make a better picture. He could shift trees, or substitute withered stumps for spreading oaks, or vice versa. He could alter a hillock, a cottage, a road, or a hedge, which might indeed be altered tomorrow—but he might not plant a great castle or a river where one was not. Dr Syntax makes a good satirical use of these advantages in drawing a guide-post, broken and mangled by someone into 'an uninforming piece of wood':

But as my time shall not be lost
I'll make a drawing of the post;
And though your flimsy taste may flout it,
There's something *picturesque* about it.
'Tis rude and rough without a gloss
And is well cover'd o'er with moss;
And I've a right—(who dares deny it?)
To place yon group of asses by it.
Aye! this will do: and now I'm thinking
That self-same pond where Grizzle's drinking,
If hither brought 'twould better seem,
And faith I'll turn it to a stream
I'll make this flat a shaggy ridge
And o'er the water throw a bridge:
I'll do as other sketchers do
Put anything into the view. . . .
Thus tho' from truth I haply err,
The scene preserves its character.

Wordsworth talked of 'the inferior wonders of an artist's hand' when, according to Christopher Hussey, author of *The Picturesque*, 'gravely deliberating the spiritual motives that could possess that good friend of his but essentially picturesque painter Sir George Beaumont when he had the impertinence to paint an imaginary castle in one of Wordsworth's favourite scenes'. Dorothy, on the other hand, seemed to share the picturesque desire to shift objects when she observed the castles along the banks of the Rhine in 1820. 'What a dignity does the Form of an ancient castle or tower confer upon a precipitous woody or craggy eminence! Well might this lordly River spare one or two of his castles, which are too numerous for the most romantic fancy to hang its legends round each and all of them—well might he spare, to our purer and more humble streams and lakes, one solitary ruin for the delight of our Poets of the English mountains!'

Gilpin's principles of picturesque beauty led later to painters' aids, such as, for instance W. H. Pyne's encyclopaedia of above a thousand subjects (with aquatints, 1845) of *Picturesque Groups for the Embellishment of Landscape*. Volume I covered, amongst others,

Army, Banditti, Brickmakers, Butchers, Camp Scenes, Carts, Ferry Boats, Fire Engines, Games, Gypsies, Gleaners, Gravel Diggers, Grinders. Volume II contained Post Chaises, Racing, Ropemakers, Rustics, Smugglers, Statuary, Threshing, Timber Wagons, Toll-gates, Travellers Reposing, Trucks, Wheelwrights and Woodmen.

Behind these artifices can be seen the same aesthetic and social curiosity that created Wordsworth's marvellous studies of beggars and soldiers met in the road, or Constable's casual delineations of rural occupations. The apparently repellent occupation of the butchers was vouched for by Rembrandt's marvellous studies of ox carcasses—to which I shall return.

Besides encyclopaedias there was equipment. A dead painter found after an accident on Helvellyn in 1805 caused much local gossip, and gave rise to poems by Scott and Wordsworth. The Wordsworths retailed to Sir George Beaumont the contents of his pockets, which included 'a Gold Watch, Silver Pencil, Claude Lorraine glasses etc.'.

The Claude glass was a plano-convex mirror of about 4 inches diameter on a black foil and bound up like a pocket book. It was used to determine the tonal values of planes and reflected scenes in tiny pictures, accentuating the tones by reducing the colours to a lower ratio. The poet Gray carried one on his tours. Thomas West recommends in his *Guide* that travellers take a telescope to look at inaccessible summits and a 'landscape mirror'—he offers detailed instructions for its use:

> Where the objects are great and near, it removes them to a due distance, and shews them in the soft colours of nature, and in the most regular perspective the eye can perceive, or science demonstrate.
>
> The mirror is of the greatest use in sunshine; and the person using it ought always to turn his back to the object that he views. It should be suspended by the upper part of the case, holding it a little to the right or left (as the position of the parts to be viewed require) and the face screened from the sun.
>
> The mirror is a plano-convex glass, and should be the segment of a large circle; otherwise distant and small objects are not per-

ceived in it; but if the glass be too flat the perspective view of great and near objects is less pleasing, as they are represented too near. These inconveniences may be provided against by two glasses of different convexity. The dark glass answers well in sunshine; but on cloudy and gloomy days the silver foil is better.—Whoever uses spectacles upon other occasions, must use them in viewing landscapes in these mirrors.

Philippe De Loutherbourg, whose *Avalanche* in the Tate Gallery creates an atmosphere akin to Coleridge's romantic tale, *The Old Man of the Alps*, with simple tragedy amidst the vast forces of Nature, created the Eidophusikon, in 1781—a lit up scene of four-dimensional pictures which has been called the forerunner of *son et lumière*. There were five scenes—dawn, noon, sunset, moonlight, storm at sea and shipwreck—with, as an alternative finale, the region of the fallen angels with Satan arraying his troops on the banks of the Fiery Lake. A contemporary record suggests how much this must have appealed to the taste for the wild and unlimited. In the foreground of a vista was seen 'stretching an immeasurable length between mountains ignited from their bases to their lofty summits with many-coloured flame, a chaotic mass rising in dark majesty, which gradually assumed form until it stood, the interior of a vast temple of gorgeous architecture, bright as molten brass, seemingly composed of unconsuming and unquenchable fire. In this tremendous scene the effect of coloured glasses before the lamp was fully displayed.' It was accompanied by sounds and peals of thunder and horrid groans, and may well have had the same effect on the poets as John Martin's similar paintings which might have been thought to appeal to them. But Wordsworth concurred with Lamb's use of Martin as an example of the poverty of imagination in modern art, and Coleridge said 'It seems to me that Martin never looks at nature except through bits of stained glass. He is never satisfied with any appearance that is not prodigious.' He enjoyed the 'transparencies'—another product of the pictorial imagination—continuous designs on thin paper, rolled in front of a lamp showing figures moving in landscapes, as toys for feast-days. I have already referred to Coleridge's

An Avalanche in the Alps, by P. de Loutherbourg

transparency of Napoleon's defeat. Mrs Coleridge and the Southeys celebrated this memorable event with transparencies too.

Wordsworth, who said that picturesque analysis of scenes 'was never much my habit', nevertheless wrote his *Guide to the Lakes* originally as an introduction to the *Select Views* of the Reverend Joseph Wilkinson, printed by Ackermann in 1810, although he felt himself impelled to apologize to his knowledgeable friends for the poor artistic quality of the prints themselves—he preferred the works of William Green (*78 Studies from Nature, 1809*). His *Guide* itself is a remarkable piece of descriptive prose, accurate, immediate, beautifully constructed and evocative. He shows a keen knowledge both of Burke, and of Gilpin, although he condemns the picturesque 'craving for prospects', and his description, for instance, of the small lakes and their edges combines the eye of the visual analyst with the language of the aesthetic theorist, and, more than that, a sense of the history and present solidity of the earth he is looking at, and the psychology of his own response to it:

> As the comparatively small size of the lakes in the North of England is favourable to the production of variegated landscape, their *boundary-line* also is for the most part gracefully or boldly indented. That uniformity, which prevails in the primitive frame of the lower grounds among all chains or clusters of mountains where large bodies of still waters are bedded, is broken by the *secondary* agents of nature, ever at work to supply the deficiencies of the mould in which things were originally cast. Using the word *deficiencies*, I do not speak with reference to those stronger emotions which a region of mountains is peculiarly fitted to excite. The bases of these huge barriers may run for a long space in straight lines, and these parallel to each other; the opposite sides of a profound vale may ascend as exact counterparts or in mutual reflection like the billows of a troubled sea; and the impression be, from its very simplicity, more awful and sublime.
>
> Sublimity is the result of Nature's first great dealing with the superficies of the earth; but the general tendency of her subsequent operations is towards the production of beauty by a multiplicity of symmetrical parts uniting in a consistent whole.

His visual accuracy is unassuming and striking:

> Among minuter recommendations will be noticed especially along bays exposed to the setting-in of strong winds, the curved rim of fine blue gravel, thrown up in course of time by the waves, half of it perhaps gleaming from under the water, and the corresponding half of a lighter hue.

Or the casually appropriate simile for the larger island on Rydal-mere:

> The line of the grey rocky shore of that island, shaggy with variegated bushes and shrubs, and spotted and striped with purplish brown heath, indistinguishably blending with its image reflected in the

still water, produced a curious resemblance, both in form and colour, to a richly-coated caterpillar, as it might appear through a magnifying-glass of extraordinary power.

Wordsworth used his *Guide* as a weapon in the battle he saw himself engaged in against artists and improvers and businessmen for the preservation of the landscape. He particularly disliked three things—the erection of artistic buildings or pillars to decorate landscapes in the style of paintings, the introduction of new houses, particularly white-washed ones, which did not blend with the landscape, and the planting of trees which were not natural inhabitants of that part of the world.

Thomas West argues enthusiastically *for* 'placing objects on the eminences' in the Lakes. '*Columns, obelisks, temples* etc.' attract the eye and 'nothing sets off the beauties of nature so much as elegant works of art'. Therefore they appeal to 'anyone who has a taste for moral beauty' and, moreover, 'the practice is certainly patriotic; for such elegant ornaments will at least naturally contribute to diffuse a serenity and cheerfulness of mind into every beholder; and thence (if we may be pardoned the figure) like electrical conductors they may be supposed to bring down a little of the happy placidity of better regions, to add to the natural quantity shooting about on the earth . . .'. Obelisks and properly formed summer-houses (octagonal) are recommended, or a series of columns through which the setting sun could be seen, fitting in with the 'sublimity of the surrounding mountains'. 'Perforated doors and windows, in the imitation of old Gothic ruins, it is true, could yield part of this effect; but their gloomy and irregular appearance renders them, in the case before us, generally improper.'

Wordsworth, in this context, if he saw Nature with the eyes of art did not believe the works of art added to nature. He professed himself 'disgusted with the new erections and objects about Windermere'. Dorothy, in the *Alfoxden Journal*, describes a walk round the squire's grounds at Crookham with 'quaint waterfalls about, about which Nature was very successfully striving to make beautiful what art had deformed—ruins, hermitages etc. etc. In spite of all these things the dell romantic and beautiful, though everywhere planted with unnaturalised trees. Happily we cannot shape the huge hills, or carve out the valleys according to our fancy.'

Wordsworth's battle against the whitewashed houses was ever fiercer. In 1799 Coleridge was writing in his journal of this 'damn'd whitewashing'. In 1805 Dorothy Wordsworth wrote to Lady Beaumont complaining of various desecrations of Grasmere. The Dale 'has not yet been intruded on by any of the Fancy-builders— there is only one offensive object, the house of Mr Mounsey, the King of Patterdale, and that is chiefly ugly from the colour which has been so cried out against that he intends to change it next summer. ... You may remember that I spoke of the white-washing of the church, and six years ago a trim Box was erected on a hill-side; it is surrounded with fir and Larch plantations that look like a blotch or scar on the fair surface of the mountain. Luckily these deformities are not visible in the grand view of the Vale—but alas poor Grasmere! The first object which now presents itself after you have clomb the hill from Rydale is Mr Crump's newly-erected large mansion, staring over the Church Steeple . . . Then a farm-house opposite to ours . . . has been taken by a dashing man from Manchester who, no doubt, will make a *fine place* of it, and as he has taken the Island too, will probably erect a Pavilion upon it, or, it may be, an Obelisk. This is not all. . . .' She goes on to complain of a hideous *sunk fence* and of Sir Michael Fleming, who not only had decided to axe all his trees but 'has been building a long high wall under the grand woods behind his house which cuts the hill in two by a straight line; and to make his doings visible to all men, he has whitewashed it, as white as snow. One who could do this wants a sense which others have. To him there is no "*Spirit in the Wood*".'

Wordsworth's objections to white colouring are strictly picturesque, but also on the grounds of unnaturalness:

The objections to white, as a colour, in large spots or masses in landscape, especially in a mountainous country, are insurmount-able. In Nature, pure white is scarcely ever found but in small objects, such as flowers; or in those which are transitory, as the clouds, foam of rivers, and snow. Mr Gilpin, who notices this, has also recorded the just remark of Mr Locke, of N—, that white destroys the *gradations* of distance; and, therefore, an object of pure white can scarcely ever be managed with good effect in landscape-painting. Five or six white houses, scattered over a valley, by their obtrusiveness, dot the surface and divide it into triangles, or other mathematical figures, haunting the eye, and disturbing that repose which might otherwise be perfect. I have seen a single white house materially impair the majesty of a mountain; cutting away, by a harsh separation, the whole of its base, below the point on which the house stood.

He himself, he continued, particularly disliked the effect of white objects at twilight:

> The solemnity and quietness of Nature at that time are always marred, and often destroyed by them. When the ground is covered with snow, they are of course inoffensive; and in moonshine they are always pleasing—it is a tone of light with which they accord: and the dimness of the scene is enlivened by an object at once conspicuous and cheerful.

Neither a 'cold, slaty colour' nor a 'flaring yellow' were suitable alternatives: the safest was 'something between a cream and a dust-colour, commonly called stone colour'. His admiration for the humble Lakeland cottages was partly picturesque—they had 'so little formality' and much 'wildness and beauty', and had the appropriate surfaces of rough, unhewn stone and lichens, mosses, ferns and flowers. They were, like his ideal work of art, organic in appearance, they might 'rather be said to have grown than to have been erected', and, in their very form calling to mind the processes of Nature 'do thus, clothed in part with a vegetable garb, appear to be received into the bosom of the living principle of things, as it acts and exists among the woods and fields; and by their colour and their shape, affectingly direct the thoughts to that tranquil course of Nature and simplicity, along which the humble-minded inhabitants have, through so many generations, been led.'

He particularly disliked larch trees also, whether planted for ornament or profit—they made excellent pit-props. They were too vivid a green in spring, and in autumn 'a spiritless, unvarying yellow'. He wanted the native, deciduous trees to be left alone, particularly in the valleys—oak, holly, hazel and ash. If larch *must* be planted, let the 'vegetable manufactories' be 'confined to the highest and most barren tracts where their "dreary uniformity" would be broken by rocks, and the winds would imprint upon their shapes a wildness congenial to their situation'.

Wordsworth's views on the whole controversy being conducted at this time about the right and proper way to 'improve' gardens and estates were extreme though sensible. The current fashion for the 'English garden', he told Sir George Beaumont, would be really valuable if it led people to stop 'improving' in any manner and, as Sir George had declared his intention of doing with his own house, leaving it to Nature so that 'your House will belong to the Country and not the Country be an appendage to your House'. Improvements to parks, gardens, and houses were very much the fashion, as *Mansfield Park* and, later, George Eliot's *Scenes from Clerical Life* bear witness. The 'English' garden derived from the reaction against the landscape sculpturing of 'Capability' Brown. Addison had written 'Our British gardeners . . . instead of humouring nature, love to deviate from it as much as possible. Our trees rise in cones, globes, and pyramids. We see the marks of the scissors on every plant and bush. I do not know whether I am singular in my opinions but for my part I would rather look upon a tree in all its luxuriancy and diffusion of boughs and branches than when it is thus cut and trimmed into a mathematical figure. . . .' Sir William Temple, Swift's patron, in *The Gardens of Epicurus* (1685) introduced the idea of Chinese *Sharawadgi*— 'artificial rudeness'—and the 'Chinese' irregular garden led to the landscape park. Pope laid down three conditions for an irregular garden—'surprise, variety, concealment'. This entailed, among other things *winding* paths and vistas which led the eye away from the path travelled by the feet. Thomas West applies these gardening principles to Lakeland views:

What charms the eye in wandering over the vale is, that not one straight line offends. The roads all serpentize round the mountains, and the hedges wave with the inclosures. Everything is thrown into some path of beauty or agreeable line of nature.

The dale-landers, according to West, were all 'men of taste' and decorated their villages with 'natural elegance'. 'Not one formal avenue or straight-lined hedge or square fishpond offends the eye in all this charming vale.' The fashion went too far, and attracted satirical and commonsense adverse comment. Thomas Love Peacock, in *Headlong Hall* in 1812, wrote a parody of a picturesque discussion in which Marmaduke Milestone, representing that great landscape gardener and designer of Regent's Park, Humphry Repton, depresses the pretensions of a profound critic who adds *unexpectedness* to the picturesque and the beautiful as qualities required in the laying out of grounds.

'Pray Sir,' said Mr Milestone 'by what name do you distinguish

Sir George Beaumont's house at Coleorton, Leics

this character when a person walks round the grounds for a second time?' Wordsworth read and approved *Some Observations on Gardening* 'by the Author of the Democrat'. This condemns the improver of the 'Capability' Brown school who tries

> ... to make his domain appear park-like, and down goes every hedge within a quarter of a mile of the house. The noble hedge-rows of elm and oak, which, growing in the irregular fences, give every well planted county in England the appearance of a forest, are destroyed, except a few that contrivance is able to torture into those unmeaning unnatural masses called clumps, and the whole estate that is in the view of the house is divided by sunk fences. The kitchen garden is posted half a mile off, which, till the skreen of firs grows up to hide it, has the appearance of a burying ground near a great town. And you go out of the hall door into the wet grass, unless you are indulged with an undulated gravel walk by the boundary that divides the appropriated field of the owner from the ornamented farm, if that can be called ornament which is in fact devastation.
>
> It is surely better for a person of moderate fortune to have his kitchen garden (always a busy and interesting scene) near his house. . . .

This writer was also indignant about the banishing of the lime and horse chestnut, 'trees of singular beauty . . . partly from their leaves being very early deciduous, which makes them unfit for the owner of a fine place at present, as it is now agreed that London is only pleasant in the spring and the country-seat never tolerable before the first of September; and partly from a fanciful disgust to the shape of both, one being called too formal and the other too heavy: as if natural shapeliness bordered on the deformity of the sheared yew . . .'.

Wordsworth himself designed for Lady Beaumont a winter garden based on one described by Addison in *The Spectator*, and gave much loving and detailed attention to the creation of 'the *feeling* of the place . . . of a spirit which the winter cannot touch, which should present no image of chilliness, decay or desolation, when the face of Nature everywhere else is cold, decayed and desolate'. His description of the centre of the garden is vivid and evocative:

> We are then brought to a small glade or open space, belted round with evergreens, quite unvaried and secluded. In this little glade should be a basin of water inhabited by two gold or silver fish if they will live in this climate all the year in the open air; if not any others of the most radiant colors that are more hardy: these little creatures to be the 'genii' of the pool and of the place. This spot should be as monotonous in the colour of the trees as possible. The enclosure of evergreen, the sky above, the green grass floor, and the two mute inhabitants, the only images it should present, unless here and there a solitary wild-flower.

The colourlessness of Wordsworth's winter garden was a deliberate poetic device, but it reflects what was a general trend in gardening. Picturesque painting had an immense influence on gardens, and was more concerned with surfaces and lighting than with colour, with the result that gardens were designed in Claude's golds and browns. It was not until Victorian times that gardens became colourful again.

Beyond the parks and gardens the landscape was being changed by acts of enclosure. Enclosure had been carried out intermittently throughout English history. After the Restoration the Government ceased to interfere with the enclosure of open fields by private landlords, and until George II's reign enclosure was carried out by private agreements. But from the 1750s onwards, land was enclosed by private act of Parliament in rapidly increasing quantities. There were eight private acts of enclosure in the whole of England before 1714, eighteen under George I, 229 under George II (1727–60), and in the next forty years 1,479 acts dealt with $2\frac{1}{2}$ million acres. From 1800 onwards, the high prices of the war years brought more marginal land into cultivation and the 'wastes' began to be enclosed—500 acts between 1760 and 1801 enclosed 750,000 acres of waste: during the nineteenth century another 1,300 acts took in one and a quarter million acres of heath, indiscriminately chosen. The enclosures made a visual transformation of the landscape, as well as far-reaching social changes. The old pattern of open fields, with grassy cart-roads and paths, and strips of cultivation, the commons and rough places, became a chequer board of small squarish fields enclosed by hawthorn hedges and crossed by straight, wide roads. All this happened within a relatively short time.

Reactions to the enclosures varied. Coleridge was distressed by the poverty induced by the dispossession of Scottish peasants: a gentleman touring caves in the West Riding of Yorkshire admired the solitary secluded vale and hillside of Breada-Garth, remarked that 'No monk or anchoret could desire a more retired situation for his cell, to moralize on the vanity of the world, or disappointed lover to bewail the inconstancy of his nymph', but went on to worry about the lack of use of the rich soil. Before Malthus people in general worried about *underpopulation* and the aesthetically solitary gentleman 'could not but lament that, instead of peopling the wilds and deserts of North America our fellow-subjects had not peopled the fertile wastes of the north of England. We have since then been informed, that a plan is in agitation for having them inclosed, when no doubt it will support some scores of additional families. . . .'

Visual reactions varied, too. Southey's fictional Don, travelling through 'Dorsetshire, a dreary country', remarked: 'Hitherto I had been disposed to think that the English inclosures rather deformed than beautified the landscape, but now I perceived how cheerless and naked the cultivated country appears without them. The hills here are ribbed with furrows, just as it is their fashion to score the skin of roast pork.' But there was a health argument against enclosures: 'It has been ascertained by the late census, that the proportion of deaths in the down-countries to the other parts is 66–80—a certain proof that inclosures are prejudicial to health.'

Bewick regretted the loss of the Northumberland commons: the poet John Clare wrote in his *Journal* on 29 September 1824:

Took a walk in the fields saw an old wood stile taken away from a favourite spot which it had occupied all my life the posts were overgrown with Ivy and it seemed so akin to nature and the spot where it stood as tho it had taken it on lease for an undisturbed existance it hurt me to see it was gone for my affection claims a friendship with such things but nothing is lasting in this world last year Langley Bush was destroyed an old whitethorn that had stood for more than a century full of fame the gipsies shepherds and Herdmen all had their tales of its history and it will be long ere its memory is forgotten.

His poem 'Ye injur'd fields which once were gay' is full of the same regret.

Wordsworth, writing to Sir George Beaumont in 1811, kept an open mind:

> I heard the other day of two artists who thus expressed themselves upon the subject of a scene among our Lakes. 'Plague upon those vile Enclosures!' said one; 'they spoil everything!' 'O' said the Other, 'I never *see* them.' ... Now for my part, I should not wish to be either of these Gentlemen, but to have in my own mind the power of turning to advantage, wherever it is possible, every object of Art and Nature as they appear before me.

He goes on to make a relevant and deeply interesting comparison with painting.

> What a noble instance, as you have often pointed out to me, has Reubens given to this in that picture in your possession, where he has brought as it were a whole Century into one Landscape and made the most formal partitions of cultivation; hedge-rows of pollard willows conduct the eye into the depths and distances of his picture; and thus, more than by any other means, has given it that appearance of immensity which is so striking.

Both poets at some very profound level naturally used visual images for the poetic imagination they cared so much about. I have tried to show that this was a characteristic of the thought of the time—something which led in truly visual terms to Constable's trees and moving clouds or Turner's paintings of almost pure light. But in their hands it became something new and powerful. The rest of this chapter is concerned with their *use* of the images of landscape. Here is Coleridge on Rubens's poetic imagination in a landscape with the setting sun:

> Rubens does not take for his subjects grand or novel conformations of objects; he has, you see, no precipices, no forests, no frowning castles—nothing that a poet would take at all times and a painter take in these times. No; he gets some little ponds, old tumble-down cottages, that ruinous chateau, two or three peasants, a hay-rick, and other such humble images, which looked at in and by themselves convey no pleasure and excite no surprise; but he—and he Peter Paul Rubens alone—handles these everyday in-gredients of all common landscapes as they are handled in nature; he throws them into a vast and magnificent whole, consisting of heaven and earth and all things therein. He extracts the latent poetry out of these common objects—that poetry and harmony which every man of genius perceives in the face of nature, and which many men of no genius are taught to perceive and feel after examining such a picture as this. In other landscape painters the scene is confined and as it were imprisoned—in Rubens, the landscape dies a natural death; it fades away into the apparent infinity of space.

Here are picturesque standards, in poetry and painting, used and transcended in Coleridge's vision of imaginative unity—although it is interesting to remember in this context that Constable's friend Fisher wrote to Constable that Coleridge had said *some parts* of his last picture were good. 'I told him if he had said, *all parts* of your last picture were good, it would be no compliment, unless he said the *whole* was good. Is it not strange how utterly ignorant the world is of the very first principles of painting? Here is a man of the greatest abilities, who knows almost everything, and yet he is as little a judge of a picture as if he had been without eyes.'

Wordsworth was also a shrewd analyst of the picturesque aesthetic. In 1825 he was explaining to a correspondent that when he had observed that 'many objects were fitted for the pencil without being picturesque' he had meant not the Dutch school but 'the higher order of Italian artists'. He went on to discuss the fact that the Dutch painters treated objects that 'would not by a superficial observer be deemed picturesque, nor would they with any propriety, in popular language, be termed so'—objects which tended to arouse disgust such as 'insides of stables—dung carts— dunghills and foul and loathsome situations' but on canvas could be made picturesque. This controversy about 'disgusting' objects was very much part of current discussion. Wordsworth went on to say that 'our business is not so much with objects as with the laws under which they are contemplated. The confusion incident to these disquisitions has I think arisen principally from not attending to this distinction.' Whether a thing was beautiful or not depended not on the *thing* but on the imaginative attention of observer or artist—and it was Wordsworth's attention, as observer and artist, to the primary importance of *laws* of contemplation that led to his emphasis on his 'own mind' as subject matter and the new vision of the *Lyrical Ballads* as form.

There are two connected aspects of contemporary aesthetics which I particularly want to look at in the writings of the poets themselves. One is the use of the concepts of 'sublime' landscape, particularly of infinity, by the poets in their creation of a *whole* living universe, unified in its diversity. The other is their deepening of the picturesque theorists' view that it was the structure of *light* and response to light that created the unity of a painting, and their use of light as a primary image for the imagination. The two are usually aspects of the same vision, as in Coleridge's description of the Rubens painting above, where Rubens' light and imagination, like Nature, form the landscape into a whole which becomes infinite: 'The landscape dies a natural death; it fades away into the apparent infinity of space.'

Wordsworth's 'pantheism' has been much talked about: the *Tintern Abbey* vision of 'something far more deeply interfused/ Whose dwelling is the light of setting suns/And the round ocean and the living air/And the blue sky and in the mind of man.' *Tintern Abbey* is permeated by the vision educated in the knowledge of the sublime and the picturesque. But more permanently satisfying and moving than statements about spirits is Wordsworth's living sense of the unity of matter beneath the changing and shifting forms of natural objects, man rolled round in earth's diurnal course with rocks and stones and trees, and his further sense of the unity of these in the way in which the imaginative vision sees one in the other, one form as an image of another form. In his poems, as in his *Guide to the Lakes*, and in Dorothy's beautifully written journals, the sense of the history and changing reality of concrete objects works with the sense of changing vision.

On the *Tour in Scotland* in 1803 Dorothy made many picturesque observations of Nature which suggest the atmosphere of the mystery of concrete objects and persons suggested by Wordsworth's poems. Looking from Dumbarton Castle on the Clyde she saw some sheep and a sentry in a red coat on top of a perpendicular cliff, and noted the effects of perspective and emotion together:

> The sheep, I suppose owing to our being accustomed to see them in similar situations, appeared to retain their real size, while, on the contrary, the soldier seemed to be diminished by the distance till he almost looked like a puppet moved with wires for the pleasure of children . . . I had never before, perhaps, thought of sheep and men in soldiers' dresses at the same time, and here they were brought together in a strange fantastic way. As will be easily conceived, the fearlessness and stillness of those quiet creatures on the brow of the rock, pursuing their natural occupations, contrasted with the endless and apparently unmeaning motions of the dwarf soldier, added not a little to the general effect of this place, which is that of a wild singularity, and the whole was aided by a blustering wind and a wild sky.

Here the elements of the picturesque—the *unexpected* concatenation of sheep and men, craggy rock and regular movements—combined with the artificial infinity and unrelatedness of the human component with his unnatural 'endless and apparently unmeaning motions'—produce a Wordsworthian image of man's isolation in nature which moves on in its own way—and of the poetic vision's reunifying of the scene. Her description of a sea loch at Arrochar calls up more direct echoes of another Wordsworthian image of natural and spiritual infinity:

I thought of the long windings through which the waters of the sea had come to this inland retreat, visiting the inner solitudes of the mountains, and I could have wished to have mused out a summer's day on the shores of the lake. From the foot of these mountains whither might not a little barque carry one away? though so far inland, it is but a slip of the great ocean: seamen, fishermen and shepherds here find a natural home.

Compare the *Immortality* ode:

> Hence in a season of calm weather
> Though inland far we be,
> Our Souls have sight of that immortal sea
> Which brought us hither,
> Can in a moment travel thither,
> And see the Children sport upon the shore,
> And hear the mighty waters rolling evermore.

Wordsworth's own description in his *Guide* of the tarns combines a picturesque opening with the Wordsworthian vision of the sublime and the Wordsworthian sense of the history of the solid objects around him to recall another great poem

One of these pools is an acceptable sight to the mountain wanderer; not merely as an incident that diversifies the prospect, but as forming in his mind a centre or conspicuous point to which objects, otherwise disconnected or unsubordinated, may be referred. Some few have a varied outline, with bold heath-clad promontories; and, as they mostly lie at the foot of a steep precipice, the water, where the sun is not shining upon it, appears black and sullen; and round the margin, huge stones and masses of rock are scattered; some defying conjecture as to the means by which they came thither; and others obviously fallen from on high—the contribution of ages! A not unpleasing sadness is induced by this perplexity, and these images of decay; while the prospect of a body of pure water unattended with groves and other cheerful rural images by which fresh water is usually accompanied, and unable to give furtherance to the meagre vegetation around it—excites a sense of some repulsive power strongly put forth and thus deepens the melancholy natural to such scenes. Nor is the feeling of solitude often more forcibly or more solemnly impressed than by the side of one of these mountain pools; though desolate and forbidding it seems a distinct place to repair to; yet where the visitants must be rare.

This is the setting for *The Leech-gatherer*, another image of human solitude amongst the timeless change and decay of Nature: in the poem the man, and the still water, and the mysterious stones like sea-beasts crawled out into the sun are all somehow seen as *one*, providing an image of a kind of persisting sublime poverty, an 'apt admonishment' to Wordsworth troubled by melancholy thoughts of 'mighty poets in their misery dead'. It is an image again of eternity in change and decay.

Other images, different and complex, could be produced almost endlessly from Wordsworth's work. In *The Prelude* Wordsworth combines social and political concern with a vision of infinity in his description of 'the windings of a public way'. He imagined that the 'disappearing line' that

> crossed
> The naked summit of a far off hill
> Beyond the limits that my feet had trod
> Was like an invitation into space
> Boundless, or guide into eternity.

And the 'wanderers of the earth', solitary beggars met on it, have 'the depth of human souls/Souls that appear to have no depth at all/To casual eyes'. The water image for the infinity of the soul casually buried here is explicitly elaborated in many other places. In *The Excursion* in the mountain retreat of the solitary, human life is likened to

> a mountain brook
> In some still passage of its course . . . [the visitor sees]
> Within the depths of its capacious breast,
> Inverted trees, rocks, clouds and azure sky;
> And on its glassy surface, specks of foam

And conglobated bubbles undissolved,
Numerous as stars; that, by their onward lapse,
Betray to sight the motion of the stream
Else imperceptible.

Through what perplexing labyrinths, abrupt
Precipitations, and untoward straits,
The earth-born wanderer hath passed. . . .

The earlier description of the alpine pass quoted above (p. 244) is another example of the same use of water to suggest infinite change and infinite sameness, and Coleridge in a letter to Sara Hutchinson describes the Waterfall that divides Great Robinson from Buttermere Halse Fell in the same terms. He describes the water rushing over a ground

so fearfully savage, and black, and jagged, that it tears the flood to pieces. . . .
What sight it is to look down on such a Cataract!—the wheels, that circumvolve in it—the leaping up and plunging forward of that infinity of Pearls and Glass Bulbs—the continual *change* of the *Matter*, the perpetual *Sameness* of the *Form*—it is an awful Image and Shadow of God and the World.

The famous passage in *Biographia* in which Coleridge describes the original intention of the *Lyrical Ballads* uses a natural image of light on landscape for the imagination:

During the first year that Mr Wordsworth and I were neighbours our conversations turned frequently on the two cardinal points of poetry, the power of exciting the sympathy of the reader by a faithful adherence to the truth of nature, and the power of giving the interest of novelty by the modifying colours of imagination. The sudden charm which accidents of light and shade, which moonlight or sunlight diffused over a known and familiar landscape, appeared to represent the practicability of combining both. These are the poetry of nature.

Throughout Dorothy Wordsworth's Journals the accidents of light and shade constantly create other worlds within the known world. In a Highland hut she is amazed by the beauty of the rafters, in which the hens perched, seen through gusts of smoke:

> They had been crusted over and varnished by many winters till, where the firelight fell upon them, they were as glossy as black rocks on a sunny day cased in ice. . . . They had a bright fire, which I could not see; but the light it sent up among the varnished rafters and beams, which crossed each other in almost as intricate and fantastic a manner as I have seen the under-boughs of a large beech-tree withered by the depth of the shade above, produced the most beautiful effect that can be conceived. It was like what I should suppose an underground cave or temple to be, with a dripping or moist roof, and the moonlight entering in upon it by some means or other, and yet the colours were more like gems.

Or crossing Westminster Bridge in 1802 'The houses were not overhung by their cloud of smoke, and they were spread out endlessly, yet the sun shone so brightly, with such a fierce light, that there was even something like the purity of one of nature's own grand spectacles.' Or in Grasmere 'I observed the glittering silver line on the ridge of the backs of the sheep, owing to their situation respecting the sun, which made them look beautiful, but with something of strangeness, like animals of another kind, as if belonging to a more splendid world.' Or the 'mountain lightness' at the top of the White Moss. 'There is more of the sky there than any other place. It has a strange effect sometimes along with the obscurity of evening or night. It seems almost like a peculiar *sort* of light.'

Gilpin saw colours like a moving vision on a mountain side. 'They are rarely permanent, but seem to be a sort of floating silky colours—always in motion—always in harmony—and playing with a thousand changeable varieties into each other. They are literally colours dipped in heaven.' Coleridge, a man fascinated by lights, chemical lights, firelight, the supernatural still and awful red that burned in the charmed water in *The Ancient Mariner* wrote again and again about it in his notebooks. A typical observation, made in October 1803 makes it clear how much the effect of light on the forms of landscape was seen by him, in terms of painting to a certain extent, as an image of the relationship between human imaginative vision and the forms of non-human life:

> Heavy masses of shapeless Vapour upon the mountains (O the perpetual Forms of Borrodale!) yet it is no unbroken Tale of dull Sadness—slanting Pillars travel across the Lake, at long Intervals— the vaporous mass whitens, in large Stains of Light—on the Lakeward ridge of that huge arm chair, of Lowdore, fell a gleam of softest Light, that brought out the rich hues of the late Autumn.— The woody Castle Crag between me and Lowdore is a rich Flower-Garden of Colours, the brightest yellows with the deepest Crimsons, and the infinite Shades of Brown and Green, the *infinite* diversity of which blends the whole—so that the brighter colours seem as *colors* upon a ground, not colored Things.

Light unifies the *vision*, the things are colours in a painting, not 'colored Things', not pure objects. The vision is informed by Coleridge's feeling, however much seen for itself.

Wordsworth had very early used light and his own feelings as a guide in the creation of imaginatively unified scenes. In the Valley of the Reuss in 1790 he saw an Alpine sunset, which he described in the *Descriptive Sketches*, with a special footnote to explain his deliberate contravention of the established rules of the picturesque:

> Whoever in attempting to describe their sublime features, should confine himself to the cold rules of painting, would give his reader but a very imperfect idea of those emotions which they have the irresistible power of communicating to the most impassive. . . . Had I wished to make a picture of this scene I had thrown much less light into it. But I consulted nature and my feeling. The ideas excited by the stormy sunset I am here describing owed their sublimity to that deluge of light; or rather of fire, in which nature had wrapped the immense forms around me; any intrusion of shade, by destroying the unity of the impression, had necessarily diminished its grandeur.

This manages to suggest the original creative *Fiat Lux*, or fire in which the world was forged—a deluge not of water that destroyed but of light that created a unified vision by drowning the landscape in unrelieved fire.

Much later at the end of *The Prelude* Wordsworth describes another vision of pure light—his own of the moon shining over hills, islands and promontories of mist over the main Atlantic, seen from Snowdon, above it, and uses it as an image of the high imagination, of

> a majestic intellect, its acts
> And its possessions, what it has and craves,
> What in itself it is and would become
> There I beheld the emblem of a mind
> That feeds upon infinity, that broods
> Over the dark abyss, intent to hear
> Its voices issuing forth to silent light
> In one continuous stream; a mind sustained
> By recognitions of transcendent power
> In sense conducting to ideal form. . . .

Again this vision of imaginative infinity has its corollary in Dorothy's description—this time of a view in Scotland:

We had not climbed far before we were stopped by a sudden burst of prospect, so singular and beautiful that it was like a flash of images from another world. We stood with our backs to the hill of the island, which we were ascending, and which shut out Ben Lomond entirely, and all the upper part of the lake, and we looked towards the foot of the lake, scattered over with islands without beginning and without end. The sun shone, and the distant hills were visible, some through sunny mists, others in gloom with patches of sunshine; the lake was lost under the low and distant hills, and the islands lost in the lake, which was all in motion with travelling fields of light, or dark shadows under rainy clouds. There are many hills, but no commanding eminence at a distance to confine the prospect so that the land seemed as endless as the water.

Coleridge used the image Shakespeare used of the sun of

Shakespeare's own imaginative vision, his eye which 'would have given one of his *Glows* to the first Line, and flatter'd the mountain Top with his sovran Eye'. The theorists of the picturesque were interested in the power of the eye to perceive light. In the *Dialogue* between Uvedale Price and W. Payne Knight, Price says: 'The picturesque is merely that kind of beauty which belongs exclusively to the sense of vision. . . . The eye, unassisted, perceives nothing but light, variously graduated and modified.' In the picture gallery the protagonists of the *Dialogue* look at Rembrandt and the 'blended variety of mellow tints' in his painting of the dead flesh of an ox carcass, and talk of the Dutch painters' treatment of 'ugly and disgusting objects in Nature. In the originals of these, animal disgust and the nauseating repugnance of appetite overwhelmed every milder pleasure of vision, which a blended variety of mellow and harmonious tints must *necessarily* produce on the eye, in nature as well as in art, if viewed in both with the same degree of abstract and impartial attention.' Seymour, the uninstructed *homme moyen sensuel* of the *Dialogue*, could not bring himself to this degree of abstraction—his human feelings made him remain conscious of the squalor and poverty of the subjects:

> I can imagine a man of the future, born without the sense of feeling, being able to see nothing but light variously modified, and that such a way of considering nature would be just. For then the eye would see nothing but what in point of harmony was beautiful. But that pure, abstract enjoyment of vision, our inveterate habits will not let us partake of.

Abstract. The word has not its modern meaning in art and aesthetics and yet it foreshadows it, as picturesque theory, and much more intensely Wordsworth's and Coleridge's vision of light *on* the landscape foreshadows the use of light by Turner and the Impressionists, the steady shift of aesthetic interest which led to the use of light, and of the artist's own visual responses as the subject matter of paintings, as the poet's imagination became the subject matter of poems, until painting at least was as inconceivably 'abstract' as Mr Seymour foresaw.

I may here be making an impermissable verbal connection,

but it does seem that this painters' interest in 'abstraction' is related to Coleridge's own linguistic intérest in abstract thoughts and abstract words. We have seen in the political and literary chapters of this book how important it was to the poets to shift the interest from the generalizing abstract *concepts* of the eighteenth century to the particular—the particular problem, the concrete image, the actual landscape. Coleridge was sharp with Rousseau's Reason, Pitt's abstraction, Walter Scott's visual and literary vagueness. But at the same time, as we have seen in the introductory chapter, he knew his own 'abstract' habit of mind to be in some ways a mode of connecting himself to the deepest roots and underlying patterns of behaviour, language and expression. What was required was a mode of vision which would combine the particular life of individual vision with the sense of underlying form and unity that could be 'abstracted'. Between the eighteenth-century interest in ideal vision and generalizations and the twentieth-century abstract interest in the analysis of the mind, the eye, which led to abstract art, the Romantics were uneasily searching for a viable compromise. They were fortunate and un-fortunate—unfortunate because, as Hazlitt saw, they came to have to rely far too heavily on their own individual personal vision as an authority and a guarantor of true feeling, fortunate because they were not limited by a constricting theory but really confronted their experience and tried to see what it was they saw. There is an extremely profound piece of aesthetics in a letter written by Coleridge to an unknown correspondent after Wordsworth had criticized his *Hymn before Sunrise in the Vale of Chamouny* as a Specimen of the Mock Sublime:

> I could readily believe that the mood and Habit of mind out of which the Hymn rose—that differs from Milton's, and Thomson's and from the Psalms, the Source of all three, in the Author's addressing himself to individual Objects actually present to his Senses, while his great Predecessors apostrophize *classes* of Things, presented by the Memory and generalized by the understanding—I can readily believe, I say, that in this there may be too much of what our learned Med'ciners call the *Idiosyncratic* for true Poetry.

For from my very childhood I have been accustomed to *abstract*
and as it were unrealize whatever of more than common interest
my eyes dwelt on; and then by a sort of transfusion and trans-
mission of my consciousness to identify myself with the Object.

The idiosyncratic mountain, that is, lacks a value perhaps
inherent in Milton's, the Psalms', Thomson's generalized *classes*
of things, and conferred by Coleridge's sense of the identity between himself and the thing seen which he called '*abstract* and as
it were unrealize(d)'. This kind of abstraction *deeper* than the
recognition of the concrete idiosyncrasy of objects is also recog-
nizable in Wordsworth's description of the 'abyss of idealism' he
experienced in childhood which is recalled in the glorious light
images of the *Immortality Ode*:

> I was often unable to think of external things as having external
> existence, and I communed with all that I saw as something not
> apart from, but inherent in, my own material nature. Many times
> while going to school have I grasped at a wall or a tree to recall
> myself from this abyss of idealism to the reality.

It was the tension between the identity of subject and object,
eye and light, and the sense that the outer world *was* outer and
other, between the 'blank misgivings of a creature moving about
in worlds not realized' and the individual mountains that created
their greatest poetry: Wordsworth's descriptions of the forms of
mountains in and out of the child's mind in *The Prelude*, or 'the
earth and that uncertain heaven received/Into the bosom of the
steady lake'. In *Peele Castle* the picturesque light is the 'light that
never was on sea or land/The consecration and the Poet's dream',
but reality is different. In the *Dejection Ode* the imagination is 'a
light, a glory, a fair luminous cloud/Enveloping the Earth—'
and must come from the poet's own soul:

> It were a vain endeavour
> Though I should gaze for ever
> On that green light that lingers in the west:
> I may not hope from outward forms to win
> The passion and the life whose sources are within.

The strain of creating one's own values, and indeed one's own surroundings as their aesthetic implied, is tremendous, and it is significant that both the *Immortality Ode* and the *Dejection Ode* express among other emotions regret for the lost unifying vision:

> All this long eve, so balmy and serene,
> Have I been gazing on the western sky,
> And its peculiar tint of yellow green:
> And still I gaze and with how blank an eye!
>
> I see, not feel, how beautiful they are!
>
> The sunshine is a glorious birth
> But yet I know, where 'er I go
> That there hath past away a glory from the earth.
>
> Whither is fled the visionary gleam
> Where is it now, the glory and the dream?

To study the use of visual imagery, the *meaning* of painting and landscape and aesthetic theory in the period is to make both poets' achievement in *realizing* their worlds seem more gigantic, and the sense of loss of visual intensity and increase of abstraction of the wrong kind in the *Dejection Ode* more important and more poignant.

Selected Reading List

BIOGRAPHY AND LETTERS
MARY MOORMAN *William Wordsworth. A Biography* (Clarendon Press, 1957)
WALTER JACKSON BATE *Coleridge* (Weidenfeld and Nicolson, 'Masters of World Literature', 1968) An illuminating, if short, biography.
WILLIAM AND DOROTHY WORDSWORTH *The Letters*, ed. Ernest de Selincourt (Oxford, 1935–9): *The Early Years* rev. by Chester L. Shaver (Oxford University Press, 1967)
DOROTHY WORDSWORTH *Journals*, ed. Ernest de Selincourt (Macmillan, 1941)
S. T. COLERIDGE *Collected Letters*, ed. Earl Leslie Griggs (Clarendon Press, 1956)
S. T. COLERIDGE *Notebooks*, ed. ed. Kathleen Coburn (Routledge, 1957)

DAILY LIFE
ROBERT SOUTHEY *Letters from England*, ed. Jack Simmons, (Cresset Press, 1951)

THE STRUCTURE OF SOCIETY
ASA BRIGGS The Age of Improvement, (on the years 1784–1867) (Longmans, 1959, Vol. 8 of the *History of England*)
JOHN A. COLMER *Coleridge: Critic of Society* (Clarendon Press, 1959)
BRIAN INGLIS *By the Sweat of thy Brow: Poverty in the Industrial Revolution* (Hodder and Stoughton)
F. D. KLINGENDER *Art and the Industrial Revolution*, 1947 revised and ed. Arthur Elton, London; (Evelyn, Adams and MacKay, 1968)
R. J. WHITE *From Waterloo to Peterloo* (Peregrine Books)

POLITICS
ed. R. J. WHITE *The Political Thought of Samuel Taylor Coleridge* (Jonathan Cape, 1938)
ed. R. J. WHITE *Political Tracts of Wordsworth, Coleridge and Shelley* (Cambridge University Press, 1953)
C. CRANE BRINTON *The Political Ideas of the English Romanticists* (Oxford University Press, 1926)
A. B. C. COBBAN *Edmund Burke and the Revolt against the Eighteenth Century* (Allen and Unwin, 1960)

EDUCATION AND CHILDHOOD
COVENEY, PETER *Poor Monkey*, The Child in Literature (Rockliff, London, 1957)

THE LITERARY WORLD
JOHN GROSS *The Rise and Fall of the English Man of Letters* (Weidenfeld and Nicolson, 1969)
WILLIAM HAZLITT *The Spirit of the Age* (Oxford University Press, World's Classics Series)
W. L. RENWICK *English Literature 1789–1815* (Oxford History of English Literature, vol. 9)

LANDSCAPE
CHRISTOPHER HUSSEY *The Picturesque* (Frank Cass and Co., 1967) (I am deeply indebted to this book throughout Chapter 7)
EDMUND BURKE *A Philosophical Enquiry into the Origin of our Ideas of the Sublime and Beautiful*, ed. J. T. Boulton (Routledge & Kegan Paul, 1958)

General Index

NOTE: References to works are by author only, unless the author's name is not given in the text. Italic figures refer to illustrations.